The Dynamics of Entrepreneurial Ecosystems

T0300224

This book aims to provide new approaches to analysing and thinking about how entrepreneurial ecosystems develop and evolve over time as well as shed light on the relatively unexplored area of entrepreneurship ecosystem dynamics.

The concept of entrepreneurial ecosystems has emerged as a framework to understand the nature of places in which entrepreneurial activity flourishes. Time is fundamental to the analysis of the dynamics of an entrepreneurial ecosystem. New firm creation, survival, growth and demise all occur within a temporal context that is, over and within time. Systems approach to research invariably models the influential effects of the actors and elements that shape, re-shape, maintain, shift and change the system itself. An entrepreneurial ecosystem point of view, therefore, is inherently time-dependent and provides an analytical framework that reveals how the number and diversity of entrepreneurial actors situated in a place and time influence the creation of new firms, their survival, growth, and ultimately the stability of markets and industry in a time and place. Whether for better or worse, the historic and present time dimensions underpin the functioning and trajectory of entrepreneurial ecosystem performances and how they are shaped over time.

Each chapter in this edited volume outlines a particular perspective and/or a unique case drawn from a range of countries that collectively reveal the dynamics of an ever-changing entrepreneurial ecosystem.

The chapters were originally published as a special issue of the journal, *Entrepreneurship and Regional Development*.

Allan O'Connor is Associate Professor in Enterprise Dynamics at the University of South Australia, Australia.

Colin Mason is Professor of Entrepreneurship at the University of Glasgow, UK.

Morgan P. Miles is Professor of Entrepreneurship at Charles Sturt University, Australia.

David Audretsch is Distinguished Professor at Indiana University, USA.

The Dynamics of Entrepreneurial Ecosystems

Edited by
Allan O'Connor, Colin Mason,
Morgan P. Miles and David Audretsch

Routledge
Taylor & Francis Group

LONDON AND NEW YORK

First published 2022
by Routledge
2 Park Square, Milton Park, Abingdon, Oxon, OX14 4RN

and by Routledge
605 Third Avenue, New York, NY 10158

Routledge is an imprint of the Taylor & Francis Group, an informa business

© 2022 Taylor & Francis

British Library Cataloguing-in-Publication Data
A catalogue record for this book is available from the British Library

ISBN13: 978-1-032-15616-3 (hbk)
ISBN13: 978-1-032-15617-0 (pbk)
ISBN13: 978-1-003-24496-7 (ebk)

DOI: 10.4324/9781003244967

Typeset in Myriad Pro
by codeMantra

Publisher's Note
The publisher accepts responsibility for any inconsistencies that may have arisen during the conversion of this book from journal articles to book chapters, namely the inclusion of journal terminology.

Disclaimer
Every effort has been made to contact copyright holders for their permission to reprint material in this book. The publishers would be grateful to hear from any copyright holder who is not here acknowledged and will undertake to rectify any errors or omissions in future editions of this book.

Contents

Citation Information

The chapters in this book, except Chapter 4, were originally published in the journal *Entrepreneurship & Regional Development*, volume 33, issue 1-2 (2021). Chapter 4 was originally published in a different issue of the same journal. When citing this material, please use the original page numbering for each article, as follows:

Chapter 1
Time and the dynamics of entrepreneurial ecosystems
David Audretsch, Colin Mason, Morgan P. Miles and Allan O'Connor
Entrepreneurship & Regional Development, volume 33, issue 1-2 (2021) pp. 1–14

Chapter 2
From orchards to chips: Silicon Valley's evolving entrepreneurial ecosystem
Stephen B. Adams
Entrepreneurship & Regional Development, volume 33, issue 1-2 (2021) pp. 15–35

Chapter 3
The role of MNEs in the genesis and growth of a resilient entrepreneurial ecosystem
Paul Ryan, Majella Giblin, Giulio Buciuni and Dieter F. Kogler
Entrepreneurship & Regional Development, volume 33, issue 1-2 (2021) pp. 36–53

Chapter 4
Meeting its Waterloo? Recycling in entrepreneurial ecosystems after anchor firm collapse
Ben Spigel and Tara Vinodrai
Entrepreneurship & Regional Development, DOI: 10.1080/08985626.2020.1734262

Chapter 5
Degrees of integration: how a fragmented entrepreneurial ecosystem promotes different types of entrepreneurs
Katharina Scheidgen
Entrepreneurship & Regional Development, volume 33, issue 1-2 (2021) pp. 54–79

Chapter 6
The injection of resources by transnational entrepreneurs: towards a model of the early evolution of an entrepreneurial ecosystem
Aki Harima, Jan Harima and Jörg Freiling
Entrepreneurship & Regional Development, volume 33, issue 1-2 (2021) pp. 80–107

Chapter 7

Unhelpful help: The state of support programmes and the dynamics of entrepreneurship ecosystems in Ethiopia
Ashenafi Biru, David Gilbert and Pia Arenius
Entrepreneurship & Regional Development, volume 33, issue 1-2 (2021) pp. 108–130

For any permission-related enquiries please visit:
http://www.tandfonline.com/page/help/permissions

Notes on Contributors

Stephen B. Adams, Department of Management & Marketing, Franklin P. Perdue School of Business, Salisbury University, USA.

Pia Arenius, School of Management, RMIT University, Melbourne, Australia.

David Audretsch, School of Public and Environmental Affairs, Indiana University, Bloomington, USA.

Ashenafi Biru, School of Management, RMIT University, Melbourne, Australia.

Giulio Buciuni, Trinity Business School, Trinity College Dublin, Ireland.

Jörg Freiling, LEMEX, University of Bremen, Germany.

Majella Giblin, J.E. Cairnes School of Business & Economics, National University of Ireland, Galway, Ireland.

David Gilbert, Monash Business School, Monash University, Melbourne, Australia.

Aki Harima, LEMEX, University of Bremen, Germany.

Jan Harima, LEMEX, University of Bremen, Germany.

Dieter F. Kogler, School of Architecture, Planning & Environmental Policy, University College Dublin, Ireland.

Colin Mason, Adam Smith Business School, University of Glasgow, UK.

Morgan P. Miles, School of Management and Marketing, Charles Sturt University, Bathurst, Australia.

Allan O'Connor, School of Management' (now defunct) with 'UniSA Business', University of South Australia, Adelaide, Australia.

Paul Ryan, Trinity Business School, Trinity College Dublin, Ireland.

Katharina Scheidgen, Technische Universität Berlin, Department of Sociology, Sociology of Organization, Berlin, Germany.

Ben Spigel, University of Edinburgh Business School, United Kingdom.

Tara Vinodrai, Department of Geography and Planning, University of Toronto, Canada.

Time and the dynamics of entrepreneurial ecosystems

David Audretsch, Colin Mason, Morgan P. Miles and Allan O'Connor

ABSTRACT

In this article, we are primarily concerned with the influence and role of time on an entrepreneurial ecosystem (EE). Hence, the dynamics incorporated into the conception of the EE comes into focus. The recent work on this aspect has generally observed time as an evolutionary element for shaping and forming the context for entrepreneurial outcomes or that time is related to the change in entrepreneur and network profiles within a region. Other scholars have also noted how certain aspects of an EE will be affected by dimensions of size over time or that the profile of resources will alter the EE attractiveness for entrepreneurs. Time itself as a dynamic influence has not been explicitly examined and here we seek to draw out the multiple perceptions of time that influence the different rates of start-up, firm growth, change and evolution. We conclude by drawing attention to the simultaneous interaction of the different perceptions of time and outline the contributions to this Special Issue on the dynamics of the entrepreneurial ecosystem.

The fundamental impulse that sets and keeps the capitalist engine in motion comes from the new consumers' goods, the new methods of production or transportation, the new markets, the new forms of industrial organization that capitalist enterprise creates.

Schumpeter 1942, 72-73

Introduction

Building on the ecological concepts formulated by organizational theorists (see Hannan and Freeman 1977), the entrepreneurial ecosystem (EE) concept has been gaining prominence since at least the early nineteen-nineties. While the term EE is still considered relatively new (Spigel 2017; Shepherd 2015), the concept of an ecosystem is anything but novel. The economist Joseph Schumpeter, as quoted above, in building his case for the waves of change known as creative destruction, implicitly connects the enterprise to the dynamics among levels of analysis that produce new forms of industrial organization acting as a fuel for the capitalist engine.

One of the earliest and more explicit references to an ecological perspective of entrepreneurship can be found with Aldrich (1990), who, in an interdisciplinary forum, offered the ecological perspective as an alternate way to consider the 'rates' of business founding occurring within a given environment. When borrowed, adapted, and applied to entrepreneurship, Aldrich argued that an ecological conception of entrepreneurship, when viewed as business founding, gave focus to the dynamics, the ability to account for differing scales of social interactions, and the potential to produce new and interesting hypotheses. Since then, an increasing number of works have examined and categorized the contexts for entrepreneurship that span organizational, institutional, industrial, social, and regional forms of definition (Autio et al. 2014).

One of the glaring limitations of the extant literature is that entrepreneurial ecosystems have generally been analysed from a static perspective (Stam and van de Ven 2019; Bhawe and Zahra 2019). While a plethora of important insights have been garnered about the structure and interactions characterizing entrepreneurial ecosystems, little is known about how they develop and evolve over time. The purpose of this special issue is to address this striking gap in the literature by focusing on the dynamics of entrepreneurial ecosystems. The concept of entrepreneurial ecosystems (EEs) has emerged in recent years as a framework to understand the nature of places in which entrepreneurial activity flourishes. Spigel (2017, 50) defines entrepreneurial ecosystems as follows: 'combinations of social, political, economic, and cultural elements within a region that support the development and growth of innovative start-ups and encourage nascent entrepreneurs and other actors to take the risks of starting, funding, and otherwise assisting high-risk ventures'.

However, the existing literature has several shortcomings. Despite some progress (Acs et al. 2017b), the concept is under-theorized. While it is evident that the entrepreneur is central to an EE perspective, it remains unclear how entrepreneurial ecosystems bring about distinctive performances over time from other concepts that seek to explain the geographical concentration of entrepreneurial activity (e.g. clusters, learning regions, regional innovation systems). Much of the literature comprises 'superficial generalisations ... rather than rigorous social science research' (Stam and Spigel 2017, 408). Specifically, empirical studies are static rather than dynamic which does not capture the genesis and evolution of EEs (Mason and Brown 2014; Mack and Mayer 2016; Alvedalen and Boschma 2017). There is little consideration of the context in which entrepreneurial ecosystems emerge (Mack and Meyer 2016). The network of interactions of individual elements in the EEs has not been sufficiently explored (Motoyama and Watkins 2014). And the causal mechanisms are weak: it is not clear how the various elements in entrepreneurial ecosystems enhance entrepreneurship (Alvedalen and Boschma 2017; Stam and Spigel 2017).

In this special issue, we are primarily concerned with the dynamics of EEs, and therefore it follows that we need to take into account the influence and role of time. The recent work on this aspect has generally treated time as an evolutionary element for shaping and forming the EE (Autio et al. 2018). For instance, Thompson, Purdy, and Ventresca (2018) articulate the time-dependent pattern of ecosystem formation. Others have suggested that time is related to the change in entrepreneur and network profiles within a region, although the dynamics as such have not been explicitly examined (Cowell 2018). Some scholars have also noted how EEs are affected over time by increases in degrees of such things as intentions, coherence, and resources (Roundy, Bradshaw, and Brockman 2018). Furthermore, over time the changing sources and profile of resources (e.g., entrepreneurial knowledge, financial capital, mentors, etc.) will also alter the EE attractiveness for entrepreneurs (Mason, Cooper, and Harrison 2002; Spigel and Harrison 2018). Apart from the explicit reference to evolution of the EE, these various observations about time have not particularly examined and contextualized the specific effect of time as it intersects with the various levels of analysis.

Entrepreneurship is a multi-level phenomenon, and the EE can be considered as a composite construct that fits within an eclectic paradigm of entrepreneurship reflecting theories of behaviour, organization, and performance (Audretsch, Kuratko, and Link 2015). Through the behavioural lens, actors, being individuals with motivations and traits, and organizations with cultures and intent, each play a role in shaping the nature of the EE from the inside. Organizational theories of people, teams, and firms provide the relational and interactional understandings between these actors and how they transact entrepreneurship. To this we can add the institutional setting (Denzau and North 1994; North 1990; Scott 1987) that comprises the political, social, and legal formal and informal 'rules' that contribute to new venture creation, opportunity, support and legitimacy, shaping and influencing the mental models of actors (Lim et al. 2010). The organization does not occur isolated from the institutional settings found in places or contexts. Performance theories can only be exhibited over time through the objective outcomes of entrepreneurs and firms, typically measured as new firm formations, firm growth and/or innovation, and socio-economic contribution (Audretsch, Kuratko, and Link 2015). While multi-level understanding and methods of analysis are needed, we argue that an EE is not only a multi-level phenomenon but also a multi-temporal one whereby the levels themselves are subject to different perceptions of time horizons; historic, present and future. In contrast to the extant literature, we invited authors to examine more particularly the dynamics of the EE as it is influenced by time.

The extant EE literature tends to assume that time hosts entrepreneurial activity by actors. We adopt an alternate view, that time is an instrument of entrepreneurial actors and their activity that, over time, evolves the ecosystem. This alternate concept accepts that entrepreneurial activity is in the hands of entrepreneurial actors be they at micro, macro or meso levels. In this framing, time is a concept that works for and/or potentially against the entrepreneurial actor. The entrepreneurial actor will be both influenced by and influence time in the past, present and future. Time for the ecosystem is established by the pace of the actors rather than the pace of the ecosystem determining the time for entrepreneurial activity. The ecosystem is conceptually inert but representational of the actors and activities that give it life and dynamics. The EE does not have volution or action, but the actors have both, and the pace of their interactions determines the profile, the intensity, the rate of output, and, ultimately, the outcomes of the EE.

This is a major departure from previous conceptions of the EE, whereby the focus of an EE study has been on how the EE stimulates additional entrepreneurial activity. We suggest instead that entrepreneurial activity is the driver of the ecosystem, and this conception is consistent with Schumpeter's original framing of economic development (Schumpeter 1942). This does not debase the idea that entrepreneurial activity is important, but it places the outcomes of EE in the hands of the entrepreneurial actors and their interactivity (Harrison, Cooper, and Mason 2004). By default, actors are inside the ecosystem, and the entrepreneurial activity is not dependent on the ecosystem, but the EE is a framing of interdependent entrepreneurial activity. This conceptualization is consistent with the earlier views proposed by Van de Ven (1993, 211–212), who argued that individual entrepreneurs 'construct and change the industrial infra-structure' and that 'infrastructure does not emerge and change all at once by the actions of one or even a few key entrepreneurs. Instead, it emerges through the accretion of numerous institutional, resource, and proprietary events that co-produce each other over an extended period'. Entrepreneurship observed through the lens of an EE is not just about new firm creation, but holistically it is about the disruption and change of the ecosystem, and the primary concern is how actors may vary the pattern of interaction to alter the entrepreneurial outcomes.

The remainder of this paper includes the following sections. The next section undertakes a brief definitional analysis to make apparent the consistencies and contrasts that exist within various versions of the EE definition. This is followed by an exploration of related ecosystem concepts to draw out the distinctive attributes of the EE viewpoint. A discussion then ensues to articulate various approaches to defining what might be in or out of the analysis of the EE. It is proposed that temporal boundaries need to define the levels of analysis of the EE. We then present a conclusion that suggests EE research has strong relevance to 'how' and 'why' questions of entrepreneurship as they are relevant to place and time. In this way EE research is a tool of analysis rather than a field of research. When used as a tool, the variation of entrepreneurial dynamics comes into focus revealing the heterogeneity rather than the generalized and homogenized understanding of an EE that is invariably, although unintentionally, presumed to fit all. Lastly the papers in this issue are then introduced.

Time and dynamics in entrepreneurial ecosystems

The consideration of time in entrepreneurship spans a number of areas such as a focus on the entrepreneur and how they manage time and/or decisions (Lévesque, Minniti, and Shepherd 2009;

Miller and Sardais 2015; Slevin and Covin 1998), the influence of time on risk behaviour (Das and Teng 1997), how entrepreneurs allocate time in transitioning into a start-up (Lévesque and Maccrimmon 1998), and the temporal effects related to opportunity evaluation (Tumasjan, Welpe, and Spörrle 2013). For example, entrepreneurs need time to recover from failure, to make sense of the experience, deal with negative emotions and self-reflect (Byrne and Shepherd 2015). Time is also a primary concern in considerations of new venture start-up, survival, and growth reflected in studies of firm life cycles, stages, and phases (Churchill and Lewis 1983; Lichtenstein and Lyons 2008; Levie and Lichtenstein 2010). Time further features in the evolutionary perspective of entrepreneurship (Ahlstrom and Bruton 2010; Vanacker, Manigart, and Meuleman 2014; Hite 2005). However, while these perspectives deal with the dynamics imposed by time at different levels of analysis, little has been done in the EE domain to reconcile the multi-level implications of variations in time perspectives and the influence of such variations on entrepreneurship using the analytical lens of an EE. Indeed, the uncertainty of how to deal with time is raised when we consider the analysis of history – do we read it backwards – i.e. respondents explaining why they did what they did in the past, relying on retrospection, or do we read it forwards – either using contemporary documents or via series of longitudinal data collection exercises, to illustrate a trajectory. In either case the reliability and stability of findings must be questioned when time is taken into account (Mason and Harvey 2013).

Bygrave and Hofer once said of entrepreneurship research that 'good science starts with good definitions' (1991, 13). Examining a number of more recent definitions of EE (see Table 1), it can be seen that a time dimension is implied by terms such as 'dynamic', 'interact and influence', 'support and facilitation', 'that combine', 'coalesce to connect, mediate, and govern', 'heightened levels of entrepreneurial activity', 'new ventures form and dissolve over time', 'development and growth', and 'enable'. The often implicit inference is that the analysis of the activity and interactivity of the range

Table 1. Definitional approaches to an entrepreneurial ecosystem.

Author (alphabetical order)	Definition
Acs et al. (2017a, 479)	A National System of Entrepreneurship is the dynamic, institutionally embedded interaction between entrepreneurial attitudes, ability, and aspirations, by individuals, which drives the allocation of resources through the creation and operation of new ventures.
Audretsch and Belitski (2016)	We define systems of entrepreneurship (further ecosystem) as institutional and organizational as well as other systemic factors that interact and influence the identification and commercialization of entrepreneurial opportunities. Systems of entrepreneurship are geographically bounded ...
Cohen (2006, 3)	Sustainable entrepreneurial ecosystems are defined as an interconnected group of actors in a local geographic community committed to sustainable development through the support and facilitation of new sustainable ventures.
Isenberg (2010, 43)	The entrepreneurship ecosystem consists of a set of individual elements – such as leadership, culture, capital markets, and open-minded customers – that combine in complex ways.
Mason and Brown (2014, 5)	A set of interconnected entrepreneurial actors (both potential and existing), entrepreneurial organizations (e.g. firms, venture capitalists, business angels, banks), institutions (universities, public sector agencies, financial bodies) and entrepreneurial processes (e.g. the business birth rate, numbers of high growth firms, levels of 'blockbuster entrepreneurship', number of serial entrepreneurs, degree of sell-out mentality within firms and levels of entrepreneurial ambition) which formally and informally coalesce to connect, mediate and govern the performance within the local entrepreneurial environment.
Regele and Neck (2012, 25)	... the interaction of people, roles, infrastructure, organizations, and events creates an environment for heightened levels of entrepreneurial activity.
Roundy, Bradshaw, and Brockman (2018, 5)	Is a self-organized, adaptive, and geographically bounded community of complex agents operating at multiple, aggregated levels, whose non-linear interactions result in the patterns of activities through which new ventures form and dissolve over time?
Spigel (2017, 50)	Entrepreneurial ecosystems are combinations of social, political, economic, and cultural elements within a region that support the development and growth of innovative start-ups and encourage nascent entrepreneurs and other actors to take the risks of starting, funding, and otherwise assisting high-risk ventures.
Stam (2015, 1765)	The entrepreneurial ecosystem is a set of interdependent actors and factors coordinated in such a way that they enable productive entrepreneurship.

of entrepreneurial actors is undertaken across a window of time. Overall, while a number of these authors would likely argue that culture is shaped by history (Walsh and Winsor 2019), and hence the historic time perspective is tacitly included, the dimension of time is mostly implicit and mostly acknowledged as 'time' in the present as it influences business foundation activity, development, and growth. That is, time is considered as it unfolds and reveals the outputs that are observed by cross-sectional accounts of firm formation, entrepreneurial activity, and allocation of resources.

The definitions furthermore reveal a focus on a number of different outputs from an EE, including innovative start-ups (Spigel 2017), venture creation and growth (Isenberg 2010) or venture creation and operation (Acs et al. 2017a), or heightened entrepreneurial activity (Regele and Neck 2012) or, more particularly, new sustainable ventures (Cohen 2006). Roundy, Bradshaw, and Brockman (2018) go beyond the new venture formation to include firms that also dissolve. Audretsch and Belitski (2016) suggest the identification and commercialization of entrepreneurial opportunities, while Mason and Brown (2014) highlight entrepreneurial processes as an output. These conceptions suggest the importance of a cross-sectional view or snapshot of the outputs at a specific moment in time that can account for an EE.

Extending beyond outputs to outcomes draws attention to the inclusion of macroeconomic views of resource allocation (Acs et al. 2017a) or, more specifically, productive entrepreneurship (Stam 2015). Mason and Brown (2014), by contrast, assume the type of general performance as an outcome. Four of the nine definitions are silent on this aspect, presumably preferring to focus on the output. The specification and scope of outcome remains unclear, which further complicates the study of EEs. More importantly, for this article, the various outputs and outcomes are subject to variations in time, scope and scale which invariably all are occurring simultaneously. However, we find that the concept of time in its historical and future contexts has received less attention.

Exploring related ecological links

The concept of the EE borrows from a branch of the biological sciences that deals with the relations between organisms and their environment (Aldrich 1990). The first use of the term 'ecosystem' in a business context is often attributed to Moore (1993), who drew upon the term to explain business innovation in an article where he argued that businesses do not evolve as isolated entities but develop through interaction with suppliers, financiers, and customers. In this way, the *relational* view among the business entities is highlighted, drawing attention to industrial organization theories.

Also worth noting is that ecology has meaning and a derivative within the sociological sciences as a branch that deals specifically with human ecology being a 'consideration of the relations of individuals to their surroundings, their habits, and modes of life [that] include almost all aspects of what are now seen as *contextual effects*' (author added emphasis, Appold 2007, I-444). The ecological view, therefore, is not as foreign as may first appear as the EE refers to relations in a specific context and of a specific form that is reiteratively influencing and is influenced by the contextual effects.

These conceptions of the ecosystem also lend credence to the earlier observation that relational elements could be defined as factors and processes. Adopting the view of Aldrich (1990), three types of processes are highlighted. The first is between the actors and the historical context, and the second is between the various actors and organizations within the current situational context. Third, factors are also highlighted as institutional, and therefore these institutional factors combine as a composite to define a set of processes shaping the contextual setting. In Aldrich's view, the ecosystem becomes the combination of these three forms of processes that to various extents affect the resources available to new venturing in the defined region. These processes shape the historical context and 'experience' of entrepreneurship, the competitive and collaborative influences on resource availability, and the composite of institutional factors that influence the types and forms of new ventures created.

Around the same time as Aldrich's work, the application of an ecological perspective was also being applied to industrial and manufacturing process design, which became known as industrial ecology (Graedel 1994). Frosch and Gallopoulos (1989, 144) noted that

> "The industrial ecosystem would function as an analog of biological ecosystems. (Plants synthesize nutrients that feed herbivores, which in turn feed a chain of carnivores whose wastes and bodies eventually feed further generations of plants.) An ideal industrial ecosystem may never be attained in practice. But both manufacturers and consumers must change their habits to approach it more closely if the industrialized world is to maintain its standard of living – and the developing nations are to raise theirs to a similar level – without adversely affecting the environment."

It is interesting to also note that industrial ecology examines how economic systems work in concert with other surrounding systems (Graedel 1994). This view suggests that adopting an ecological perspective does not intend to isolate a single system as an ecosystem but looks at how a set of systems interact to optimize resource factors within that set of systems (O'Rourke, Connelly, and Koshland 1996). It may be particularly instructive to note these original salient points that the borrowing from biological ecology was considered a means to understand and improve socio-economic systems and that an ecosystem perspective is an interactive view of multiple systems that can lead to resource optimization (Autio et al. 2018).

The ecological perspective of ecosystems also alerts us to other distinct conceptualizations of the EE (McKenzie and Sud 2009). First, a perspective that assumes an ecosystem maintains equilibrium, although vulnerable to external shocks, gives grounds to the analysis of births, deaths and survival rates of firms and how various internal and external influences may control or impact the survival of a new firm 'species'. In this case, the 'species' is the new venture, and the analysis takes into account the forming and subsequent survival of young new ventures guided by the 'entrepreneurial' actor. For instance, at an extreme, the imposition of a communist government to socialize a market-based system could completely destroy (make extinct) the species of the private firm, making the EE analysis of new firm formation redundent.

McKenzie and Sud's (2009) alternate perspective is one of ecological succession or evolution that studies populations and how they change over time, what causes the demise of some and the emergence of new populations and how some transform, mutate, or migrate. An example in today's world would be the emergence of digital technology firms and the diminution of traditional manufacturing firms among advanced economies. 'Digital technology' and 'traditional manufacturing' can be seen as different firm populations. We can also readily observe that digital and physical products and services differ in time dimensions in terms of rate of development, distribution time and the pace of customer experiences.

In brief, this exploration of the foundational concepts reveals that ecosystems are concerned with interacting systems and can be viewed through alternate perspectives that are consistent with alternate conceptualizations of entrepreneurship. The first perspective brings into focus the rates of business founding as the objective with a primary focus on the influence of the EE on firm birth rates. This view suggests that EE research is concerned with the systemic relational and institutional influences on new venture births as an indicator of entrepreneurship as a collective 'species.' A researcher working from this perspective may be concerned with the proliferation of new ventures and therefore we label this first concern of EE research entrepreneurial proliferation. The historic time that sets the pattern of firm formation along with the influence in the present combine to deliver the rate of new venture formations.

A second perspective suggests that EE may be conceptualized as the preservation of the new venture through 'healthy' creation, survival, continuity, and/or growth. This view, accepting the unit of analysis and object of study as the new firm, seeks to account for entrepreneurship as more than firm creation; it also encompasses how new firms survive and grow within a set of systemic relations. In brief, then, a researcher concerned with the influences on new venture survival beyond start-up will need to take longitudinal influences into account and examine the various effects on a new venture experienced over time until it becomes a firmly established trading entity. This second perspective of an EE we label entrepreneurial survival.

The third perspective is concerned with new venture creation that influences equilibrium and disequilibrium forces among markets and business populations, causing change and evolution, seeing the demise of some business populations and the emergence of new ones (Mason and Harrison 2006). This third viewpoint follows a structural level of analysis acknowledging the duality and reciprocity of the new firm and structural influences relative to new firms. The unit of analysis and object of study is the various categories of system interactions that influence the evolution of types and scope of firm populations. We call this third perspective entrepreneurial evolution. Time dimensions are further extended to examine the historical, to present, to future continuum with the entrepreneurial firm being either the disruptor or driver of, respectively, the established or new market equilibrium.

Distinctions in time

By examining the roots of the ecological conceptions of entrepreneurship, it is apparent that different views of time emerge; that is, the 'what' or the unit of analysis differs, which in turn imposes a different sense of time. Returning to our sample of definitions these multi-time dimensional views can also readily be observed. For instance, eight of the nine definitions make specific reference to firm creation either explicitly through terms such as creating, starting, or forming a new venture or implicitly through the reference to entrepreneurial activities, processes, or commercializing opportunities. This frames time around the individual entrepreneur and the process of firm formation. Five of the eight definitions refer to sustaining the new venture through terms such as growth, operation, sustainable, supporting development, or, perhaps ambiguously, through concerns with firms that dissolve. The unit of analysis, therefore shifts to the firm and time as relevant to the firm's survival and growth. In four of the nine definitional examples there seems to be yet longer-term or broader concerns although perhaps less explicitly stated. These views can be observed through references to outcomes of sustainable development, productive entrepreneurship, allocation of resources, and innovative start-ups. Each of these terms reveals a concern with the broader state of the economy or community resources or the disruptiveness and growth of innovative firms that may influence socioeconomic status quo. Time in this broader community sense follows patterns of evolution in time frames broader again.

EE analysis, therefore, is not only a static cross-sectional 'snapshot' account of the start-up community actors and inter-relationships with interests in the start of new ventures (the proliferation or birth rate of new ventures) in a specific point in time. Although this information is important, it does not account for the more inclusive influences that are responsible for the births and deaths or demise of entrepreneurial ventures or the rates of business survival and growth over sustained time periods. Furthermore, the interests of an EE analysis may also focus on how entrepreneurial actors acquire and generate different attributes that manifest as industrial evolution (phylogeny or the evolution and branching of species in ecological terms). This is represented in our definitional samples by interests in the environmentally sustainable ventures of Cohen (2006) or the innovative ventures of Spigel (2017), both specific types of ventures. This focus on types of ventures can be further extended to specific industry identifications, for example, digital, defence, creative, or manufacturing. In these interests the EE analysis narrows to the specific types of new ventures and tends, therefore, to look at evolutionary perspectives of the EE, considering the emergence and demise of different sub-species among the general species of new ventures. These sub-species may affect and influence the larger social and economic systems and evolution of our human societies and communities.

It should not be ignored that all three perspectives – proliferation, survival, and evolution – are acting concurrently and new venture founding, or start-up, is insufficient as a measure for any defined geo-socio-political performance. We must have evidence of new ventures (and the form of these is a point for further discussion beyond the scope of this article) in an EE, but they also must survive and grow after founding (Brown and Mason 2017). Stam (2015) goes one step further, describing the new ventures as outputs of an EE and new value created as outcomes, thus signalling the evolutionary interests. Hence, for analysis purposes, there are three specific time horizons that one may specify in researching an EE. The first is the formational time involved in business founding that examines the historical and contextual influences on new venture births (Aldrich 1990); the proliferation of new ventures. The second perspective focus is on longer periods of time to allow for new venture survival and growth that addresses, for instance, the sufficiency of resources to sustain new ventures through their initial cycle of development (Brown and Mason 2017). While the third perspective is that the longer-term evolutionary time phase of the ecosystem itself traces the development and demise of species as may be accounted for in terms of economic transitions through industry sectors (Auerswald and Dani 2017); for example, agrarian to industrial or manu-facturing to knowledge economies; the evolutionary effect of new and growing firms. Evolutionary perspectives are important as the over-reliance of a region on one particular industry has the effect of stifling diversification, hence the region then lacks the resilience to adapt when a dominant industry declines. This situation has been superbly exemplified for Glasgow by Checkland (1976). Figure 1 isolates the EE and depicts the three temporal boundary specifications that may distinguish the three distinct perspectives that may be relevant to EE analysis.

Discussion

The extant research has generally focused on EEs as distinct and as an alternative to or substitute for the more established and familiar ecosystems, such as the regional system of innovation. By contrast, this paper considers the EE as a complementary and interactive concept. Perhaps oddly from a systems perspective, in trying to understand the concept, its analysis, why it is important, and how it can be applied, it has been necessary to de-construct the EE into time dependent conceptual pieces. In doing so it is not intended to convey that the EE concept can be analysed particularly well through the lens of only one of its conceptual pieces. Ecosystems of any form operate as a set of systems, each being deeply embedded within supra-systems and dependent to some extent on sub-systems and related systems. In this article, an attempt has been made to draw out the layers of systemic effects and show the inter-relationships between the layers of time within the ecosystem analysis.

To illustrate, if the analysis of the EE intends to target the rate of start-ups in a defined boundary space, then one would need to consider that the start-up rates are affected and perhaps dependent upon other sub, supra, or related systems. For instance, these could be the institutional effects such as the education system or the banking and finance system or the entrepreneurial support system. The rate of founding itself, if it is to be understood in a system sense, is not simply a count of firm births, but it is an account of the historic and present systemic influences on firm births or the 'species' called new firms. The conceptual development undertaken in this introductory paper to this Special Issue illustrates however that a focus on the counts of new firms is based on a very limited understanding of the scope of an EE.

It is also essential to state that the temporal boundaries of an EE analysis are fuzzy, and this is largely unavoidable. For example the truncated idea to new business formation analysis at the decision level of business founding may not detect the multiple influences on the new venture idea but instead may focus on access to networks, family experience, financial accessibility, and available support infrastructures such as local incubators. This may overlook the influence of either the university or business sectors on a broader temporal scale. The decisions taken by the limited view of the ecosystem analysis can suppress identification of influences. A decision to change either the geo-socio-political or time boundary conditions would add new information. In turn, the degree of complexity of the business founding analysis increases with the broader time span identifying the

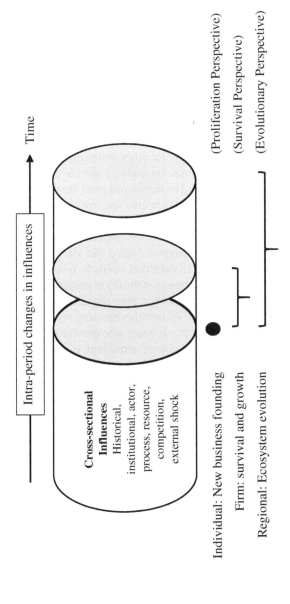

Figure 1. The three temporal perspectives of an entrepreneurial ecosystem.

influences on the idea that shaped the new venture creation and hence introducing more influencers over the time span of analysis.

To comprehend the entire EE, a layered analysis anchored on each specific time perspective described here, to first distinctly and then to overlay the influences identified to eliminate duplication and note the variation of the influence over time, is required. To address the evolutionary case, the surrounding knowledge and business ecosystems need to be accounted for through other institutional and organizational influences. Lastly, depending on the industry level specification the related ecosystems that intersect with the EE – whether that be the health care ecosystem for a biomedical start-up or the effects of the education ecosystem on skilled labour for robotics manufacturing or the transport and logistics ecosystem for food processing industries – all need to be considered – the broader the specification parameters, the more complex the system and its analysis.

Conclusion

While research on EEs is relatively new and replete with a plethora of views and definitions of what actually constitutes a bona fide EE, a common trait of extant research is the attempt to differentiate the EE concept as an alternative to or substitute for other more conventional and established system concepts, such as regional innovation systems. Reviewing a sample of past definitions revealed the diversity of views on what constitutes an EE. The definitions were conflicted on the unit of analysis as to whether the entrepreneurial actor, the new firm creation, the early-stage start-up, and growth or the socioeconomic system was the focus of the analysis. There were observable variations in boundaries and purpose. These differing perspectives impede the empirical development of the concept. Hence this paper examined the ecological origins and identified three temporal variations that have been embedded in the research to date that needs to be reconciled in an EE analysis.

Entrepreneurship is a concept that has inherent difficulty in empirical analysis. Over the years, the field has flip-flopped over whether the entrepreneur, their organization, the process of new venture creation, or whether opportunity is centric to entrepreneurship research. The rise of an EE view amplifies this uncertainty making it difficult to pin down who or what is influenced and is influencing in an EE research design. This article sets out an argument that suggests an EE has multiple conceptualizations, including the act and process of new venture creation, the subsequent survival, and growth of new ventures and the impact these new ventures have on the socioeconomic evolution. Moreover and importantly for this Special Issue, we contend that the dynamics among these place and time dependent layers mean that there is no basis for a 'one size fits all' approach to an EE.

EE research, therefore, needs to account for conflicts in influence that vary in and over time and is essentially a tool or framework of analysis that examines the entrepreneurial effects across time and levels. This is the polyrhythm effect whereby within an EE, the pace of entrepreneurship in proliferation, survival, and evolution are occurring simultaneously but differently, creating cross-variation in rhythm each affected by the other. In this article we have considered that the analysis is concerned with the relatively cross-sectional substantiation of new venture creation, the longer view of survival and growth of new ventures, or the generational time view to account for industry transitions and transformations.

Gartner (1988) proposed that the 'who is an entrepreneur' question should be replaced with questions about what entrepreneurs do embracing the behavioural research design. Shane and Venkataraman (2000) shifted the emphasis towards the opportunity space in entrepreneurship. This has ultimately led entrepreneurship research full circle back towards its origin in economic interests (Minniti and Lévesque 2008) to an appreciation that it is 'an important mechanism to explain the outcome of economic systems' (Acs et al. 2017b, 2). In other words, the questions that EE research brings into focus are both 'how' and 'why' questions. Grappling with the 'how' question means acknowledging that entrepreneurship, as new venture creation, is influenced by factors beyond any particular entrepreneur, notwithstanding that the entrepreneur is a central character. But more importantly, coming to grips with the 'why' question means dealing with the fundamental alignment of perhaps the more neglected side of Shane and Venkataraman's (2000) definition of entrepreneurship research to ask, with what effect? This special issue and its conceptual framework of EEs offer researchers a useful way to conceptualize alignment between the entrepreneur, time, and the ultimate socioeconomic effect.

Special issue papers

To shed light on the relatively unexplored area of entrepreneurship ecosystem dynamics, the papers included in the special issue provide new approaches to analysing and thinking about how entrepreneurial ecosystems develop and evolve over time. In 'From orchards to chips: Silicon valley's evolving Entrepreneurial ecosystem' Stephen B. Adams examines how entrepreneurial ecosystems evolve and adapt over time to the changing needs of industry. He reminds us that the region that is now known as Silicon Valley has long established roots. By the 1960s – well before scholars first started to write about the region – it was already a leading high technology region based around electronics and telecommunications that was supported by an existing ecosystem of institutions – which was more geographically extensive than the contemporary ecosystem – and by the repurposing of capital from previous industrial activity. This paper reveals the evolutionary perspective of EE dynamics.

Paul Ryan, Majella Giblin, Giulio Buciuni and Dieter F. Kogler examine the role of multinational enterprise (MNE) subsidiaries in the genesis and evolution of entrepreneurial ecosystems. Their longitudinal study of Galway in the Republic of Ireland shows how two MNE subsidiaries specializing in medical devices that located in the region several decades ago, attracted by government financial incentives, have evolved from manufacturing plants into advanced R&D centres of excellence. This shift to higher value-added and knowledge-based activities has led to them becoming catalysts for the emergence of an entrepreneurial ecosystem as employees have drawn upon the market and technical knowledge that they accrued while working in the companies to start new 'born global' ventures, initially in related technologies but subsequently in unrelated technologies. Some of these firms have become incubators for further business formation. The authors argue that the resulting technological heterogeneity has produced a more resilient entrepreneurial ecosystem. The framing of this paper illustrates how the analysis over time is necessary to uncover the roles and influences of elements within an EE on its evolution.

The paper by Ben Spigel and Tara Vinodra offers novel insights into the process of entrepreneurial recycling as a stimulus for business creation. By analyzing the career paths and transistions of the human capital dimension of the Waterloo, Canada entrepreneurial ecosystem this study explores the temporal dynamics of entrepreneurial recycling on the development of an EE through the lens of the Blackberry's former employees. Prior to 2008 the Waterloo EE was driven primarily by Blackberry which, similar to Fairchild's role in the development of Silcon Valley (Agarwal, Audretsch, and Sarkar 2007), was the anchor that developed the Waterloo EE. The paper deals more specifically with the interplay effects of firm demise and creation when longer time periods are drawn into the analysis.

In Degrees of integration: How a fragmented entrepreneurial ecosystem promotes different types of entrepreneurs Katharina Scheidgen challenges the view that entrepreneurial ecosystems are necessarily highly integrated, suggesting that they may, in fact, be fragmented. Focusing on how entrepreneurs make use of the entrepreneurial ecosystem to acquire resources, her study of Berlin identifies that its entrepreneurial ecosystem comprises two sub-systems comprising different types of entrepreneurs who have different resourcing practices. The paper exposes the multiple system effects that simultaneously occur within an EE to influence its development over time.

The final two papers each focuses on the role of government programmnes to support the emergence and growth of entepreneurial ecosystems. They each show how institutional interventions shape and influence the EE leaving residual effects that either positively or negatively influence EE productivity with respect to new firm creation, survival, growth and entrepreneurial evolution. Aki Harima, Jan Harima, and Jörg Freiling investigate how a region without a rich resource base – 'fertile soil' (Mason and Brown 2014) – can use the injection of external resources, specifically transnational entrepreneurs, to facilitate the emergence and growth of entrepreneurial ecosystems. The paper looks at the case of Start Up Chile – a government programme that attracts transnational entrepreneurs – albeit often on a temporary basis – with incentives to create an ecosystem. They identify several positive impacts: a change in the Chilean perception towards entrepreneurship, creating an entrepreneurial culture, stronger entrepreneur mindsets, the elevation of the social status and image of entrepreneurs, strengthened interactions and the emergence of autonomous networks, and building regional confidence, all of which increase the legitimacy of the local entrepreneurial ecosystem. However, the downside of the over-reliance on policy instruments to achieve these outcomes has created a dependency relationship which has prevented the region from transforming into a self-sustaining and resilient entrepreneurial ecosystem.

Finally, Ashenafi Biru, David Gilbert and Pia Arenius, in 'Unhelpful help: The state of support programs and the dynamics of entrepreneurship ecosystems in Ethiopia' provides insights into the interrelationship of entrepreneurship support programmes and the development of EEs in a developing economy. Their analysis focuses on how the structure and implementation of entrepreneurship support programmes in Ethiopia influence firm behaviour within the context of an ecosystem. In particular, they find that entrepreneurship support programmes that do not prioritize innovative and competitive firms when distributing resources actually deter entrepreneurial behaviour and impede the development of the entrepreneurial ecosystem.

Time is fundamental to the analysis of the dynamics of an EE. New firm creation, survival, growth and demise all occur within a temporal context. Systems approaches invariably model the influential effects of the actors and elements that shape, re-shape, maintain, shift and change the system itself. An EE point of view therefore is inherently time dependent and provides an analytical framework that reveals how the number and diversity of entrepreneurial actors situated in a place and time influence the creation of new firms, their survival, growth, and ultimately the equilibrium dynamics of markets and industry. Whether for better or worse, the historic and present time dimensions underpin the trajectory of and future of EE performances regardless of how they are measured.

Disclosure statement

No potential conflict of interest was reported by the authors.

References

Acs, Z., D. Audretsch, E. Lehmann, and G. Licht. 2017a. "National Systems of Innovation." *The Journal of Technology Transfer* 42 (5): 997–1008. doi:10.1007/s10961-016-9481-8.

Acs, Z., E. Stam, D. Audretsch, and A. O'Connor. 2017b. "The Lineages of the Entrepreneurial Ecosystem Approach." *Small Business Economics* 49 (1): 1–10. doi:10.1007/s11187-017-9864-8.

Agarwal, R., D. Audretsch, and M. B. Sarkar. 2007. "The Process of Creative Construction: Knowledge Spillovers, Entrepreneurship, and Economic Growth." *Strategic Entrepreneurship Journal* 1 (3-4): 263–286. doi:10.1002/sej.36.

Ahlstrom, D., and G. D. Bruton. 2010. "Rapid Institutional Shifts and the Co-evolution of Entrepreneurial Firms in Transition Economies." *Entrepreneurship Theory and Practice* 34 (3): 531–554. doi:10.1111/etap.2010.34.issue-3.

Aldrich, H. E. 1990. "Using an Ecological Perspective to Study Organizational Founding Rates." *Entrepreneurship Theory and Practice* 14 (3): 7–24. doi:10.1177/104225879001400303.

Alvedalen, J., and R. Boschma. 2017. "A Critical Review of Entrepreneurial Ecosystems Research: Towards A Future Research Agenda." *European Planning Studies* 25 (6): 887–903. doi:10.1080/09654313.2017.1299694.

Appold, S. J. 2007. "Human Ecology." In *21st Century Sociology*, edited by C. D. Bryant and D. L. Peck, I-444-I-454. Thousand Oaks: SAGE Publications, Inc. doi:10.4135/9781412939645.n45.

Audretsch, D. B., and M. Belitski. 2016. "Entrepreneurial Ecosystems in Cities: Establishing the Framework Conditions." *Journal of Technology Transfer*. (accessed December 2016). doi:10.1007/s10961-016-9473-8.

Audretsch, D. B., D. F. Kuratko, and A. N. Link. 2015. "Making Sense of the Elusive Paradigm of Entrepreneurship." *Small Business Economics* 45: 703–712. doi:10.1007/s11187-015-9663z.

Auerswald, P. E., and L. Dani. 2017. "The Adaptive Lifecycle of Entrepreneurial Ecosystems: The Biotechnology Cluster." *Small Business Economics* 49: 97–117. doi:10.1007/s11187-017-9869-3.

Autio, E., M. Kenney, P. Mustar, D. Siegele, and M. Wright. 2014. "Entrepreneurial Innovation: The Importance of Context." *Research Policy* 43: 1097–1108. doi:10.1016/j.respol.2014.01.015.

Autio, E., S. Nambisan, L. D. W. Thomas, and M. Wright. 2018. "Digital Affordances, Spatial Affordances, and the Genesis of Entrepreneurial Ecosystems." *Strategic Entrepreneurship Journal* 12 (1): 72–95. doi:10.1002/sej.1266.

Bhawe, N., and S. A. Zahra. 2019. "Inducing Heterogeneity in Local Entrepreneurial Ecosystems: The Role of MNEs." *Small Business Economics* 52: 437–454. doi:10.1007/s11187-017-9954-7.

Brown, R., and C. Mason. 2017. "Looking inside the Spiky Bits: A Critical Review and Conceptualisation of Entrepreneurial Ecosystems." *Small Business Economics* 49 (1): 11–30. doi:10.1007/s11187-017-9865-7.

Bygrave, W. D., and C. W. Hofer. 1991. "Theorizing about Entrepreneurship." *Entrepreneurship Theory and Practice* 16 (2): 13–22. doi:10.1177/104225879201600203.

Byrne, O., and D. A. Shepherd. 2015. "Different Strokes for Different Folks: Entrepreneurial Narratives of Emotion, Cognition, and Making Sense of Business Failure." *Entrepreneurship Theory and Practice* 39 (2): 375–405. doi:10.1111/etap.12046.

Checkland, S. 1976. *The Upas Tree, Glasgow, 1875–1975: A Study in Growth and Contraction*. Glasgow: University of Glasgow Press.

Churchill, N. C., and V. L. Lewis. 1983. "The Five Stages of Small Business Growth." *Harvard Business Review* 61 (3): 30–50.

Cohen, B. 2006. "Sustainable Valley Entrepreneurial Ecosystems." *Business Strategy and the Environment* 15 (1): 1–14. doi:10.1002/()1099-0836.

Cowell, F. 2018. *Microeconomics: Principles and Analysis*. Oxford University Press.

Das, T. K., and B. S. Teng. 1997. "Sustaining Strategic Alliances: Options and Guidelines." *Journal of General Management* 22 (4): 49–64. doi:10.1177/030630709702200404.

Denzau, A. T., and D. C. North. 1994. "Shared Mental Models: Ideologies and Institutions." *Kyklos* 47 (1): 3–31. doi:10.1111/kykl.1994.47.issue-1.

Frosch, R., and N. Gallopoulos. 1989. "Strategies for Manufacturing." *Scientific American*, Sep 144–152. doi:10.1038/scientificamerican0989-144.

Gartner, W. B. 1988. "'Who Is an Entrepreneur?' Is the Wrong Question." *American Journal of Small Business* 12 (4): 11–32. doi:10.1177/104225878801200401.

Graedel, T. 1994. "Industrial Ecology: Definition and Implementation." In *Industrial Ecology and Global Change*, edited by R. Socolow, C. Andrews, F. Berkhout, and V. Thomas, 23–42. Cambridge, UK: Cambridge University Press.

Hannan, M. T., and F. Freeman. 1977. "The Population Ecology of Organizations." *American Journal of Sociology* 82 (5): 929–964. doi:10.1086/226424.

Harrison, R. T., S. Y. Cooper, and C. M. Mason. 2004. "Entrepreneurial Activity and the Dynamics of Technology-based Cluster Development: The Case of Ottawa." *Urban Studies* 41 (5–6): 1045–1070. doi:10.1080/00420980410001675841.

Hite, J. M. 2005. "Evolutionary Processes and Paths of Relationally Embedded Network Ties in Emerging Entrepreneurial Firms." *Entrepreneurship Theory and Practice* 29 (1): 113–144. doi:10.1111/etap.2005.29.issue-1.

Isenberg, D. 2010. "How to Start an Entrepreneurial Revolution." *Harvard Business Review*, June 41–50.

Lévesque, M., and K. R. Maccrimmon. 1998. "On the Interaction of Time and Money Invested in New Ventures." *Entrepreneurship Theory and Practice* 22 (2): 89–110. doi:10.1177/104225879802200207.

Lévesque, M., M. Minniti, and D. Shepherd. 2009. "Entrepreneurs' Decisions on Timing of Entry: Learning from Participation and from the Experiences of Others." *Entrepreneurship Theory and Practice* 33 (2): 547–570. doi:10.1111/etap.2009.33.issue-2.

Levie, J., and B. B. Lichtenstein. 2010. "A Terminal Assessment of Stages Theory: Introducing A Dynamic States Approach to Entrepreneurship." *Entrepreneurship Theory and Practice* 34 (2): 317–350. doi:10.1111/()1540-6520.

Lichtenstein, G. A., and T. S. Lyons. 2008. "Revisiting the Business Life-cycle: Proposing an Actionable Model for Assessing and Fostering Entrepreneurship." *The International Journal of Entrepreneurship and Innovation* 9 (4): 241–250. doi:10.5367/000000008786208759.

Lim, D. S., E. A. Morse, R. K. Mitchell, and K. K. Seawright. 2010. "Institutional Environment and Entrepreneurial Cognitions: A Comparative Business Systems Perspective." *Entrepreneurship Theory and Practice* 34 (3): 491–516. doi:10.1111/j.1540-6520.2010.00384.x.

Mack, E., and H. Meyer. 2016. "The Evolutionary Dynamics of Entrepreneurial Ecosystems." *Urban Studies* 53 (10): 2118–2133. doi:10.1177/0042098015586547.

Mason, C., and R. Brown. 2014. "Entrepreneurial Ecosystems and Growth Oriented Entrepreneurship." *Final Report to OECD*. Paris. Accessed May 2015. http://lib.davender.com/wp-content/uploads/2015/03/Entrepreneurial-ecosystems-OECD.pdf

Mason, C., and C. Harvey. 2013. "Entrepreneurship: Contexts, Opportunities, and Processes." *Business History* 55: 1–8. doi:10.1080/00076791.2012.687542.

Mason, C. M., S. Y. Cooper, and R. T. Harrison. 2002. "Venture Capital in High Technology Clusters: The Case of Ottawa." In *New Technology Based Firms in the New Millennium*, edited by R. Oakey, W. During, and S. Kauser, 261–278. Oxford: Pergammon.

Mason, C. M., and R. T. Harrison. 2006. "After the Exit: Acquisitions, Entrepreneurial Recycling, and Regional Economic Development." *Regional Studies* 40 (1): 55–73. doi:10.1080/00343400500450059.

McKenzie, B. M., and M. Sud. 2009. "Prolegomena to a New Ecological Perspective in Entrepreneurship." *Academy of Entrepreneurship Journal* 15 (1): 43–60.

Miller, D., and C. Sardais. 2015. "Bifurcating Time: How Entrepreneurs Reconcile the Paradoxical Demands of the Job." *Entrepreneurship Theory and Practice* 39 (3): 489–512. doi:10.1111/etap.2015.39.issue-3.

Minniti, M., and M. Lévesque. 2008. "Recent Developments in the Economics of Entrepreneurship." *Journal of Business Venturing* 23: 603–612. doi:10.1016/j.jbusvent.2008.01.001.

Moore, J. 1993. "Predators and Prey: A New Ecology of Competition." *Harvard Business Review* 71 (3): 75–86.

Motoyama, Y., and K. K. Watkins. 2014. *Examining the Connections within the Startup Ecosystem: A Case Study of St. Louis*. Kauffman Foundation Research Series on City: Metro, and Regional Entrepreneurship.

North, D. C. 1990. *Institutions, Institutional Change, and Economic Performance*. Cambridge, UK: Cambridge University Press.

O'Rourke, D., L. Connelly, and C. P. Koshland. 1996. "Industrial Ecology: A Critical Review." *International Journal of Environment and Pollution* 6 (2/3): 89–112.

Regele, M. D., and H. M. Neck. 2012. "The Entrepreneurship Education Sub-ecosystem in the United States: Opportunities to Increase the Entrepreneurial Activity." *Journal of Business and Entrepreneurship Winter* 23 (2): 25–47.

Roundy, P. T., M. Bradshaw, and B. K. Brockman. 2018. "The Emergence of Entrepreneurial Ecosystems: A Complex Adaptive Systems Approach." *Journal of Business Research* 86: 1–10. doi:10.1016/j.jbusres.2018.01.032.

Schumpeter, J. A. 1942. *Capitalism, Socialism, and Democracy*. New York: Harper & Brothers.

Scott, W. R. 1987. "The Adolescence of Institutional Theory." *Administrative Science Quarterly* 32: 493–511. doi:10.2307/2392880.

Shane, S., and S. Venkataraman. 2000. "The Promise of Entrepreneurship as a Field of Research." *The Academy of Management Review* 25 (1): 217–226.

Shepherd, D. A. 2015. "Party On! A Call for Entrepreneurship Research that Is More Interactive, Activity Based, Cognitively Hot, Compassionate, and Prosocial." *Journal of Business Venturing* 30 (4): 489–507. doi:10.1016/j.jbusvent.2015.02.001.

Slevin, D. P., and J. G. Covin. 1998. "Time, Growth, Complexity, and Transitions: Entrepreneurial Challenges for the Future." *Entrepreneurship Theory and Practice* 22 (2): 53–68. doi:10.1177/104225879802200205.

Spigel, B. 2017. "The Relational Organization of Entrepreneurial Ecosystems." *Entrepreneurship Theory and Practice* 41 (1): 49–72. doi:10.1111/etap.12167.

Spigel, B., and R. Harrison. 2018. "Toward a Process Theory of Entrepreneurial Ecosystems." *Strategic Entrepreneurship Journal* 12 (1): 151–168. doi:10.1002/sej.2018.12.issue-1.

Stam, E. 2015. "Entrepreneurial Ecosystems and Regional Policy; A Sympathetic Critique." *European Planning Studies* 23 (9): 1759–1769. doi:10.1080/09654313.2015.1061484.

Stam, E., and B. Spigel. 2017. "Entrepreneurial Ecosystems and Regional Policy." In *SAGE Handbook for Entrepreneurship and Small Business*, edited by R. Blackburn, D. de Clercq, J. Heinoen, and Z. Wang, 407–422. Thousand Oaks, CA: SAGE Publications.

Stam, E., and H. van de Ven. 2019. "Entrepreneurial Ecosystem Elements." *Small Business Economics*. doi:10.1007/s11187-019-00270-6.

Thompson, T. A., J. M. Purdy, and M. J. Ventresca. 2018. "How Entrepreneurial Ecosystems Take Form: Evidence from Social Impact Initiatives in Seattle." *Strategic Entrepreneurship Journal* 12 (1): 96–116. doi:10.1002/sej.2018.12.issue-1.

Tumasjan, A., I. Welpe, and M. Spörrle. 2013. "Easy Now, Desirable Later: The Moderating Role of Temporal Distance in Opportunity Evaluation and Exploitation." *Entrepreneurship Theory and Practice* 37 (4): 859–888. doi:10.1111/etap.2013.37.issue-4.

Van de Ven, H. 1993. "The Development of an Infrastructure for Entrepreneurship." *Journal of Business Venturing* 8 (3): 211–230. doi:10.1016/0883-9026(93)90028-4.

Vanacker, T., S. Manigart, and M. Meuleman. 2014. "Path-dependent Evolution versus Intentional Management of Investment Ties in Science-based Entrepreneurial Firms." *Entrepreneurship Theory and Practice* 38 (3): 671–690. doi:10.1111/etap.2014.38.issue-3.

Walsh, J., and B. Winsor. 2019. "Socio-cultural Barriers to Developing a Regional Entrepreneurial Ecosystem." *Journal of Enterprising Communities: People and Places in the Global Economy* 13 (3): 263–282. doi:10.1108/JEC-11-2018-0088.

From orchards to chips: Silicon Valley's evolving entrepreneurial ecosystem

Stephen B. Adams

ABSTRACT

The initial development of Silicon Valley and its indigenous start-ups relied on various endowments, including abundant resources and a set of institutions and know-how inherited from previous industrial activity. This article identifies the entrepreneurial ecosystem that supported key tech start-ups on the San Francisco Peninsula prior to the 1960s, shows how the ecosystem developed and how it evolved. By 1940, a far-flung ecosystem—from Santa Clara County to San Francisco to Washington, DC – was in place, well before the arrival of the Valley's first venture capitalists in 1959 and the establishment of the region's first high-tech law firm in 1961. Federal agencies and laws provided revenue and risk reduction. Local universities provided brainpower. San Francisco-based banks and their Peninsula branches provided financing. San Francisco law firms drafted organizational agreements and protected intellectual property. Without such institutional support, there would be no Silicon Valley as we know it. Silicon Valley's early high-tech start-ups were supported by an ecosystem that was developed for the agriculture, extractive, and trans-portation industries. That ecosystem was repurposed for defence-based electronics and telecommunications, and then transformed for the con-sumer world of calculators, video games and personal computers. The "master cluster" benefitted from being in the right place at the right time, and by inheriting the right ecosystem.

Introduction

In 1958, the Palo Alto Chamber of Commerce counted more than 120 tech firms in the two counties (San Mateo and Santa Clara) just south of San Francisco that would constitute the heart of Silicon Valley.(Gillmor 2004, 328; Saxenian 1994, xii) This was the year before the establishment of the region's first venture capital firm, and three years before the inception of the Palo Alto law practice that would become the largest tech law firm in the world. In the latter part of the 20th century, venture capital firms and law firms devoted to helping tech firms became standard features of entrepreneurial, high-tech regions. Yet without the benefit of either local venture capital or tech law firms, a cluster of electronics and telecommunications firms developed on the San Francisco Peninsula worthy of state visits by Soviet premier Nikita Khrushchev in 1959 and French president Charles De Gaulle in 1960. (Findlay 1992, 192) Before the local arrival of venture capitalists and high-tech law firms, what was the nature of the Valley's entrepreneurial ecosystem and how did it come to be?

Central aspects of Silicon Valley's entrepreneurial ecosystem, which scholars first wrote about in the 1980s and 1990s, have been sufficiently spatially concentrated to convey an impression of the Valley as a self-sufficient entity. (Braun and McDonald 1982; Hanson 1982; Rogers and Larsen 1984; Malone 1985; Leslie 1993; Saxenian 1994) That spatial concentration and appearance of self-sufficiency has shaped the nature of questions asked about the Valley, resulting in limited emphasis on the role of external factors in the region's development.

Yet the mid-1980s was a distinctive time in the Valley's history. Firms in semiconductors and other industries were increasingly dispersing their manufacturing around the globe. Most of the region's tech enterprise involved commercial and consumer products (in sharp contrast to the period before 1960). Most of the region's high-tech employees worked for firms headquartered in the Valley, as opposed to the 1960s and much of the 1970s, when a majority worked at branches of firms based elsewhere. (Adams 2011a) By 1985, much of the region's venture capital and legal capabilities were close at hand but had been based in the Valley for little over a decade. Once there, venture capital firms adopted what Josh Lerner terms a 'parochial view,' which means 'wishing only to invest in firms within a few miles of their office' (Lerner 2009, 28). The self-contained portrayal from the 1980s would shape accounts of earlier developments in the Valley.

In this article, I will show that the Peninsula's pre-1960 cluster of electronics and telecommunications firms was supported by a far-flung ecosystem – from Santa Clara County to San Francisco to Washington, DC – that was in place by 1940. The initial development of Silicon Valley, and its indigenous start-ups, relied on existing institutions – federal defence agencies, Bay Area universities, San Francisco-based banks and law firms. These institutions and multiple contexts enabled the start-ups to begin, to survive, to grow, and to matter.

In addition to a portrayal of the pre-1960 ecosystem in action, I will show its decades-old roots. Even before the coming of electronics, the San Francisco Bay Area was already an innovative region and San Francisco was a major financial centre – serving agriculture, lumber, mining, oil, railroads, and shipping. Finally, I will show how the ecosystem serving the Peninsula's tech industry in the 1940s and 1950s underwent what scholars call a 'phase transition,' evolving into the one familiar to those observing the Valley during the last two decades of the 20th century. (Thompson, Purdy, and Ventresca 2018) The case of Silicon Valley demonstrates how ecosystems can adapt to the changing needs of industries. Overall, this story shows that an entrepreneurial high-tech region relies on adaptation not just by entrepreneurs but also by supporting organizations and industries. (Schafer and Henn 2018)

Methods and approach

A consensus is forming among leading scholars of entrepreneurship, such as Acs and Mueller (2008) and Shane (2009), to pay particular attention to high-growth enterprise rather than giving equal attention to all start-ups and small business. This is one of the distinctions that characterizes the literature on entrepreneurial ecosystems, such as Mason and Brown (2014). Indeed, in regions such as Silicon Valley, venture capitalists seek to invest in what Thomas Hellman calls 'infant giants' rather than small firms. (Hellman 2000, 277) The focus of this article aligns with that sensibility. Therefore, the primary data points are the region's largest, most rapidly growing electronics and telecommunications firms of the 1940s and 1950s

As of 1959, the seven major telecommunications and electronics firms on the San Francisco Peninsula were Ampex (recording equipment), Hewlett-Packard (instruments to test electronic systems), Dalmo Victor (airborne antennas), Lenkurt (telecommunications equipment), Litton Industries and Eitel-McCullough (tube makers), and Varian Associates (adding magnetic resonance imaging to tube making). As of 1940, only two of these firms existed, and the larger of the two employed twenty people. By 1960, the workforces of the seven firms ranged in size from 900 to more than 5,000.

These firms not only grew rapidly, but they attracted the attention of institutions with financial resources. During the 1950s, each of the seven had a major liquidity event (made an initial public offering or were acquired by another firm). Stuart and Sorenson demonstrate that such events show investors that there is serious money to be made in the relevant industry and location, and they may 'induce nascent entrepreneurs.' The result is new firm formation. (Stuart and Sorenson 2003) Eitel-McCullough (1953), Varian Associates (1954), Ampex Corporation (1956), and Hewlett-Packard (1957) had initial public offerings on San Francisco's Pacific Coast Stock Exchange. Litton Industries was acquired by Electro-Dynamics in 1953; Dalmo Victor was acquired by Textron in 1954; and Lenkurt was acquired by General Telephone and Electric (GTE) in 1959. I will use the development of these firms to show contributions of each feature of the entrepreneurial ecosystem to the region's post-1940 takeoff.

One of the advantages of paying particular attention to high-growth firms rather than to an entire population of start-ups is that it affords a fine-grained longitudinal approach – including more specificity regarding antecedents–and enables the acknowledgement of grey areas that the coding of a large-scale quantitative study may not. My findings regarding the Peninsula's high-growth firms and their entrepreneurial ecosystem are based on archival records of government, industry, universities, and financial institutions. I examined correspondence, meeting minutes, reports, contracts, patent filings, financial statements, memoirs, and oral histories. I also consulted secondary sources.

Increasing attention has been paid to entrepreneurial ecosystems by economists, policy scholars, and geographers, providing entrepreneurial studies with a sense of place. A nascent field of study often has multiple definitions of central terms, and entrepreneurial ecosystems is no exception, with different (but overlapping) definitions from Kenney and Patton (2005); Feld (2012); and Spigel (2017). I adapt Daniel Isenberg's definition, which includes six 'domains,' for use in pre-1960 Silicon Valley. (Isenberg 2011) For this article, I explore four of the domains of the region's ecosystem in relation to its leading start-ups:

(1) Sources of revenue and risk reduction: During the pre-1960 period, the government played multiple roles. A start-up becomes a going concern only with a sufficient customer base. In the absence of large local markets for electronics, the Valley's key start-ups found lead users in the federal government's armed services – especially with 1940 mobilization for World War II and the subsequent Cold War. All seven firms had government contracts; for six of the seven, federal government agencies represented either the majority of or the initial source of their business. In addition, both the federal and state governments acted as rule makers, and three of these rules especially helped the Peninsula's tech firms: two federal laws helping ameliorate risk for defence contractors, and a California state law helping them obtain financing from banks.

(2) Sources of brainpower. This can centre in universities, research laboratories, or in branches of established firms based elsewhere. (Adams 2011a) I focus on Stanford University, which acted as a magnet for and processor of brainpower and helped shape the behaviour of other members of the ecosystem. I refer to Stanford as an academic anchor, a version of what Agrawal and Cockburn call an 'anchor tenant,' and what Colombelli, Paolucci, and Ughetto call a 'mediator.' (Agrawal and Cockburn 2003; Colombelli, Paolucci, and Ughetto 2019)

(3) Sources of financing. In recent years, Silicon Valley's focus has been on venture capital and angel investors. Prior to the arrival of modern venture capital, commercial banks provided much of the capital for start-ups. By the 1930s, California's branch banking system allowed Peninsula start-ups to simultaneously form relationships with local bankers and gain access to funds from big San Francisco banks.

(4) Sources of legal services. During the pre-1960 period, the primary legal support for the Peninsula's tech start-ups came from San Francisco. One set of attorneys served business needs, such as establishing partnerships and corporations and handling securities matters. Another set of attorneys handled intellectual property matters, including patents.

Since the late 20th century, economists, policy scholars, geographers, and scholars of clusters and industrial districts have made great strides in providing entrepreneurial studies with a sense of place. One of the major gaps identified in the literature, which scholars of entrepreneurial ecosystems have attempted to rectify, has been that most such studies have been static rather than dynamic, lacking a time dimension, sequencing, and an acknowledgement of historical and institutional influence. The result of the attempt to remedy this gap has been an emphasis on studies that show the creation and evolution of entrepreneurial ecosystems (Audretsch et al. 2018; Feldman and Braunerhjelm 2006; Mack and Mayer 2016; Simmie and Martin 2010; Ter Wal and Boschma 2011; Wolfe and Gertler 2006). For many scholars, this has meant exploring the notion of a life cycle for these systems. (Colombelli, Paolucci, and Ughetto 2019; Brown and Mason 2017; Spigel 2017; Martin & Sunley 2006, 2011)

This study, which ends before Silicon Valley even received its name, more directly addresses the question of how entrepreneurial ecosystems come to be. One of the lingering questions for scholars of entrepreneurial ecosystems involves the 'chicken and egg' (entrepreneur first or ecosystem?). (Mason and Brown 2014; Brown 2000) Contributors to two edited volumes about Silicon Valley address that question with respect to the Valley's ecosystem (Lee et al. 2000; Kenney 2000a). Kenney and von Burg posit that the Valley's defining feature is a form of entrepreneurial ecosystem they call 'Economy Two,' an 'institutional complex specialized at creating new firms,' primarily venture capitalists and high-tech law firms (Kenney and von Burg 2000, 222) Yet they suggest that the entrepreneurs came first: 'In the 1950s there were start-ups, but not a discernible set of institutions to support them' (Kenney and von Burg 2000, 229). I will show that there was a set of supporting institutions and how these institutions coalesced into an adaptive entrepreneurial ecosystem.

Sources of revenue and risk reduction: the lead customer

A growing literature describes how events in Washington have influenced what happened in Silicon Valley. Ann Markusen delineates possible government roles with respect to individual industries: 'as rule maker, as producer and consumer of goods and services, and as underwriter of innovation' (Markusen 1996, 295). Scholarship on the Valley demonstrates the relevance of each of those roles. Stuart Leslie shows the federal government's role in underwriting innovation at Stanford University. (Leslie 1993) Christophe Lécuyer shows how the military, as consumer, 'influenced the development of electronics component technologies.' (Lécuyer 2007, 2) Margaret O'Mara shows the government's role as rule maker (nationally) with respect to dispersion of defence industry and (locally) with respect to land use (O'Mara 2005). Missing from this literature, however, are explicit accounts of the relationship between defence agencies and entrepreneurship. In this section, I will discuss the federal government's role as customer, rule maker, and reducer of risk for the region's indigenous firms.

What did individual companies receive in exchange for meeting the military's needs? Time. Scholars of entrepreneurship have found that half of all start-ups fail during their first five years, and that, for various reasons (such as learning curve), casualty rates drop considerably during subsequent years (Shane 2010). The collective challenge faced during the first five years, known as the 'liability of newness,' is one reason for the popularity of start-up incubators (Stinchcombe 1965). The idea is that if it has support during a particularly vulnerable period, the fledgling company will later be able to build the relationships, pipeline of products, and organization necessary to stand on its own. During the period 1909–1959, defence contracts not only helped sustain Silicon Valley start-ups during their formative years, but allowed them to grow rapidly.

Such opportunities appeared in the wake of a change in America's global role. The modern U.S. military-industrial complex grew out of ambitions for American power to match its economic might. (Zakaria 1999) In the wake of the 1898 Spanish American War, U.S. expansion evolved from 'manifest destiny' (limited to the western hemisphere, and accompanied by the promise of state-hood) to a network of military installations that helped protect American overseas interests, including access to markets. (Merk 1963: 259; Bacevich 2004, 25) America's new empire had technological needs. The U.S. military's twentieth-century needs included cutting-edge capabilities in telecommunications (especially radio and radar), instrumentation, and electrical components that would enhance systems capabilities. The San Francisco Bay Area, with its military installations and radio hobbyists, got in on the ground floor. (Lécuyer 2007; Adams 2017)

The original business model for the region's first major high-tech firm in 1909 involved a commercial telegraphy alternative to Western Union in the United States. The path to competitive advantage was via one of the original promises of wireless: cheaper rates made possible through cost reduction (Douglas 1989, 26). When that model did not provide anticipated profitability for the Federal Telegraph Company (FTC), the company was saved by defence business. Representatives of the Mare Island Naval Shipyard kept tabs on research and manufacturing developments at FTC's Palo Alto facility, and in 1913 the company received its first Navy contract. Blessed with government work, FTC became a going concern. Within six years, the company did more than USD 2 million of business with the U.S. Navy alone (Adams 2017). Thus began a pattern of relationships between Valley firms and defence agencies, with the federal government representing what Martin Kenney calls a 'price insensitive lead customer' (Kenney 2000, 5).

The availability of defence contracts ebbs and flows, however, based on international geopolitics. The early development of Silicon Valley reflects that ebb and flow. By the mid-1930s, in addition to the Federal Telegraph Company, the San Francisco Peninsula had produced telecommunications/ electronics firms such as short-wave radio maker Heintz and Kaufman, Inc. (founded in 1923); electronic tube equipment maker Litton Engineering Laboratories (founded in 1932); and transmission tube maker Eitel-McCullough (founded in 1934). Yet a period of American isolationism and reduction in military spending in the 1920s and 1930s reduced demand for the region's technical capabilities. As Carroll Pursell put it, 'Never had [the army and navy) received such a small share of the federal budget.' (Pursell 1972, 7) By 1939, FTC was gone; Heintz and Kaufman had been acquired by San Francisco's Dollar Steamship Company; Litton Engineering Laboratories employed only five machinists; and Eitel-McCullough wasn't much larger (Lécuyer 2007, 34).

As of 1940, San Mateo County, initial home to six of the seven largest tech firms in the area that would become Silicon Valley, employed fewer than 100 people in electrical machinery and communications. (Shapiro 1966, 49) World War II and the subsequent Cold War changed that.

1940 proved to be a watershed year for defence contracting, and cemented Washington, DC's role in Silicon Valley's entrepreneurial ecosystem for decades to come. In the spring of 1940, Nazi Germany invaded the Low Countries and defeated France. By June, with Russia and Germany having created an alliance the previous year, England stood alone – and America began to systematically mobilize for war with the establishment of the National Defense Advisory Commission (NDAC). Among the greatest needs were telecommunications, particularly radar, to detect enemy attacks. That need played to the strengths of the Peninsula's knowledge base. That alone, however, does not guarantee a proliferation of start-ups.

Systematic efforts to stimulate entrepreneurship typically involve strategies to ameliorate risk. In this case, the lead customer not only alleviated the liability of newness, but also reduced risks for its suppliers. Defence contracts can be situation specific, and the possibility of contract cancellation presented huge risk for the contractor. In addition, firms engaged in high-tech commercial business are ever vigilant about potential patent infringement suits filed by larger companies. E. I. 'Tim' Moseley had established the Dalmo Manufacturing Company, a San Francisco machine shop, in 1921, and then moved his business to San Carlos. In the late 1930s, Dalmo Manufacturing declared bankruptcy after losing a patent infringement suit.

How could the government entice industry to meet its needs? One way to assure a sufficient stable of contractors during a national emergency is through legal protection. In 1918, at the behest of Assistant Secretary of the Navy Franklin D. Roosevelt, Congress had decreed that patent infringement suits related to government contracting would be directed against the government rather than against the individual firm. (Welch 1968, 39–42)

In 1941, Moseley's firm emerged from bankruptcy as the Dalmo Victor Company. As a defence contractor, Dalmo Victor was on firmer ground. By the end of the war it was America's leading manufacturer of airborne antennas. (Sturgeon 2000, 42–43).

The payoff to electronics start-ups on the San Francisco Peninsula of involvement in national defence was enormous. San Mateo County employment in electrical manufacturing rose from fewer than 100 in 1940 to about 2,500 in 1943/44. (Shapiro 1966, 49) The size of Eitel-McCullough grew particularly as the customer base for its tubes shifted from radio amateurs and airlines to the defence contractors RCA and Western Electric. (Lecuyer 2007, 36–40) Growth also came to Santa Clara County, where instrument maker Hewlett-Packard (founded in 1938) grew rapidly after it began work on both prime- and sub-contracts for defence agencies. From 1940 to 1945 (the end of the war), the company grew from 10 to 200 employees. (Packard 1995, 52)

Ampex was founded during World War II, and its initial revenues came from defence contracts. Dalmo Victor lacked sufficient electric motors and generators to provide the volume of antennas the navy needed. In 1944, Tim Moseley convinced one of his employees, Alexander M. Poniatoff, to form a company to supply them: Ampex (the founder's initials plus 'ex' for excellence).

After World War II, defence contracting dipped briefly, causing some of the region's companies to shrink. San Mateo County employment in electrical machinery and communications fell from its wartime peak to less than 500 in 1946/47. (Shapiro 1966, 49) From 1943 to 1947, Eitel-McCullough's revenue shrank by about 70 percent. Commercial applications for magnetic tape (such as recording Bing Crosby's radio programme) attracted some business for Ampex, but as late as 1950, the company's revenues were less than USD 400,000 a year. After the Soviet Union tested an atomic bomb in 1949 and the Korean War broke out in 1950, the budgets of America's defence agencies grew, and Ampex garnered government work. Its audio recorder became the standard for the National Security Agency and it also was a contractor for the Air Force and CIA. From 1954 to 1957, government contracts as a percentage of the company's business increased from 32% to 62%, and during the last five years of the decade never dropped below 45% (Ampex Corporation 1956). Thanks in no small part to defence work, the company's revenue grew to USD 73 million in 1960.

The 1950s were also big years for telecommunications components makers. Spurred by demand for radar system components (as Eitel McCullough had experienced), Charles Litton had established Litton Industries in 1945 to mass produce vacuum tubes. Litton Industries grew dramatically – from revenue of USD 700K in 1950 to USD 3.5 million in 1953, when the company was acquired by Electro-Dynamics. During much of the 1950s, Litton's work was entirely with the federal government. Varian Associates, founded in 1948, was another tube maker spurred by defence work. By 1950, 91% of the company's business was with the government. Varian grew rapidly, with revenues rising from USD 208,000 in 1949 to more than USD 38 million in 1959, 90% of which was from defence work. (Lécuyer 2007, 192)

The most significant firms founded in the late 1950s also relied heavily on government contracts. The Valley's first successful semiconductor maker, Fairchild Semiconductor, was established in 1957 (weeks before the Soviet launch of Sputnik, the world's first artificial satellite) as a spin-off from Shockley Semiconductor (founded in 1955). As of 1959, 99% of Fairchild's work was with the government. (Lécuyer 2007: 337, F/N 54) Fairchild's revenue grew from USD 500,000 in 1958 to USD 21 million in 1960. (Lécuyer 2007, 162) In short, six of the seven largest tech firms on the Peninsula in the 1950s (Lenkurt was the other), plus the fastest growing firm at the outset of the 1960s, either began with defence contracts or were sustained by them.

The federal government helped catalyse the early development of Silicon Valley – but its scope in doing so was not as broad as some scholarship suggests. Stuart Leslie refers to the federal government as 'The Biggest "Angel" of Them All' (meaning angel investor), and AnnaLee Saxenian writes, 'venture capital replaced the military as the leading source of financing for Silicon Valley start-ups by the early 1970s.' (Leslie 2000, 48; Saxenian 1994, 26) Suggesting that the government invested in Silicon Valley start-ups conflates revenue, which the defence agencies provided, with equity investments, which they did not. What the military provided was revenue and shelter from risk, not financing.

Financing came from other sources. Even government contractors need capital; most progress payments come *after* work has been done and working capital expended. In a later section, I will show that during the early years of Silicon Valley, financing for start-ups came from angel investors and commercial banks headquartered in San Francisco. This is not to suggest that defence contracts to industry and shelter from risk represented the extent of the federal government's contribution to the early development of Silicon Valley. The government also supported the region's academic anchor, Stanford University.

Sources of brainpower: the entrepreneurial university

In November 1963, Stanford provost Frederick Terman observed, 'Industry is finding that for those activities that involve a high level of scientific and technological creativity, a location in a center of brains is more important than a location near markets, raw materials, transportation, or factory labor.' (Terman 1963, 2). In so doing, Terman anticipated the coming of the knowledge economy. He suggested the potential for the modern research university to stand at the centre of a 'community of technical scholars,' and provided two examples. 'The largest and best defined such modern community of technical scholars is in the Boston area. Here one has the Massachusetts Institute of Technology and Harvard ... ' The second example Terman provided was closer to home: 'On the San Francisco Peninsula around Stanford University.' (Terman 1963, 2–3) Terman fostered relationships with government officials and industry executives, and helped Stanford become the academic anchor of the world's foremost tech region. More than any other individual, Terman played the role of mediator within the region's pre-1960 ecosystem. In so doing, he became known as the 'Father of Silicon Valley.'

The literature on entrepreneurial ecosystems suggests that universities have played little role in spinning off high-growth firms. This was the case with Stanford University and Silicon Valley during the period ending in 1969. Terman's community of scholars was more about innovation than about entrepreneurship. Yet Stanford has come to be known as an 'entrepreneurial university.' That has meant becoming more of an engine of economic development (Etzkowitz 2002; Leslie 1993). Indeed, in October 2012, Charles Eesley and William F. Miller published *Impact: Stanford University's Economic Impact via Innovation and Entrepreneurship*. A survey of Stanford alumni found that if the companies founded by Stanford graduates were treated as a separate country, its economy would be the world's tenth largest. (Eesley and Miller 2012, 6) The report goes further, stating on page 13 that Stanford played a role as an incubator of start-ups. This contrasts with the findings of Arnold C. Cooper in his 1971 *The Founding of Technologically-Based Firms*. (Cooper 1971) In a study of the approximately 250 tech firms founded on the San Francisco Peninsula from 1960 to 1969, Cooper found that only four of those firms were spun off from Stanford (meaning that the founder or founding team came directly from the university. (Cooper 1971, 32)

Here are two quantitative studies, done forty years apart, with dramatically different results. Granted, by the 21st century, Stanford had established a technology licencing office and an expanded entrepreneurship curriculum (which Arnold Cooper had recommended in 1971). (Cooper 1971, 62) Yet the 21st century surveys did not demonstrate cause-and-effect regarding the university and start-ups. In any case, my pre-1960 findings align more with those of Cooper.

In this section I will show that while Stanford's formal outreach programmes from the 1950s became part of the region's system of innovation, the university's support of tech start-ups was ad hoc and primarily involved two of the seven major 1950s firms: Hewlett-Packard (directly) and Varian Associates (indirectly). Stanford's role as an entrepreneurial university had more to do with building the university itself than incubating high-tech start-ups.

After World War II, Stanford established programmes where resources typically flowed to the university. This is because a prolonged budget crisis catalysed Stanford's administrators to generate institutional means of support (Adams 2009). The deepest pockets of all were those of the federal government. During the early stages of the Cold War, Terman sought to make Stanford a key research source as the United States built technological capabilities for defence (Pursell 1972, 338). He succeeded. After having been what Stuart Leslie terms a 'benchwarmer' during the war, in 1946 the university had government contracts worth USD 127,000, which included Stanford's first contract with the Office of Naval Research (ONR) (Leslie 1993, 45). By the mid-1960s, Stanford's defence contract total had swelled to USD 13 million (including contracts with the Army Signal Corps and the Air Force), in addition to USD 50 million from the Atomic Energy Commission for the Stanford Linear Accelerator (Leslie 1993, 45–46). Increased flows of defence money from the federal government helped Stanford create key laboratories and hire important faculty members (Leslie 1993, 44–75; 102–132; 160–187).

Stanford also attracted resources from established firms based outside of the Valley (Adams 2005). Firms such as Sylvania, General Electric, IBM, and Lockheed established manufacturing and/or research facilities in the Valley in the 1950s. They added to the region's knowledge base and workforce. Yet the impact of the branch operations on spin-off creation and their managerial capabilities came largely after 1959: the spin-off of Memorex from IBM in 1961, of Electronic Systems Laboratories from Sylvania in 1964, and most notably, spinoffs of dozens of semiconductor firms from Fairchild (Adams 2011a; Leslie 1993, 66–67; Lécuyer 2007). Until the 1960s, the primary impact of external firms on the ecosystem was through Stanford, particularly its Honors Cooperative Program (which gave the university double tuition for graduate work by employees of local firms, including plants of large firms based elsewhere), the Affiliates Programs (annual stipends from firms wishing to hire Stanford high-tech graduates and seeking early access to Stanford-developed technology), and the Stanford Industrial Park (rents from primarily high-tech firms). There has been a misconception that the Stanford Industrial Park incubated start-ups. (Eesley and Miller, 2012, 13; O'Mara 2005, 98, 122) Not so. The tenants prior to 1960 either were unrelated to tech (such as publishers), were branches of firms based elsewhere (such as Lockheed, Eastman Kodak, and GE), or were established local firms (such as H-P and Varian). (Stanford 1960) They had resources to begin with.

One of the primary steps start-ups must take is organization building. Looking at the Valley's seven leading firms of the 1950s, only Hewlett-Packard assembled its team on campus. Hewlett-Packard went public in 1957, and its first annual report was very revealing. The president (David Packard), the executive vice president (William Hewlett), the vice president of manufacturing (Noel Porter), and the vice president of research & development (Barney Oliver) had met a quarter century earlier at Stanford, where they were all students of Terman (who later served on H-P's board) and began discussions to start a firm. (Gillmor 2004, 122). In July 1938, at the same Stanford laboratory where Cyril Elwell had launched the Federal Telegraph Company, Hewlett developed H-P's first major product, an audio oscillator (the prototype of which he had earlier built as a student in Terman's seminar) (Gillmor 2004, 127).

The Stanford connection helped in other ways. After David Packard spent four years in the east working for General Electric, Charles Litton (class of 1924) made possible a USD 1,000 fellowship that Terman used to entice Packard back to Stanford. Packard worked at Litton's laboratory in the evenings after attending class and working with Hewlett on their start-up during the day. (Packard 1995, 35) Overall, without a stated policy regarding start-ups, Stanford had acted as an incubator for H-P.

H-P was later active in Stanford's formal outreach programmes, but more as a contributor than as a recipient. Not until it was a 15-year-old company with revenues of more than USD 10 million did H-P became the leading indigenous participant in the Honors Cooperative Program, an anchor tenant at Stanford Industrial Park, and a member of Stanford's Affiliates Program. Terman served on H-P's Board of Directors, and Packard served on Stanford's Board of Trustees – chairing it from 1958 to 1960. (Gillmor 2004, 326) This set of formal relationships all occurred well after H-P's incubation.

Varian Associates was also an endeavour of Stanford graduates – but was directly a spin-off of the Sperry Gyroscope Company. The first three presidents of Varian Associates, from the 1940s until the 1970s, were Russell Varian, Myrl Stearns, and Ed Ginzton – all Stanford graduates (Stearns and Ginzton were students of Terman). (Gillmor 2004, 159) Varian earned a BA and an MA in physics at Stanford in the 1920s. In 1937, working in a Stanford laboratory, Russell and his brother Sigurd developed the klystron, a tube with applications for radar. As part of an agreement with Stanford and the Varians, Sperry Gyroscope invested resources into the project in exchange for royalties, and then moved the operation to Long Island in 1940. The klystron team, including several Stanford people, returned to the Peninsula in 1946 and established Varian Associates in San Carlos in 1948. Varian Associates later contributed to Stanford's formal programmes, becoming the first tenant in Stanford Industrial Park in 1953 and an active participant in the Honors Cooperative Program.

Stanford's primary role in entrepreneurship was less direct than as an incubator. Founders of Litton Industries and Dalmo Victor attended Stanford, as did important early members of the Ampex team. All seven of the large companies hired Stanford graduates.

Stanford may have been at the centre of a cluster of tech companies by the 1960s, but proximity to a top technological research institution was not sufficient to grow an entrepreneurial, high-tech region. (Feldman and Desrochers 2003)

If all you needed to succeed was a high-quality research university and government contracts/ sponsorship, then the geography of tech regions would be quite different. The area around Ithaca, New York, for one, would have become a major engine of economic development. Necessities for a high-tech entrepreneurial ecosystem – proximity to sources of financing and guides for the protection of intellectual property – help distinguish the suburban Stanford from the rural Cornell. Otherwise, history might have followed a different path.

In the mid-1880s, when Leland Stanford decided to establish a university south of San Francisco, he visited Johns Hopkins, Harvard, MIT, and Cornell. Of the four, Cornell best fit Stanford's desired balance between, on the one hand, 'applied sciences, engineering, and agriculture' and, on the other hand, the humanities. Leland Stanford offered Andrew D. White, Cornell's current (and founding) president, the top job at his new university. (Jordan 1922, 368–369) White turned Stanford down, but referred him to Cornell alumnus David Starr Jordan, who served as Stanford's president for more than 20 years. Jordan was succeeded by his Cornell classmate John C. Branner. (Jordan 1922, 56–58, 455).

Cornell University was, like Stanford and the University of California, one of the original 14 members of the American Association of Universities. The only private land grant institution of the 14, Cornell had, as Leland Stanford recognized, a practical bent – just like Stanford and MIT. Yet, as of 1959, Tompkins County, which surrounds Ithaca, had 71 total manufacturing facilities (a minority of which were technology related) with a total of fewer than 6,000 employees. Ampex alone had nearly as many. (County Business Patterns 1959, 181; Dun and Bradstreet 1961, 154) Why did a significant tech cluster not grow up around Cornell, the way it did around MIT and Stanford? Even if Cornell focused on technology for emerging industries as effectively as MIT and Stanford did, its chances of creating a tech cluster like Route 128 or Silicon Valley were slim because of geographical limitations. Stanford and MIT both grew up in close proximity to major financial centres, with all the related resources and services – including attorneys well versed in intellectual property law. In Boston and San Francisco, earlier industrial activity provided capital and expertise to repurpose for the needs of telecommunications and electronics.

I will show in the next two sections that during the period ending in 1959, key aspects of Silicon Valley's entrepreneurial ecosystem originated in San Francisco. The city was important, wealthy, and innovative before the coming of electronics and before the first major spin-off from Stanford more than a century ago. For Cornell, benefits of engineering location near a major financial centre had to wait until 2011, when the university won a bidding war to establish a Cornell Tech on Manhattan's Roosevelt Island – beating out Stanford.

Sources of financing before the advent of venture capital

An enduring allusion regarding Silicon Valley's development is to the 'Valley of Heart's Delight,' the pre-1950 Santa Clara County of orchards and farmland. As late as 1940, Santa Clara County had about 100,000 acres of orchards and, notes AnnaLee Saxenian, 'accounted for one-third of California's annual crop of plums, cherries, pears, and apricots.' (Saxenian 1983, 7) Everett Rogers and Judith Larsen note that Silicon Valley 'in 1950 was the prune capital of America … Today the fruit trees have disappeared.' (Rogers and Larsen 1984, 28) Michael Malone writes, 'What had been the Valley of Heart's Delight had been bulldozed and paved out of existence' (Malone 1985, 428). Margaret O'Mara writes, 'Over the second half of the twentieth century, this region evolved from a primarily agricultural landscape … to "Silicon Valley" … "the ultimate post-industrial city"' (O'Mara 2005, 97). That truth, combined with the accepted wisdom about the region's boundaries, has led to a major historical misconception.

If the Silicon Valley saga were entirely a Santa Clara County story, then what happened there would have been nothing less than an economic miracle. In a few decades, the region went from orchards to chips, from agrarian to post-industrial, from rural to suburban – and with a competitive advantage to boot. Saxenian suggests, 'Unhampered by the constraints imposed by pre-existing industrial traditions, the region's founders created a distinctive technological community.' (Saxenian 1994, 12) Who could fault distant observers for seeing in the region a geographic version of the Horatio Alger myth?

Such an interpretation of local history ignores the role earlier industrial activity played in the development of the region's electronics industry. Before it is possible to suburbanize tech, creating a 'city of knowledge,' you need to first have an urban centre. San Francisco played that role for Silicon Valley.

In matters of financing, the literature on Silicon Valley has emphasized the development of local venture capital. (Kenney and Florida 2000; Berlin 2014; Reiner 1989) Before the arrival of VC firms, where had start-up capital come from? From nearby San Francisco, the leading financial centre west of the Mississippi River, where capital had accumulated from the agriculture, extractive, and transportation industries. For the region's indigenous firms, much of the capital investment was repurposed from one economy to the next. The Valley was therefore a beneficiary of the bounty from the region's legacy industries.

We do not often associate commercial banks with start-ups, and for good reason. Commercial banks are conservative institutions and therefore are most likely to make loans when the borrower provides collateral. Few start-ups have collateral to provide; hence the need for funding from family, friends, angel investors, and, most prominently, venture capital, whose higher expected returns compensate for higher levels of risk. Yet commercial banks did lend to the Valley's key start-ups in the 1940s and 1950s, helping them grow rapidly. Commercial banks were able to play a large role thanks to changes in government policy.

In 1940, the National Defense Advisory Commission (NDAC) encountered difficulty in expanding the American mobilization effort to include small firms and start-ups. One of the main reasons was financing. Because of working capital needs, even firms with government contracts face potential liquidity problems. Having a big backlog, or even having begun work on government contracts, does not necessarily help a start-up make payroll. In response to a proposal from the NDAC, in October 1940 Congress approved the Assignment of Claims Act, which allowed commercial banks to use government contracts as collateral for loans. (T., K. V. 1941, 692–698; Smith 1991, 221)

On the San Francisco Peninsula, almost all of the pre-1960 electronics firms relied on contracts from the U.S. Navy, Army, Air Force, NSA, CIA, or NASA. The Assignment of Claims Act was used by Eitel-McCullough and Hewlett-Packard during World War II, and by Litton Industries and Varian Associates during the Korean War to obtain financing to rapidly expand their businesses in response to government demand.

The Act was helpful, but alone it would not have been sufficient to finance rapid growth of tech companies on the San Francisco Peninsula. A bank's willingness to lend to a defence contractor would matter little if the company were not nearby. This is where location in the state of California proved advantageous to pre-1960 Silicon Valley.

Margaret O'Mara notes that the development of Silicon Valley was part of a broader trend: the suburbanization of technology in America. The coming of the knowledge economy, where the principal assets of the tech firms were brains rather than machinery, meant that the desires of engineers increasingly mattered in industrial location decisions. After World War II, aided and abetted by America's love affair with the automobile, engineers favoured suburbs – and nowhere was car culture more warmly embraced than in California. From the early decades of the 20th century to the postwar period, a tech diaspora occurred from cities, including San Francisco, to suburbs. This might have caused financing problems for growth firms locating outside of San Francisco, except for California's Banking Act of 1909, which enabled urban banks to either create branches within the same city or elsewhere, or to acquire established banks and to deploy them as branches.

The principal architect of California's branch banking system was A. P. Giannini, founder of the Bank of Italy (predecessor of the Bank of America). Based in San Francisco, Giannini's first string of branches (in 1910) ran down the peninsula to San Jose – the future path of Silicon Valley. That path originally had nothing to do with electronics, however, and everything to do with the region's earlier proliferation of orchards and identity as the Valley of Heart's Delight. A native of San Jose, Giannini came to banking from the produce business, and therefore knew that California's farmers needed better access to capital. Branch banking, then, was an innovation designed to help one industry that would make a tremendous difference for another.

Within two decades of passage of the Banking Act, California had become the nation's epicentre of branch banking. A 1932 report from the Federal Reserve Board indicated that 'California is the only State in the Union in which modern inter-community branch banking has had a considerable development' (Goldenweiser 1932, 1). This mattered to the Valley's key early firms. Thanks to being in California, founders of firms on the Peninsula did not need to make the trip to the big city often. Instead, they could do most of their banking business in their headquarters town, but because the local branch was part of a much larger bank, these founders had access to far more funds when needed.

It was an advantage for Silicon Valley that it was located on a peninsula where the total distance from San Francisco, to the north, and San Jose, to the south, was just shy of fifty miles. California's system of branch banking helped shrink the gap, emboldening firms to locate closer to Stanford University, and then in proximity to other firms, without distancing themselves from a local source of loans. (Adams, Chambers, and Schultz 2018)

Large Silicon Valley firms with major 'liquidity events' (acquisitions or initial public offerings) by 1959 had developed relationships with branch banks in their early years before tapping the resources of large San Francisco banks. This was true of Eitel-McCullough (Bank of America) in San Bruno, Litton Industries (American Trust) and Ampex (First National Bank of San Mateo County) in Redwood City, and Varian Associates and Hewlett-Packard (Anglo California Bank) in Palo Alto. Why didn't the Peninsula's start-ups in the 1940s and 1950s skip the local branch and go directly to a major San Francisco bank? When these start-ups first sought financing, they were small fry operating under the radar of bank executives. It was the job of branches to support and vet the start-ups before their needs expanded to reach the domain of San Francisco bank vice presidents.

The case of Hewlett-Packard is instructive. David Packard had brought instant local legitimacy to the Palo Alto National Bank. The manager remembered Packard as a football hero from the 1930s at nearby Stanford University. A local bank is fine for a small business but not for a start-up both on the make and in potential danger. H-P grew rapidly during World War II, from USD 34,000 in sales in 1940 to USD 1,540,000 in 1944. With growth came risks, such as sudden contract termination. As the tide turned in favour of the Allies, the major concern of many firms shifted from the challenge of obtaining defence contracts to the risk of their possible cancellation. Indeed, by June 1943, the

War Department alone had directed cancellation of more than 3,700 contracts. (Smith 1991, 623) Abrupt cancellation could dramatically change the financial outlook for a firm and strain its cash flow.

In 1945, the Anglo California Bank acquired the Palo Alto National Bank and turned it into a branch. Years of responsible business practice, which H-P had demonstrated by the end of World War II, meant more to Anglo California than local celebrity. The Anglo California relationship, along with the resources of the Wells Fargo Bank, came in handy when the company was faced with cancellation of contracts for which the company had deployed 'hundreds of thousands of dollars [for] labor and materials.' As a defensive measure to insure the company's liquidity, H-P arranged for a 'T' [termination] loan of up to USD 300,000, secured by H-P's government contracts (Hewlett-Packard 1945) H-P's cashier expressed the 'hope [that the loan would] be unnecessary,' and it turned out that it was. (Cavier 1945; Packard 1946). Yet the ability to plan for contingencies is crucial to any firm, and branch banking allowed H-P to do just that.

Eitel-McCullough (Eimac) had grown more rapidly during the war than H-P had, from USD 200,000 of sales in 1940 to more than USD 17 million in 1943 (Eitel-McCullough 1947). In January 1943, the company obtained USD 2.5 million of revolving credit from the Anglo California Bank, using its defence contracts as collateral. (Eitel-McCullough 1943) The company did not have the same postwar soft landing as H-P, shrinking from 3,600 employees in 1943 to 390 in 1945. The line of credit helped make a big difference to Eimac, keeping it afloat until its fortunes turned again in 1947. The company remained independent until its 1965 acquisition by Varian Associates. (Lécuyer 2007, 46)

Branch banking helped Peninsula electronics firms in the Korean War as well. In 1952, when Litton Industries was a USD 600,000 firm with only 57 employees, it needed a USD 700,000 loan from American Trust to execute its first job with the Air Force, a USD 2 million fixed-price contract. The loan was collateralized by the contract. Discussions with Litton officials began at the local bank branch but concluded twenty miles north, at American Trust's San Francisco offices, in a meeting with vice president Ransom Cook, who later became president of Wells Fargo (Moore and Woenne 1973, 22–23). The loan and contract launched Litton Industries on a trajectory into the ranks of major industrial enterprise.

Varian Associates found assistance at the national and local level. Only two years after its 1948 founding, Varian had annual sales just shy of USD 500,000, and employed approximately 100 people. The company's financing was primarily through bank loans of USD 120,000 from the Palo Alto branch of the Anglo California Bank (Varian Associates 1950). That changed in a hurry. Less than one year later, thanks to contracts related to the Korean War, the company required working capital of about USD 2.7 million, and needed to expand its production facilities.

In September 1951, Varian resolved these interrelated issues. The company agreed to a 99-year lease to become the first tenant in Stanford Industrial Park. The building Varian planned to construct acted as collateral for a USD 1.52 million loan from the Reconstruction Finance Corporation (RFC). Meanwhile, the company's bank loans (secured by receivables and government contracts) with Anglo California had increased to more than USD 500,000, and the company's revolving credit agreement, guaranteed by the U.S. Air Force, grew to USD 600,000 by October. In short, the company had financing of more than USD 2.5 million guaranteed or collaterized by the U.S. government. It's a good thing they did. By the following April, executives anticipated working capital needs would reach USD 2.7 million (Varian Associates 1952). Having the relationship with a large San Francisco bank mattered when the RFC ceased operations in 1954: Anglo California took over Varian's RFC loan (Varian Associates 1954). The Varian story shows the confluence of university, commercial banking, and government – three key nodes of the Valley's early entrepreneurial ecosystem.

Banks were not the only San Francisco organizations that helped Peninsula start-ups. In addition to financing, tech start-ups needed intellectual property protection, and, just as with financing, they turned to San Francisco for assistance. Prior to the 1960s, there was a major difference between these two nodes of the ecosystem. As we have seen, once a start-up formed a relationship with a branch bank, as the company's size and needs grew, there was no need to change institutions. Instead of dealing with the branch manager, the executive dealt with the manager's superiors in San Francisco. In the next section, we will see that the legal node was different. Start-ups worked with separate law firms for business matters, protection of intellectual property, and government matters.

Sources of legal services

As measured by the significance of innovations, the extent of start-up creation to produce innovation, and the amounts of venture capital invested to support the start-ups, Silicon Valley is the world's foremost entrepreneurial high-tech region. The Valley phenomenon represents an extension (albeit an extreme one) of America's innovation take-off in the late 19th century. During the period 1862 to 1890, the number of patents issued in the United States per year rose from 3,829 to 26,232. (Hughes 1989, 14) As Thomas Hughes notes, 'By the beginning of World War I, American inventors had helped to establish the United States as the most inventive of all nations.' (Hughes 1989, 7)

The innovativeness of Silicon Valley is also an extension of a California phenomenon. California was among America's most innovative regions, even before the 20th century electronics revolution. During the late 19th century, California's highly mechanized farming operations and application of scientific methods to extractive industry had involved much technical innovation (David and Wright 1997; Nash 1972). Such innovation, necessitated by high transportation costs – which hindered importation of machinery from the rest of the country – reinforced what Alan Olmstead and Paul Rhode call the 'cumulative and reinforcing character of the invention and diffusion process' (Olmstead and Rhode 1988, 87). This attracted skilled machinists to California and resulted in a greater number of patents per capita than all but one other state in the union during the first two decades of the twentieth century (Carlton and Coclanis 1995, 322–323).

San Francisco became a legal centre of note for technological issues. It was home of the Ninth Circuit Court, which in the late nineteenth century was known for rulings friendly to western defendants in patent infringement cases. (Usselman 2018) The promise of protection of intellectual property, and defence from litigation, provided an important incentive to anyone attempting to use technology to build a company in the region.

Thanks to the area's historical support for innovation, when local electronics firms sought protection for their intellectual property or guidance on how to avoid infringing on the patents of others, San Francisco-based attorneys were ready to help. Prior to the 1960s, high-tech firms on the peninsula used leading patent attorneys such as Paul D. Flehr and Donald Lippincott, based in San Francisco (Sturgeon 2000, 31, 35, 40; Flehr 1989). The careers of Flehr, Lippincott, and other attorneys from Silicon Valley's early years demonstrate the variety of networks involved in the development of the region's entrepreneurial ecosystem. Whereas much of the development of technology and founding of Peninsula start-ups was done by Stanford graduates, much of the legal support for the tech cluster came from graduates of UC Berkeley.

Flehr represents a legal link between California's early industries and its high-tech takeoff. After working for the U.S. Patent Office, in 1925 Flehr joined the San Francisco firm of White, Prost, and Evans. William White's previous firm, Miller & White, had performed the Federal Telegraph Company's initial patent search in 1911. (Miller and White 1911). Before his engagement with Federal, White's work had involved agriculture and oil – two of California's initial big-ticket industries requiring innovation. Flehr's early career preceded the takeoff of electronics on the Peninsula, so he also worked with clients in agriculture and extractive industries. His practice later became most closely associated with electronics. Of the four tech firms on the San Francisco Peninsula making initial public stock offerings in the 1950s, founders of three of the four (Hewlett-Packard, Ampex, and Varian Associates) had been clients of Paul Flehr. (Flehr 1989)

When William Hewlett and David Packard established a partnership on 1 January 1939, legal assistance was close at hand (Packard 1995, 195). In June 1939, Packard wrote to his father (an attorney based in Pueblo, Colorado), requesting help in licencing the foreign rights to H-P's first product, as well as obtaining the U.S. patent for another. (D. Packard 1939) Sperry Packard's advice was: 'What you need now in your work is legal advice from some competent patent attorney in San Francisco, or if possible, in Palo Alto.' (S. Packard 1939) Within two days, Paul Flehr was working with H-P. (Flehr 1939a).

H-P's entrée to Flehr was probably overdetermined. During the 1938–1939 and 1939–1940 academic years, Packard worked with Charles Litton, who had provided Stanford with the funds for Packard's two-year fellowship. Flehr had recently defended Litton and the future founder of Ampex (Alexander Poniatoff) on a patent infringement case brought by Eastman Kodak. (Flehr 1938, 1939b)

Another possible path from H-P to Flehr was through another San Francisco attorney, William Hewlett's father-in-law, Joseph S. Lamson. The firm Byrne, Lamson, and Jordan wrote H-P's partnership agreements (Lamson 1941, 1944). Indeed, partner Paul S. Jordan turned down an offer to become H-P's corporate counsel in the 1940s.

Donald Lippincott was another prominent San Francisco patent attorney during the 1930s and 1940s. Whereas Paul Flehr's path to defending electronics intellectual property ran through agriculture and extractive industry, Lippincott's career focused on electronics from the beginning. A 1913 graduate of the University of California, Lippincott worked in the electronics industry for several years (including as chief engineer at Magnavox, a spin-off of Federal Telegraph) before earning a law degree in the late 1920s. In the 1930s, Lippincott represented San Francisco inventor Philo Farnsworth in his legal battle with RCA over the rights to television and introduced Farnsworth to Russell Varian (Varian 1983, 135). He also represented Stanford's Frederick Terman on legal aspects of his radio research, especially dealing with International Telephone and Telegraph, whose liaison with Terman was Harold Buttner, a classmate of Lippincott's at Cal. (ITT). During World War II, Lippincott was chief patent officer for the U.S. Signal Corps, whose suppliers included firms from the San Francisco Peninsula such as Dalmo Victor, Eitel McCullough, and Hewlett-Packard. Lippincott's law firm later handled the patenting of the integrated circuit for Fairchild Semiconductor. (Lecuyer and Brock 2010, 141)

San Francisco attorney Richard Leonard pursued a path similar to that of Paul S. Jordan with H-P, drafting agreements for Varian Associates at its 1948 inception. Leonard and his law partner Stuart Dole were both graduates of UC Berkeley's law school. Their entree to the Valley's entrepreneurial ecosystem came via yet another network. In an era of coders who rarely see the light of day, it is hard to comprehend that in the mid-20th century, the interest shared by many of the region's entrepreneurs, lawyers, and accountants was the outdoors. A half century before Richard Florida coined the phrase 'creative class,' influential individuals in the Peninsula's entrepreneurial ecosystem shared a love of hiking, rock climbing, fishing, and skiing. (Florida 2002) Certainly education and training programmes helped attract and develop professional talent to the region, per the pattern Storper and Scott identify. (Storper and Scott 2009, 162) Yet this is an example where various nodes of the Valley's ecosystem (university, industry, and professional support) coalesced thanks to factors beyond the regional demand for specialized talent.

'There is no question that a shared love of the outdoors strengthened our friendship,' wrote David Packard about his relationship with William Hewlett, 'and helped build a mutual understanding and respect that is at the core of our successful business relationship.' (Packard 1995, 22–23) Hewlett literally climbed the walls at Stanford; he had learned to rock climb in high school. The Varians were also outdoorsmen. When Russell Varian was accepted by Stanford in 1919, he backpacked the 225 miles north from home to the university. (Morgan 1967, 131)

Charles Litton prided himself on being the first to try mountain roads before the spring thaw. (Lécuyer 2007, 62) William Shockley, co-inventor of the transistor and founder of the Valley's first semiconductor enterprise, was an enthusiastic and competitive climber. Francis Farquhar, who served as the Federal Telegraph Company's first accountant in 1911 and then as initial accountant and board member at Varian Associates beginning in 1948, served as president of the Sierra Club from 1933 to 1935 and from 1948 to 1949. Richard Leonard became a Sierra Club director in 1938 and served as president from 1953 to 1955. Leonard and Dole came into the orbit of Russell and Sigurd Varian as outdoorsmen rather than behind closed doors. (Varian 1983, 227)

Richard Leonard's role with Varian Associates represented an important step from a transactional model (crafting agreements) to a relationship model. As Varian's general legal counsel and a board member, Leonard was present and participated in key strategic decision-making, not just called upon when it appeared that legal expertise was required. One of the activities Leonard left to Varian's executives was securing capital for the firm. Ironically, by the 1970s, bringing together capital and technology became a primary role of the leading Silicon Valley law firms.

As legal counsel to Varian, Granger Associates, and others in the 1950s, Leonard and Dole was poised to be the go-to law firm of the Valley. Yet with Leonard and Dole both living in Berkeley, and with the growing traffic congestion, it became increasingly difficult for them to serve clients in Santa Clara County (40 miles south of San Francisco). Consequently, the firm abandoned its early mover advantage in the Valley, and left the door open for Valley-based firms to seize what Wilson Sonsini's Jeffrey Saper termed a 'home-field advantage.' (Saper 2001). By the 1960s, the firm of Leonard and Dole no longer oversaw Varian's law department. (Dole 2005) The decade also saw a new model for the legal node in the Valley's entrepreneurial ecosystem.

An ecosystem transformed

A general division of labour between the Peninsula (manufacturing and R&D) and San Francisco (finance and law) existed for half a century. The nexus of high-tech activity gradually headed south, attracted by developments at and around Stanford University, but still tethered to San Francisco's financial resources and legal expertise (Adams, Chambers, and Schultz 2018). Many high-tech firms founded prior to 1950 clustered in San Mateo County (south of San Francisco but north of Santa Clara Valley), situated to maximize accessibility to both centres. Subsequently, the nexus of high-tech activity moved from Redwood City in San Mateo County past Stanford University to the city of Santa Clara. (Adams, Chambers, and Schultz 2018)

As the centre of high-tech activity headed southward, the region experienced a transportation revolution. Most of the major tech firms founded prior to 1950 were located near train stations (Federal Telegraph, 1909: Palo Alto; Litton Engineering Laboratories, 1932: San Carlos; Eitel McCullough, 1934: San Bruno; Hewlett-Packard, 1938: Palo Alto; Dalmo Victor, 1941: San Carlos; Ampex, 1944: San Carlos; Varian Associates, 1948: San Carlos). Employees could easily travel to San Francisco to meet with the firm's lawyer, accountant, or bank executive. In 1951, one reason Stanford University chose the southeast corner of the campus as the site for the Stanford Industrial Park was because train tracks ran through it. By 1959, however, the tracks were gone and Stanford Industrial Park had become a transportation model for the rest of the Valley: easily accessible only by automobile. The suburbanization of tech in the Valley was complete.

At the same time, the relationships to the Valley of four major ecosystem nodes changed. Stanford was not the only player in the higher education game on the Peninsula, nor did its administrators want it to be. It was a relatively small university, and its engineering school did not pursue a comprehensive staffing strategy. Instead, the school sought to develop what Frederick Terman called 'steeples of excellence,' a few fields in which its faculty's research was internationally competitive. This resulted in a division of labour in which Stanford focused on graduate education, leaving much of the training of undergraduates to other universities. Along the way, Stanford fostered development of San Jose State's engineering programme, which opened its doors in 1946. When UC Berkeley failed to provide a local graduate engineering programme in Silicon Valley, Santa Clara University and San Jose State met the need. San Jose State has since been a leading supplier of engineers for the Valley's workforce. Its engineering programme represents one of Stanford's most important spin-offs (Adams 2011b). The establishment of Foothill Community College in 1958 provided more vocational support.

While the 1960s brought an increased division of labour in higher education, the legal segment of the Silicon Valley ecosystem shifted in the opposite direction – from a division of labour among firms to the creation and growth of one-stop shops. As we have seen, prior to 1960 one set of San

Francisco firms (such as Byrne, Lamson and Jordan or Leonard and Dole) handled business matters for start-ups, while San Francisco patent attorneys (such as Paul Flehr or Don Lippincott) dealt with intellectual property matters.

Yet by the mid-1960s, that had begun to change. In 1966, Larry Sonsini (another UC Berkeley law graduate) contemplated working for a San Francisco law firm. His mentor, Professor Richard Jennings, suggested that Sonsini consider something different: becoming a securities lawyer for local entrepreneurs and venture capitalists. (Sonsini 2011, 3–4) John Wilson of the Palo Alto-based firm McCloskey, Wilson, Mosher, and Martin convinced Sonsini that the future was in the Valley. Sonsini helped make that happen as the firm became Wilson, Sonsini, Goodrich, and Rosati (WSGR). In the mid-1970s, no Valley-based law firm had more than twelve attorneys, and most of the region's largest companies had San Francisco-based representation. That changed because proximity mattered. By the late 1980s, Wilson Sonsini had more than 150 attorneys and, as Mark Suchman notes, 'the share of Silicon Valley business being performed in San Francisco had dwindled to negligible proportions.' (Suchman 2000, 74) Instead, San Francisco-based firms opened offices in the Valley in the 1980s. By then, Wilson, Sonsini had developed a new legal business model for the region: a law firm providing deal makers and counsellors, in addition to intellectual property services. In short, WSGR sought a model that would allow the firm, in the words of Sonsini, to 'build a full-scale law firm that can service a technology firm from infancy to as large as it can become.' (Sonsini 2003) Wilson, Sonsini and its competitors, Fenwick and West, and Ware and Friedenreich, acted as valuable go-betweens, bringing together providers of technology and sources of funds – including local venture capitalists.

Liquidity events in the 1950s (especially the IPOs of Varian in 1956 and H-P in 1957) demonstrated great demand for equity in the Valley's high-tech firms. (Kenney and Florida 2000, 106) In August 1959, General William H. Draper, H. Rowan Gaither, and General Frederick L. Anderson established the first venture capital firm in the region that would become Silicon Valley. Draper and Anderson brought knowledge of the Valley's primary customers at the time (the armed forces). Gaither, a San Francisco attorney, had been a leading administrator at the MIT Radiation Laboratory, the RAND Corporation, and the Ford Foundation. Along the way, he had developed a reputation as an expert at bringing together capital and technology. (Berlin 2014, 1) During the 1960s, some VCs (such as Rock and Davis) set up shop in San Francisco. Others, such as Sutter Hill and the Mayfield Fund, following in the footsteps of Draper, Gaither, and Anderson, located in the Valley. (Kenney and Florida 2000, 107–109) The balance soon tipped to VCs based in the Valley. In 1972, a developer on Sand Hill Road leased space to Kleiner Perkins, and several San Francisco-based VCs followed. By the end of the 1980s, three buildings on Sand Hill Road housed the largest collection of venture capitalists in the United States (Kenney and Florida 2000, 115).

Silicon Valley is the most noteworthy example of what Henry Etzkowitz calls the Triple Helix of university, industry, and government relations. Both the public-sector and private-sector aspects of the Triple Helix evolved in the latter third of the twentieth century. The federal government's role shifted from primarily that of customer to a greater emphasis on setting rules to help foster economic development: changes to the capital gains tax and the Prudent Man Rule (which encouraged fiduciary institutions to include private equity in their investment portfolios), enactment of the Bayh-Dole Act (which encouraged university involvement in high-tech enterprise), the Immigration Acts of 1965 and 1990 (which helped attract more talent, especially from East and South Asia), and establishment of the United States Court of Appeals for the Federal Circuit (which helped in defence of intellectual capital). Although defence work remained a mainstay in several corners of Silicon Valley through the 1980s (and surveillance work for the NSA and related agencies remains important to the present), commercial work as a percentage of the whole increased dramatically, and consumer products (including calculators, digital watches, video games, and personal computers) played an expanding role. As John Findlay notes, 'consumer goods really represented a second career for [the Valley's] high-tech businesses' (Findlay 1992, 144).

Hewlett-Packard and Ampex were leading examples of the Valley's transition from an emphasis on government contracts to consumer products, as they spun off not just companies but major segments of new industries. In the mid-1960s, H-P became a leading maker of calculators; in the 1970s, employee Steve Wozniak developed what would become the Apple I computer at H-P after hours. (Isaacson 2011, 60–61) Ampex created a government contracts division in the 1950s while doing business with the Air Force, National Security Agency, and CIA. The technology Ted Dabney and Nolan Bushnell developed at Ampex was helpful in 1971 when they co-founded Atari, launching the commercial video game industry. (Bowles 2018)

Beginning in the 1960s, the Valley turned less frequently to San Francisco for resources and guidance, and developed its own set of local institutions. Venture capital and legal capabilities became integral aspects of the local ecosystem. Silicon Valley firms would become responsible for about one-third of America's total venture capital investments, and the Valley became home to the world's pre-eminent high-tech law firm (Wilson Sonsini). San Francisco played less of a role in shaping the Valley, and the Valley played an increasing role in shaping San Francisco. The localization of the ecosystem accompanied a shift to more indigenous enterprise, and Silicon Valley's entrepreneurial ecosystem became a more geographically concentrated set of institutions.

Conclusion

"Do not regard Silicon Valley as some sort of economic machine, where various raw materials are poured in at one end and firms such as Apple and Cisco roll out at the other, but rather as a form of ecosystem that breeds companies: without the right soil and the right climate, nothing will grow."

–The Economist, 29 March 1997

The Silicon Valley of 1909–1959 was very different from the Valley we see today, and even from the Valley that received increasing attention in the 1980s. As this article has shown, during the Valley's first half century, a more far-flung innovation system was at work, one that featured financial resources and legal services from San Francisco, while the federal government provided defence contracts and helped alleviate risk. Without those resources, services, and customer base, there would be no Silicon Valley as we know it.

Silicon Valley grew up in the world's wealthiest country, in proximity to the principal financial centre west of the Mississippi River. It grew up in a region with capital to repurpose from the agriculture, extractive, and transportation industries. It grew up in a state with laws that favoured branch banking, encouraging the suburbanization of technical industry. It grew up in a region of geopolitical importance in a country that was becoming the world's leading military power – and that provided financial and legal support to defence contractors. It grew up near one of the primary nodes in the world's top system of research universities. The first half century (1909–1959) of this high-tech region's development was a process reliant upon an abundance of supporting institutions and accessible resources.

Michael Porter systematically delineated and mapped industry clusters in the United States. In so doing, he argued that in the 21st century, economic prosperity would be created through innovation rather than inherited through factor endowments, such as natural resources. (Porter 1998a, 1998b). Silicon Valley inherited a different set of endowments, by virtue of its location. In this article, I have shown that during Silicon Valley's first fifty years, entrepreneurship was made possible by an existing ecosystem of institutions and by the repurposing of capital from previous industrial activity. Seeds of success in high-tech were planted on fertile soil: a path leading from the agriculture, extractive, and transportation industries. Policy makers in other regions who attempt to build an entrepreneurial ecosystem need to know the extent to which the 'master cluster' benefitted from being in the right place at the right time, and by inheriting the right ecosystem.

Acknowledgments

The article benefitted from the comments of two anonymous reviewers. I also thank Henry Etzkowitz, Martin Kenney, Gavin Wright, and attendees at the Stanford Humanities Center Approaches to Capitalism Workshop and the National Museum of American History's Lemelson Center Colloquium for helpful comments on earlier versions of the manuscript, and Jack Wenstrand for arranging access to the Hewlett-Packard papers.

Disclosure Statement

No potential conflict of interest was reported by the author.

References

Acs, Z., and P. Mueller. 2008. "Employment Effects of Business Dynamics: Mice, Gazelles, and Elephants." *Small Business Economics* 30 (1): 85–100. doi:10.1007/s11187-007-9052-3.

Adams, S. B. 2005. "Stanford and Silicon Valley: Lessons on Becoming a High-tech Region." *California Management Review* 48 (1): 29–51. doi:10.2307/41166326.

Adams, S. B. 2009. "Follow the Money: Engineering at Stanford and UC Berkeley during the Rise of Silicon Valley." *Minerva* 47: 367–390. doi:10.1007/s11024-009-9138-y.

Adams, S. B. 2011a. "Growing Where You are Planted: Exogenous Forces and the Seeding of Silicon Valley." *Research Policy* 40 (3): 368–379. doi:10.1016/j.respol.2010.12.002.

Adams, S. B. 2011b. "Their Minds Will Follow: Big Business and California Higher Education, 1954–1960." *Paper presented at the Business History Conference.* St. Louis.

Adams, S. B. 2017. "Arc of Empire: The Federal Telegraph Company, the U.S. Navy, and the Beginnings of Silicon Valley." *Business History Review* 91 (2): 329–359. doi:10.1017/S0007680517000630.

Adams, S. B., D. Chambers, and M. Schultz. 2018. "A Moving Target: The Geographic Evolution of Silicon Valley, 1953–1990." *Business History* 60 (6): 859–883. doi:10.1080/00076791.2017.1346612.

Agrawal, A., and I. M. Cockburn. 2003. "The Anchor Tenant Hypothesis: Exploring the Role of Large, Local R & D-intensive Firms in Regional Innovation Systems." *International Journal of Industrial Organizations* 2 (19): 1227–1253. doi:10.1016/S0167-7187(03)00081-X.

Audretsch, D., C. Mason, M. P. Miles, and A. O'Connor. 2018. "The Dynamics of Entrepreneurial Ecosystems." *Entrepreneurship & Regional Development* 30 (3–4): 471–474. doi:10.1080/08985626.2018.1436035.

Bacevich, A. J. 2004. *American Empire: The Realities and Consequences of U.S. Diplomacy.* Cambridge, MA: Harvard University Press.

Berlin, L. 2014. "The First Venture Capital Firm in Silicon Valley." In *Making the American Century*, edited by B. J. Schulman, 155–170. New York: Oxford University Press.

Bowles, N. 2018. "Ted Dabney, a Founder of Atari and a Creator of Pong, Dies at 81." *New York Times*, May 31.

Braun, E., and S. McDonald. 1982. *Revolution in Miniature.* New York: Cambridge University Press.

Brown, J. S. 2000. "Foreword." In *Understanding Silicon Valley: The Anatomy of an Entrepreneurial Region*, edited by M. Kenney, ix–xvi. Stanford, CA: Stanford University Press.

Brown, R., and C. Mason. 2017. "Looking inside the Spiky Bits: A Critical Review and Conceptualization of Entrepreneurial Ecosystems." *Small Business Economics* 49: 11–30. doi:10.1007/s11187-017-9865-7.

Carlton, D. L., and P. A. Coclanis. 1995. "The Uninventive South? A Quantitative Look at Region and American Inventiveness." *Technology and Culture* 36 (2): 302–326. doi:10.2307/3106374.

Cavier, F. 1945. Letter to F. Hewlett, June 30. Packard papers: 2, 2, 39. Keysight archives.

Colombelli, A., E. Paolucci, and E. Ughetto. 2019. "Hierarchical and Relational Governance and Life Cycle of Entrepreneurial Ecosystems." *Small Business Economics* 52: 505–521. doi:10.1007/s11187-017-9957-4.

Cooper, A. 1971. *The Founding of Technologically-based Firms.* Milwaukee, WI: Center for Venture Management.

Corporation, Ampex. 1956. *Annual Reports.* Baker Library, Harvard University..

County Business Patterns. 1959.

David, A. P., and G. Wright. 1997. "Increasing Returns and the Genesis of American Resource Abundance." *Industrial and Corporate Change* 3 (1): 203–245. doi:10.1093/icc/6.2.203.

Dole, S. 2005. *Interview with the Author January 12, Berkeley, CA.*

Douglas, S. J. 1989. *Inventing American Broadcasting, 1899–1922.* Baltimore: Johns Hopkins University Press.

Dun and Bradstreet. 1961. *Metalworking Directory.* New York: Dun and Bradstreet.

Eesley, C., and W. F. Miller. 2012. *Impact: Stanford University's Economic Impact via Innovation and Entrepreneurship.* Stanford, CA: Stanford University.

Eitel-McCullough. 1943. "Directors Minutes." *Eitel-McCullough Papers, 77/110c, Carton 7, Folder "Minutes Oct. 1934-Oct. 1945*, January 30. Bancroft Library, University of California.

Eitel-McCullough. 1947. "Eitel-McCullough Inc. v. Commissioner."

Etzkowitz, H. 2002. *MIT and the Rise of Entrepreneurial Science*. New York: Routledge.

Feld, B. 2012. *Startup Communities: Building an Entrepreneurial Ecosystem in Your City*. Hoboken, NJ: Wiley.

Feldman, M., and Braunerhjelm. 2006. "The Genesis of Industrial Clusters." In *Cluster Genesis: Technology-based Industrial Development*, edited by P. Braunerhjelm and M. Feldman, 1–13. New York: Oxford University Press.

Feldman, M., and P. Desrochers. 2003. "Research Universities and Local Economic Development: Lessons from the History of the Johns Hopkins University." *Industry and Innovation* 10: 5–24. doi:10.1080/1366271032000068078.

Findlay, J. M. 1992. *Magic Lands: Western Cityscapes and Culture after 1940*. Berkeley, CA: University of California Press.

Flehr, P. 1938. Letter to Charles V. Litton, November 30. Litton papers, 75/7c. Box 3, folder "Paul D. Flehr 1938–44." Bancroft Library, University of California.

Flehr, P. 1939a. Letter to Hewlett, August 1. Packard papers, 1, 1, 2. Keysight archives.

Flehr, P. 1939b. Letter to Charles V. Litton, July 28. Litton papers, 75/7c. Box 3, folder "Paul D. Flehr, 1938-44." Bancroft Library, University of California.

Flehr, P. D. 1989. *Inventors and Their Inventions: A California Legacy Seen through the Eyes of A Patent Attorney*. San Francisco: Pacific Book Publishers.

Florida, R. 2002. *Rise of the Creative Class*. New York: Basic Books.

Gillmor, C. S. 2004. *Fred Terman at Stanford: Building a Discipline, a University, and Silicon Valley*. Stanford, CA: Stanford University Press.

Goldenweiser, E. A. 1932. *Branch Banking in California*. Washington, D.C.: Federal Reserve Board.

Hanson, D. 1982. *The New Alchemists: Silicon Valley and the Microelectronics Revolution*. Boston: Book Service.

Hellman, T. 2000. "Venture Capitalists: The Coaches of Silicon Valley." In *The Silicon Valley Edge: A Habitat for Innovation and Entrepreneurship*, edited by C. W. Lee, W. F. Miller, M. G. Hancock, H. S. Rowan, 276–294. Stanford, CA: Stanford University Press.

Hewlett-Packard. 1945. "Provisions for Hewlett-Packard Co. 'T' Loan." March 30. 2, 2, 39.

Hughes, T. P. 1989. *American Genesis: A Century of Invention and Technological Enthusiasm*. New York: Viking.

Isaacson, W. 2011. *Steve Jobs*. New York: Simon & Schuster.

Isenberg, D. 2011. *The Entrepreneurship Ecosystem Strategy as a New Paradigm for Economic Policy: Principles for Cultivating Entrepreneurship*. Babson Park, MA: Babson College.

Jordan, D. S. 1922. *The Days of a Man, Volume One: 1851–1899*. New York: World Book Company.

Kenney, M., and U. von Burg. 2000. "Institutions and Economies: Creating Silicon Valley." In *Understanding Silicon Valley*, edited by M. Kenney, 218–240. Stanford, CA: Stanford University Press.

Kenney, M., and R. Florida. 2000. "Venture Capital in Silicon Valley: Fueling New Firm Formation." In *Understanding Silicon Valley*, edited by M. Kenney, 98–123. Stanford, CA: Stanford University Press.

Kenney, M., Ed. 2000a. *Understanding Silicon Valley: The Anatomy of an Entrepreneurial Region*. Stanford, CA: Stanford University Press.

Kenney, M. 2000b. "Introduction." In *Understanding Silicon Valley*, edited by M. Kenney, 1–12. Stanford, CA: Stanford University Press.

Kenney, M., and D. Patton. 2005. "Entrepreneurial Geographies: Support Networks in Three High-technology Industries." *Economic Geography* 81: 201–228. doi:10.1111/j.1944-8287.2005.tb00265.x.

Lamson, J. 1941. Letter to Packard, May 17. Packard papers, 1, 1, 2. Keysight archives.

Lamson, J. 1944. Letter to Packard, October 19. Packard papers, 1, 1, 3. Keysight archives.

Lécuyer, C. 2007. *Making Silicon Valley: Innovation and Growth of High Tech, 1930–1970*. Cambridge, MA: MIT Press.

Lecuyer, C., and D. Brock. 2010. *Makers of the Microchip*. Cambridge, MA: MIT Press.

Lee, C., W. F. Miller, M. G. Hancock, and H. S. Rowen, Eds. 2000. *The Silicon Valley Edge: A Habitat for Innovation and Entrepreneurship*. Stanford, CA: Stanford University Press.

Lerner, J. 2009. *Boulevard of Broken Dreams: Why Public Efforts to Boost Entrepreneurship and Venture Capital Have Failed —and What to Do about It*. Princeton, NJ: Princeton University Press.

Leslie, S. W. 1993. *The Cold War and American Science*. New York: Columbia University Press.

Leslie, S. W. 2000. "The Biggest 'Angel' of Them All: The Military and the Making of Silicon Valley." In *Understanding Silicon Valley*, edited by M. Kenney, 48–67. Stanford, CA: Stanford University Press.

Mack, E., and H. Mayer. 2016. "The Evolutionary Dynamics of Entrepreneurial Ecosystems." *Urban Studies* 53 (10): 2118–2133. doi:10.1177/0042098015586547.

Malone, M. 1985. *The Big Score: The Billion-dollar Story of Silicon Valley*. New York: Doubleday.

Markusen, A. 1996. "Sticky Places in Slippery Space: A Typology of Industrial Districts." *Economic Geography* 72 (3): 293–313. doi:10.2307/144402.

Martin, R., and P. Sunley. 2006. "Path Dependence and Regional Economic Evolution." *Journal of Economic Geography* 6: 395–437. doi:10.1093/jeg/lbl012.

Martin, R., and P. Sunley. 2011. "Conceptualizing Cluster Evolution: Beyond the Life Cycle Model?" *Regional Studies* 45 (10): 1299–1318. doi:10.1080/00343404.2011.622263.

Mason, C., and R. Brown. 2014. "Entrepreneurial Ecosystems and Growth Oriented Entrepreneurship." *Paper for OECD workshop*, November 7, 2013.

Merk, F. 1963. *Manifest Destiny and Mission in American History: A Re-interpretation*. Cambridge, MA: Harvard University Press.

Miller and White. 1911. Letter to Poulsen Wireless Corporation, January 13." In *Report on Poulsen Wireless Corporation and Federal Telegraph Company* (1914), 28–29. Federal Telegraph Company, San Francisco, CA. History San Jose.

Moore, N., and R. Woenne. 1973. "Vacuum Tube and Magnetron Development, interviewed by A. L." Norberg. Bancroft Library, University of California, Berkeley. 84/17c.

Morgan, J. 1967. *Electronics in the West: The First Fifty Years*. Palo Alto, CA: National Press Books.

Nash, G. 1972. "Stages of California's Economic Growth, 1870–1970: An Interpretation." *California Historical Quarterly* 5 (Winter): 315–330. doi:10.2307/25157401.

O'Mara, M. P. 2005. *Cities of Knowledge: Cold War Science and the Search for the Next Silicon Valley*. Princeton, N.J.: Princeton University Press.

Olmstead, A. L., and P. Rhode. 1988. "An Overview of California Agricultural Mechanization, 1870–1930." *Agricultural History* 62 (Summer): 86–112.

Packard, D. 1939. Letter to Sperry Packard, June 29. Packard papers, 1, 1, 2. Keysight archives.

Packard, D. 1946. Letter to Greiner, August 23. Packard papers, 2, 2, 39. Keysight archives.

Packard, D. 1995. *The H-P Way*. New York: Harper Business.

Packard, S. 1939. Letter to David Packard, July 4. Packard papers, 1, 1, 2. Keysight archives.

Porter, M. E. 1998a. *Competitive Advantage of Nations*. New York: Free Press.

Porter, M. E. 1998b. "Clusters and the New Economics of Competition." *Harvard Business Review*, November-December. 77–90.

Pursell, C. W., Jr. 1972. *The Military-industrial Complex*. New York: Harper & Row Publishers.

Reiner, M. L. 1989. "The Transformation of Venture Capital: A History of Venture Capital in the United States." Unpublished doctoral dissertation, UC Berkeley.

Rogers, E., and J. Larsen. 1984. *Silicon Valley Fever: Growth of High-technology Culture*. New York: Basic Books.

Saper, J. 2001. "Interview with the Author." August 26. Palo Alto, CA.

Saxenian, A. 1983. "The Genesis of Silicon Valley." *Built Environment* 9 (1): 7–17.

Saxenian, A. 1994. *Regional Advantage: Culture and Competition in Silicon Valley and Route 128*. Cambridge, MA: Harvard University Press.

Schafer, S., and S. Henn. 2018. "The Evolution of Entrepreneurial Ecosystems and the Critical Role of Migrants. A Phase-model Based on A Study of IT Startups in the Greater Tel Aviv Area." *Cambridge Journal of Regions, Economy and Society* 11: 317–333.

Shane, S. 2009. "Why Encouraging More People to Become Entrepreneurs is Bad Public Policy." *Small Business Economics* 33 (2): 141–149. doi:10.1007/s11187-009-9215-5.

Shane, S. A. 2010. *Illusions of Entrepreneurship: The Costly Myths that Entrepreneurs, Investors, and Policy Makers Live By*. New Haven, CT: Yale University Press.

Shapiro, R. L. 1966. "A Study of Trends in Occupational Needs in Manufacturing in San Mateo County." Unpublished master's thesis, UCLA.

Simmie, J., and R. Martin. 2010. "The Economic Resilience of Regions: Towards an Evolutionary Approach." *Cambridge Journal of Regions, Economy and Society* 3 (1): 27–43. doi:10.1093/cjres/rsp029.

Smith, R. E. 1991. *The Army and Economic Mobilization*. Washington, DC: Center of Military History, United States Army.

Sonsini, L. 2003. "Interview."Accessed 22 February 2019. https://silicongenesis.stanford.edu/transcripts/sonsini.htm

Sonsini, L. 2011. "Oral History Interview with Sally Smith Hughes." Regional Oral History Project, Bancroft Library, UC Berkeley.

Spigel, B. 2017. "The Relational Organization of Entrepreneurial Ecosystems." *Entrepreneurship Theory and Practice* 41 (1): 49–72. doi:10.1111/etap.12167.

Stanford. 1960. "Number of Employees and Value of Buildings in Stanford Industrial Park." *Frederick Terman papers, SC 160, box 32, folder 10*, December 7. Stanford University Department of Special Collections.

Stinchcombe, A. 1965. "The Social Structure of Organizations." In *Handbook of Organizations*, edited by J. G. March, 142–193. Chicago, IL: University of Chicago Press.

Storper, M., and A. J. Scott. 2009. "Rethinking Human Capital, Creativity and Urban Growth." *Journal of Economic Geography* 9: 147–167. doi:10.1093/jeg/lbn052.

Stuart, T. E., and O. Sorenson. 2003. "Liquidity Events and Geographic Distribution of Entrepreneurial Activity." *Administrative Science Quarterly* 48: 175–201. doi:10.2307/3556656.

Sturgeon, T. J. 2000. "How Silicon Valley Came to Be." In *Understanding Silicon Valley*, edited by M. Kenney, 15–47. Stanford, CA: Stanford University Press.

Suchman, M. C. 2000. "Dealmakers and Counselors: Law Firms as Intermediaries in the Development of Silicon Valley." In *Understanding Silicon Valley*, edited by M. Kenney, 71–97. Stanford, CA: Stanford University Press.

T., K. V. 1941. "Assignment of Claims Act of 1940." *Virginia Law Review* 27 (March): 692–698. doi:10.2307/1067295.

Ter Wal, A. L. J., and R. Boschma. 2011. "Co-evolution of Firms, Industries and Networks in Space." *Regional Studies* 47 (7): 919–933. doi:10.1080/00343400802662658.

Terman, F. 1963. "The Newly Emerging Community of Technical Scholars." Frederick Terman papers, SC 160, series VIII, box 3, folder 3, November 5. Stanford University Department of Special Collections.

Thompson, T. A., J. M. Purdy, and M. J. Ventresca. 2018. "How Entrepreneurial Ecosystems Take Form: Evidence from Social Impact Initiatives in Seattle." *Strategic Entrepreneurship Journal* 12 (1): 96–116. doi:10.1002/sej.2018.12.issue-1.

Usselman, S. 2018. "Regional Invention: Patent Litigation and Industrial Development on the Pacific Coast, 1891–1925." *Paper presented at the Johns Hopkins University Seminar on Business and Economic History*, March 15.

Varian Associates. 1950. "Minute, Special Meeting." *Farquhar papers, 73/65c, carton 1, folder 1.* November 6. Bancroft Library, UC Berkeley.

Varian Associates. 1952. "Minutes, Executive Committee Meeting." Farquhar papers, 73/65c, box 1, folder 3, April 1. Bancroft Library, UC Berkeley.

Varian Associates. 1954. "Statement of Financial Condition for 12/31/54." *Farquhar Papers, 73/65c, Box 1.* Bancroft Library, UC Berkeley.

Varian, D. 1983. *Inventor and the Pilot.* Palo Alto: Pacific Books.

Welch, J. E. 1968. "Patent Infringement in Government Procurements: GAO's Role." *William and Mary Law Review* 10 (1): 39-57

Wolfe, D. A., and M. S. Gertler. 2006. "Local Antecedents and Trigger Events: Policy Implications of Path Dependence for Cluster Formation." In *Cluster Genesis: Technology-based Industrial Development*, edited by P. Braunerhjelm and M. Feldman, 243–263. New York: Oxford University Press.

Zakaria, F. 1999. *From Wealth to Power: The Unusual Origins of America's World Role.* Princeton, NJ: Princeton University Press.

The role of MNEs in the genesis and growth of a resilient entrepreneurial ecosystem

Paul Ryan, Majella Giblin, Giulio Buciuni and Dieter F. Kogler

ABSTRACT
This article reports on a longitudinal process study of the critical role of anchor MNEs in the metamorphosis of a high-tech industrial cluster into a local entrepreneurial ecosystem. It draws on entrepreneurial ecosystem and international business literatures to frame the study of the genesis and evolutionary processes of an entrepreneurial ecosystem that emerged from two MNE subsidiaries, both of which had evolved into advanced R&D centres of excellence around a technology specialism. It shows how multiple new venture spinouts by former MNE employees introduced technological heterogeneity that catalysed into a resilient entrepreneurial ecosystem. The theoretical and policy implications that can be drawn from this case study emphasize the existence of both technology specialism and heterogeneity for resilience in an entrepreneurial ecosystem, and that reaching such a position is evolutionary in nature.

1. Introduction

Entrepreneurship is critical to the sustenance and growth of local economies. Dynamic interactions between elements of a local entrepreneurial system have been claimed to increase entrepreneurial performance of regions (Boschma 2015). These interactions evolve over time, often into what has been termed to be an 'entrepreneurial ecosystem' (Cohen 2006). After Cohen's original theoretical incarnation of an entrepreneurial ecosystem, there was a lag in academic interest in the phenomenon as the generation of theory on cluster development and life cycles pre-dominated (Menzel and Forndahl 2009; Boschma and Forndahl 2011; Martin and Sunley 2011). However, as shortcomings in cluster theory on the nature of entrepreneurship emergence and development were identified, there has been an increase of interest in the entrepreneurial ecosystem concept and the centrality of the entrepreneur and entrepreneurship to the process (Isenberg 2010; Stam 2015; Mack and Mayer 2016 ; Acs et al., 2017; Audretsch and Belitski 2017; Stam and Spigel 2017; O'Connor et al. 2018; Liguori et al. 2019).

Whilst rapid progress has been made, the processes involved in the formation and transitioning of an entrepreneurial ecosystem to different phases of development needs to be further explored, and examined as evolutionary rather than static processes (Spigel 2017; Mack and Mayer 2016; Alveldalen and Boschma, 2017; Brown and Mason 2017; Spigel and Harrison 2018; Colombo et al. 2019). As a result, further research is required on how entrepreneurial ecosystems form and evolve over time (Malecki 2018). The bulk of existing research has lacked historical and contextual nuance (Spigel and Harrison 2018) which has prevented a thorough understanding of the dynamics underlying the genesis of an entrepreneurial ecosystem. In other words, the mechanisms underpinning the formation of an entrepreneurial ecosystem have been more assumed than explained and seldom supported by in-depth empirical analysis. As a result, there are several questions which remain unanswered to date. Which actors play which roles and in which contexts? Who are the leaders, shapers and dominant players in an entrepreneurial ecosystem? Are there stages in the evolution of entrepreneurial ecosystems and, if so, are these standard or heterogeneous? These issues need to be explored across a range of entrepreneurial ecosystems to tease out the common and exceptional elements that help to develop a general theory of an entrepreneurial ecosystem with stronger explanatory power.

Within this context, we focus on two research topics which have been largely overlooked by the existing theory: 1) the explanation of the genesis of an entrepreneurial ecosystem from a longitudinal perspective; and 2) the analysis of the role of MNEs in the formation of an entrepreneurial ecosystem. The decision to focus on MNEs comes from the recognition over the last two decades of their contribution to the development and evolution of numerous industrial clusters and production regions (e.g. Buciuni and Pisano 2018; Breznitz and Buciuni 2015). More specifically, MNEs can (a) catalyse an industry cluster (Manning 2008; Giblin and Ryan 2012) or (b) tap into an existing high-tech cluster (Mudambi and Swift 2012) that may later evolve into an even more dynamic and stronger cluster (Ryan et al., 2018). What is less clear, however, is how such an MNE-anchored industry cluster can pave the way for the emergence of an entrepreneurial ecosystem. Therefore, we ask the following research question: *how do MNEs generate entrepreneurship and shape the form of innovation trajectories that can evolve in an entrepreneurial ecosystem over time?*

We address this question by means of a longitudinal study of the genesis of an entrepreneurial ecosystem and its underlying determinants. In particular, by focusing on the role played by multinational enterprises (MNEs) in the transformation of the Galway's medical devices cluster, we provide an original analysis of the micro mechanisms whereby an entrepreneurial ecosystem forms and develops. By analysing the genesis of an entrepreneurial ecosystem, we tap into a growing and yet still under-developed stream of research which focuses on the creation and shaping of favourable conditions in a region that enable a culture of entrepreneurial behaviour and new ventures formation.

The results that emerge from our analysis matter for several reasons. First, they contribute to calls for longitudinal case studies of entrepreneurial ecosystems (Spigel and Harrison 2018; Malecki 2018) and shed further light on the micro mechanisms underlying their formation. In particular, our process study shows how an idiosyncratic entrepreneurial ecosystem was catalysed by anchor MNEs that incubated entrepreneurs that went on to shape the evolution of this entrepreneurial ecosystem in terms of its configuration, dynamics and technology trajectories. They also contribute to theory by explaining the process whereby individual entrepreneurs accumulate knowledge on business model innovation and global market intelligence by working at MNEs and later utilize these competences to spin out and launch new ventures in related and unrelated technological domains. In so doing, we provide an improved understanding of the processes by which entrepreneurial ecosystems form and transform across time. This is useful as the focus of much research to date on entrepreneurial ecosystems has been on the identification of best practices rather than the broad processes we delineate in our study (Spigel and Harrison 2018).

The paper is structured as follows: the next section of the paper draws on both the entrepreneurial ecosystem and international business literatures to provide a theoretical framework for the study. This is followed by a discussion of the methodology used in the study. The following section presents the findings from the research the evolution of Galway's entrepreneurial ecosystem. This provides the basis for a discussion on how this idiosyncratic context builds theory on entrepreneurial ecosystems. Concluding remarks are drawn in the final section.

2. Theory development

2.1 The genesis of an entrepreneurial ecosystem

Over the past decade, a growing body of research has focused on the evolution of industrial regions and the manner in which such regions have reacted to globalization (e.g. Christopherson et al. 2014;

Breznitz and Buciuni 2015). In particular, Evolutionary Economic Geography theory emerged as a new discipline that sought to improve the understanding of the spatial evolution of firms and industries through an explicit dynamic perspective (Boschma and Frenken 2006; Kogler 2015; Martin and Sunley 2015). Despite recent endeavours, this discipline has fallen short by failing to take account of the micro-level dynamics as the principal drivers of regions' evolution across space and time (Boschma and Frenken 2011; Kedron, Rocchetta, and Kogler 2019). A similar criticism of incompleteness can be made of cluster analysis and theory. This is a field where the role of leading firms has been shown to profoundly affect the competitiveness of regional industries (Feldman 2003; Klepper 2010; Giblin and Ryan 2012) but which fails to adequately explain how entrepreneurial activity is nurtured and expanded. Various regional development, innovation systems and entrepreneurship scholars have sought to address these shortcomings by positioning entrepreneurship at the core of local economic development. From this, the field of entrepreneurial ecosystems (Cohen 2006; Isenberg 2010; Mason and Brown 2014) emerged at the nexus of regional development and strategic management theories (Acs et al. 2017).

Nonetheless, the entrepreneurial ecosystem literature clearly links to research on clusters (Alvedalen and Boschma 2017; Spigel and Harrison 2018; Autio et al. 2018; Malecki 2018). However, while clusters can provide opportunities for entrepreneurs (Feldman, Francis, and Bercovitz 2005; Rocha and Sternberg 2005; Delgado, Porter, and Stern 2010), cluster theory does not place the entrepreneur nor entrepreneurial thinking at the core of cluster survival and resilience (Acs et al. 2017; Spigel and Harrison 2018). Some scholars nevertheless assert that an entrepreneurial ecosystem represents a distinct or novel cluster type or may emerge and evolve from a pre-existing technology cluster (Autio et al. 2018). Others propose that entrepreneurial ecosystems have entrepreneurial dynamics that transcend an industry cluster (Malecki 2018) or cut across industries and technologies (Auerswald and Dani 2017). The defining aspect of an entrepreneurial ecosystem is that the entrepreneur and the pursuit of entrepreneurial opportunity and robust entrepreneurial spawning is central (Autio et al. 2018; Malecki 2018). The entrepreneurial ecosystem concept is therefore both broader in scope (cross or beyond industry) but narrower in the unit of analysis (entrepreneur and entrepreneurship) than cluster theory (Auerswald and Dani 2017).

Much of the early work on entrepreneurial ecosystems was policy-oriented (Isenberg 2011; Mason and Brown 2013, 2014). Academic research on developing theory on entrepreneurial ecosystems is quite nascent (Isenberg 2010; Acs, Autio, and Szerb 2014; Autio et al. 2014; Mack and Mayer 2016; Acs et al. 2017; Audretsch and Belitski 2017; Spigel 2017; Stam and Spigel 2017; O'Connor et al. 2018) but growing (Malecki 2018). Entrepreneurial activity is most usefully studied at a local context where culture is bounded, the decisions are made, firms grow and individual traits matter (Feldman and Kogler 2010; Audretsch and Belitski 2017). Entrepreneurial ecosystem theory represents a holistic approach to entrepreneurship focusing on the role of independent and interacting actors within the entrepreneurial ecosystem (Stam 2015; Audretsch and Belitski 2017; Stam and Spigel 2017) and the processes of how it is developed, adapted and sustained (Spigel and Harrison 2018). An entrepreneurial ecosystem is rooted in place and has a relatively distinct geographic boundary (Auerswald 2015; Stam 2015; Brown and Mason 2017; O'Connor et al. 2018) within which dynamic processes of diversity, resilience and adaptation are seen in play (Boschma 2015; Roundy, Brockman, and Bradshaw 2017; Malecki 2018). Such a 'place-oriented' entrepreneurial ecosystem framework determines who becomes an entrepreneur and how actors effect and shape entrepreneurial action and outcomes of the local ecosystem (Autio et al. 2014; Audretsch and Belitski 2017; O'Connor et al. 2018). A variety of actors can impact the birth and growth of an entrepreneurial ecosystem (Mack and Mayer 2016). These include the local university (Miller and Acs 2017; Cunningham, Menter, and Wirsching 2019), diaspora (Baron and Harima 2019), large anchor firms (Mason and Brown 2014; Colombo et al. 2019) and MNEs (Neck et al. 2004; Bhawe and Zahra 2019), the focus of this study. The State (Fuerlinger, Fandl, and Funke 2015) is also a critical actor, supporting organizations, both public and private, such as incubators and accelerators, that fund and mentor actors in the entrepreneurial ecosystem (Hochberg 2016). Operating alongside Government business development agencies are business and trade associations that orchestrate and nurture interactions between horizontal firm actors and coordinate collective lobbying for resources to support entrepreneurship and the growth and resilience of the entrepreneurial ecosystem. The entrepreneurial ecosystem thus comprises a set of independent and interacting components, each of which contributes to its dynamism and trajectory (Stam and Spigel 2017).

In summary, an entrepreneurial ecosystem should be considered as an evolutionary concept (Isenberg 2010; Spigel and Harrison 2018; Malecki 2018; Colombelli, Paolucci, and Ughetto 2019), within which broader contexts such as regional, temporal and social settings matter and must be accounted for in any research (Autio et al. 2014; Zahra and Wright 2011; Alvedalen and Boschma 2017). Some efforts have been made to identify the typological stages of evolution of an entrepreneurial ecosystem: 'embryonic' and 'scale-up' (Brown and Mason 2017). Mack and Mayer (2016) describe how entrepreneurial ecosystem transitions from birth to growth and on to either virtuous sustainment or insipid decline. Auerswald and Dani (2017) suggest that the evolution is not necessarily linear across stages but rather recursive as an adaptive life cycle. However, the objective of a strong entrepreneurial ecosystem is not so much to avoid dwindling into decline (Malecki 2018) but to create resilience and sustainability over time to prevent technological inertia (Narula 2002; Hassink and Dong-Ho 2005; Williams and Vorley 2014; Roundy, Brockman, and Bradshaw 2017). The sustainability of the entrepreneurial ecosystem derives from the introduction of heterogeneous variation and adaptation that can extend an entrepreneurial ecosystem's lifespan. The ultimate objective of an entrepreneurial ecosystem is its continuous renewal (Malecki 2018). This resilience of an entrepreneurial ecosystem emanates from both coherence around specialisms (Roundy, Brockman, and Bradshaw 2017; Spigel and Harrison 2018) and heterogeneity from the diversity of new firm formations across multiple technologies (Malecki 2018). Large firms within the entrepreneurial ecosystem can serve as anchors that facilitate such resilience in the entrepreneurial ecosystem (Clarysse et al. 2014).

2.2 MNE's role in the evolution of a strong entrepreneurial ecosystem

A MNE is a particular form of large firm that operates and creates value across many countries (Dunning and Lundan 2008). They have been shown to anchor entrepreneurial ecosystems (Neck et al. 2004; Spigel and Harrison 2018; Bhawe and Zahra 2019). Governments regularly offer financial and other incentives to attract MNEs to locate in particular regions to create employment, often with high wages (Berrill, O'Hagan-Luff, and van Stel 2018), and bring advanced technologies. There is a long-running 'curse or blessing' debate in the literature and amongst policy-makers as to whether the entry of MNEs to a region has positive or negative entrepreneurial spillovers (De Backer and Sleuwaegen 2003; Audretsch and Keilbach 2008; Berrill, O'Hagan-Luff, and van Stel 2018). MNEs have been shown to have a positive impact as incubators of entrepreneurship that can generate new ventures through spinouts of former employees who draw on the learning that they have gained within the MNE (Neck et al. 2004). However, MNEs have also been shown to inhibit entrepreneurship in the locations in which they are based by attracting local talent that have a preference for the high wages and job security of paid employment that MNEs can offer (Bhawe and Zahra 2019; Berrill, O'Hagan-Luff, and Van Stel 2018).

MNE subsidiaries often enter host regions as factor-seekers but evolve into innovation creators (Gupta and Govidarajan 1991; Delany 2000; Frost 2001; Cantwell and Mudambi 2005). This can result in a subsidiary's ascension to a prominent and important role within the MNE as a 'Centre of Excellence' for R&D and new product development (Holm and Pedersen 2000; Frost, Birkinshaw, and Ensign 2002). Research-intensive subsidiaries can also act as anchors in the entrepreneurial ecosystem (Feldman 2003). This increases the local footprint of the subsidiary and increases its influence with local Government and enterprise actors to take initiatives to deepen and diversify knowledge stock in the local entrepreneurial ecosystem. The research-intensive MNE is also an extremely attractive partner to local university research institutes for joint knowledge creation that further expands the region's knowledge base (Cantwell and Mudambi 2011). MNE subsidiaries also bring with them international quality standards, process and production know-how and knowledge on the international markets they serve, a global business model perspective and an international reputation in the marketplace (Giblin and Ryan 2012). These represent valuable knowledge sources for prospective and nascent entrepreneurs in the region. The concentration of MNE subsidiaries in entrepreneurial ecosystems, therefore, deepens its technology base and enhances its capacity as an incubator for entrepreneurship. These ventures are commonly in new technology domains; these can be related or unrelated to the MNE's core technology domain (Boschma and Frenken 2011; Kogler, 2017). This increased heterogeneity amplifies the resilience of the entrepreneurial ecosystem (Roundy, Brockman, and Bradshaw 2017). Moreover, it has been shown that pioneer entrepreneurs that spinout from MNEs and later successfully exit their built venture seldom exit the entrepreneurial ecosystem but rather stimulate its renewal and growth by channelling their time and energy as role models, mentors and angel financiers (Ryan et al. 2018) into the extension and growth of an entrepreneurial ecosystem in a virtuous cycle.

This discussion points to a need for deeper investigation of the activity and role of MNEs in an entrepreneurial ecosystem's genesis and dynamic evolutionary growth trajectories. We therefore explore the role of the MNE as a key actor in an entrepreneurial ecosystem. We examine its role in the emergence and evolution of the entrepreneurial ecosystem's technology trajectories, specialism embeddedness and adaptation into related branch and unrelated variety technology through the incubation of entrepreneurship inside its R&D laboratories. Specifically, this paper aims to empirically investigate how MNEs can enable the evolution of a vibrant and dynamic entrepreneurial ecosystem that enables entrepreneurship and shapes its development and sustenance in more secure technology domains.

The next section of the paper describes and explains the longitudinal case study approach methodology used in this study.

3. Research method

3.1 Study setting and research approach

Qualitative research has been deemed an appropriate way in which to develop a rich understanding of entrepreneurship and its processes in an ecosystem's spatial and temporal contexts (Karatas-Özkan et al. 2014). Since these processes drive changes that become more evident over time, a long-term examination of an entrepreneurial ecosystem's evolution is advised (Malecki 2018). Accordingly, this process-oriented study reports on a longitudinal mixed-method case study approach (Eisenhardt 1989; Yin 2003; Pettigrew 1990; Welch et al. 2011; Langley et al. 2013; Berends and Deken 2019). It uses, as the revelatory case, the entrepreneurial ecosystem around the city of Galway in the West of Ireland which has undergone a transformation from narrow industry medical devices cluster into a broad medical applications ecosystem that has become more and more agnostic to industry and technology (Autio et al. 2018; Malecki 2018). There are, of course, limitations to the research in that it only involves one idiosyncratic entrepreneurial ecosystem in a particular form and state of transition and catalysed by MNE actors. However, the aim is theory building rather than generalizability. Moreover, whereas from a methodological perspective the entrepreneurial ecosystem literature has tended to take a static and cross-sectional approach to exploration (Mack and Mayer 2016; Spiegel 2017; Alvedalen and Boschma 2017), we conduct a process study of this particularly revelatory transitioning entrepreneurial ecosystem that utilizes longitudinal data. This allows us to examine the entrepreneurial ecosystem's evolutionary processes and specifically the role of two anchor MNEs in its genesis and growth.

3.2 Data collection

Our multi-level longitudinal study draws upon both quantitative and qualitative data. Regarding the former, both patent data and an historical company database were used. Patent applications from medical technology companies based in Galway from 1980 to 2017 were collated and analysed. The

European Patent Office (EPO) PATSTAT database served as the source of relevant patent documents (i.e. information on novel products and processes). The focus of the study was on patents applied for by inventors located in the Galway entrepreneurial system and assigned to either an MNE or an indigenous company in our sample. These were analysed in two ways, first the timing of the innovative output, which has increased significantly after a moderate start since in the mid-1990 s, and the technology classifications reported in the patent document, which indicates specialization and associated diversification patterns over time. We combined this information with data collected on all known companies within the medical technology and wider ICT applications sector in Galway. This involved the generation of a company database listing companies in order of the year the company was established in the region using the Irish Company Registration Office. Given the longitudinal approach of the study, the database includes medical technology companies that have ceased trading as well as those still in operation. Data were collected on each company from FAME (the commercial company database) and from various secondary sources, in particular, Irish industrial development agencies, newspaper searches and website searches. For each company, we recorded the indigenous or foreign nature of the operation, the primary activity of the company; including area of medicine and supplier or own device/component developer, and the current operational status of the company (e.g. still live, divested, merged, acquired, joint venture). In addition, in order to track entrepreneurs the names of the founders of each of the indigenous companies is recorded in the database. Using LinkedIn (the professional social network) as well as broader internet searches, we recorded the prior work experience of each of the founders – positions held and organizations worked with prior to establishing their own company. This helped us to understand where founders developed knowledge and skills before establishing their own firm (e.g. whether from working in foreign-owned subsidiaries or indigenous enterprises) and to ascertain any patterns over time that would indicate changes in the entrepreneurial ecosystem.

Building on the first level of analysis, we used a longitudinal qualitative analysis to make sense of the quantitative data we gathered to shed light on those micro dynamics that have enabled the entrepreneurial ecosystem to generate innovations in related and unrelated domains over two decades. A total of 51 in-depth interviews with various actors belonging to and impacting the Galway entrepreneurial ecosystem (34 founders/Directors of indigenous companies and 17 stakeholders in supporting organizations) were undertaken in 2005, 2010 and 2017, a twelve-year period in which the entrepreneurial ecosystem experienced strong growth in the context of a global economic downturn and associated recovery.

For the company interviews, founders of indigenous firms were selected for interview in order to understand how the entrepreneurs had developed their knowledge, skills and network base. We selected particular companies to interview that would represent the variety of activities within the entrepreneurial ecosystem. For example, founders of supplier companies and founders of companies designing and developing their own devices were interviewed. Directors of indigenous companies that have been acquired by foreign companies were also selected for interview. Three rounds of interviews were conducted with the indigenous medical technology companies. The first set of interviews in 2005 provided an understanding of the origins of indigenous activity within the sector. Semi-structured interviews, each of one to one-half hours in duration, were conducted with the founders of five indigenous companies. Two of these companies were founded principally as component suppliers and three were involved in designing and developing their own devices for the international marketplace. The second round of interviews was conducted in 2010 and consisted of interviewing the founders of thirteen indigenous enterprises. Each interview lasted between one and two hours. For consistency, these enterprises comprised four of the companies interviewed in 2005. The other nine companies were 'born-globals' which had developed their own devices or components for devices. The third round of interviews was conducted in 2017. This involved interviews (again lasting one to two hours) with the founders of 13 indigenous enterprises. Further three interviews were carried out with Directors of companies that were indigenous companies that by 2017 had been acquired by foreign-owned enterprises. The purpose of these interviews was to gain a better appreciation of how indigenous activity has evolved in the region and to understand how entrepreneurs had acquired the necessary skills, knowledge and networks to establish their businesses. This third set of interviews consisted of five interviews with suppliers and eleven with companies that had developed their own devices, components and applications.

In addition to these company interviews, further nine interviews in 2005 and eight interviews in 2017 were carried out with organizations that support the development of the regional medical technology ecosystem. These interviews were all semi-structured in nature and lasted 45–60 min. The 2005 interviews with supporting organizations included national semi-state industrial development agencies, regional semi-state industrial development agencies, one medical technology-related research centre and the technology transfer office at the local University. In 2017, interviews were conducted with two academic Professors of Biomedical Engineering in the region that are Principal Investigators of projects undertaken in collaboration with local medical technology companies; the founder of the medical technology entrepreneurship programme – Bioinnovate – that encourages start-up activity; the Industrial Liaison Officer and the Scientific Programme Manager of a local medical technology research centre; the manager of a research facility based at the local hospital; the manager of a medical technology accelerator programme for small enterprises – BioExel; and the manager of a centre that delivers technology solutions through collaboration with industry. The aim of these interviews was to gain multiple perspectives on the development of the entrepreneurial ecosystem and the role that support organizations play in instigating and supporting new entrepreneurial opportunities in the region. For this reason, only those organizations and key stakeholders that directly support medical technology indigenous enterprises and entrepreneurs either through research, funding or mentoring were selected for interview. In Ireland, semi-state industrial development agencies (national and regional) are a major source of early-stage funding for most high-technology start-ups, given that the private venture capital infrastructure is still emerging. Therefore, such industrial bodies along with research-based organizations and those programmes directly training and mentoring medical technology entrepreneurs (i.e. Bioinnovate and BioEXEl) were selected for interview. These organizations provide an architectural view of the sector and an understanding of the local environmental conditions facilitating or hindering the entrepreneurial ecosystem's evolution.

3.3 Data analysis

Our quest was to explain the role of MNEs in the genesis and growth of an entrepreneurial ecosystem and to describe and explain the temporal evolutionary processes (Langley et al. 2013). Initially, the interviews were transcribed and data organized for analysis (Eisenhardt and Graebner 2007). In the preliminary analyses of interview data, we manually isolated themes and concepts that helped us describe and explain the phenomena we observed . In our analytical strategy, we remained highly context-sensitive (Michailova and Mustaffa 2012; Cuervo-Cazurra et al. 2016). We ordered key events and milestones chronologically and built a chain of evidence and narrative accounts of the evolution of this entrepreneurial ecosystem (Roundy, Brockman, and Bradshaw 2017). We employed triangulation of our primary qualitative data with secondary data in our analysis to deepen our interpretation of the interview data and enhance the reliability and trustworthiness of our findings (Sobh and Perry 2006; Cuervo-Cazurra et al. 2016). Specifically, we tracked and collated secondary sources on key events, critical happenings and notable milestones in the entrepreneurial ecosystem's evolution over the course of the study. This took two forms. First, we traced and kept contemporary notes in an extensive file on key events: examples include the announcement and subsequent establishment of a Centre of Excellence for Manufacturing or R&D in a case firm, the opening of a new Research Centre or Study Programme in the local university and new venture funding. To this end, we continuously monitored press releases, press articles and website announcements. Secondly, we trawled back over press and websites for events we had heard of in our interviews but might have missed in our ongoing secondary data collation.

The sequencing and interpretation of events, many critical, provided explanations of the entre-preneurial ecosystem's context and how it has changed over time (Welch and Paavilainen-Mantymaki 2014). This permitted us to develop a process-based interpretation and explanation of entrepreneurial ecosystem evolutionary dynamics over time and in distinct time periods (Langley et al. 2013). We complemented our qualitative interpretive analysis with our patent information. Combining qualitative and quantitative data allowed us to detect general patterns in the evolving context of the entrepreneurial ecosystem. We refined our analysis through successive iterations between theory and data (Ryan and Bernard 2000; Silverman 2000). This guided our development of an explanation of the role of the R&D-intensive MNEs in the evolution of this idiosyncratic entrepre-neurial ecosystem.

4. Findings

4.1. Origins of the entrepreneurial ecosystem: MNE subsidiary entrepreneurship and specialism emergence

The first activity in the field of medical technology in the Galway region was the establishment of a foreign-owned firm in the area of diagnostics in 1973. However, it was not until the arrival of CR Bard in 1982 (which was subsequently acquired by Medtronic in 1999) and Boston Scientific in 1994, attracted by IDA Ireland incentives, that a network of specialist activity around cardiovascular devices in particular began to emerge. The establishment of these facilities in Galway coincided with the rapid international expansion in the production of balloon catheter devices for use in angioplasty procedures, whereby a balloon is used to widen a narrowed artery in the heart reached using a catheter. At the time of their establishment in the region both CR Bard/Medtronic and Boston Scientific were mandated by their respective HQs to engage in the manufacture of angioplasty devices that were based on research and design undertaken elsewhere in the corporation. Having demonstrated their capabilities for meeting targets and improving efficiencies through incremental innovation, by the mid-to-late 1990s both subsidiaries had moved into R&D activity combined with manufacturing. CR Bard/Medtronic officially opened a 17.1 million euro R&D centre in its Galway facility in 1996 and in the following year Boston Scientific opened a new product development centre staffed with specialists engaging in R&D. At that point in time Boston Scientific and Medtronic collectively employed 2000 people in the region.

By the end of the 1990s and beginning of the 2000s another significant advancement in the angioplasty area emerged internationally. This was the development of a drug-eluting stent for use in a coronary angioplasty procedure that allows for the controlled release of drugs from the stent to the artery wall to prevent future blockages. The main global companies involved in drug-eluting stents were Boston Scientific, Medtronic and Johnson & Johnson/Cordis. The two subsidiaries in Galway became key players within their respective corporations in designing, developing and manufacturing these stents. As a result, Galway became known for its specialization in this area (Giblin and Ryan 2012). During the 2000s the Medtronic subsidiary received the status of becoming a designated Centre for Excellence in the development and manufacture of treatments for cardiovascular diseases. In 2013 the corporation invested in a Customer Innovation Centre in the Galway subsidiary at a cost of €7.7 million demonstrating the subsidiary's advancement. In 2009 Boston Scientific's Galway subsidi-ary won a €91 million investment in Research, Development & Innovation that allowed for early-stage innovative activity and by 2012 the Galway site was designated a Global Centre of Excellence for Drug Eluting Stents. As they had become large-scale employers focused around advanced R&D laboratories and Centres of Excellence these two subsidiaries served as anchors within the cluster and thereby deepening of the regional knowledge base and, as we will show, becoming principal catalysts for the incubation and emergence of an entrepreneurial system in the region.

The engagement in such higher-value-added activity locally by these subsidiaries was an impor-tant stimulus for the emergence of indigenous entrepreneurial activity. As Figure 1 illustrates, the first wave of indigenous activity in the 1980s and early 1990s was predominantly vertical supplier, subcontractor and service provider companies providing goods and services mainly to the local MNE subsidiaries. From the late 1990s more horizontal type entrepreneurial activity had emerged. These indigenous firms could be classed as 'born global' since from their start they produced their own devices or technological systems embedded in devices for an international marketplace. As one entrepreneur stated: 'From day one you have to be global because it's a global industry' (Indigenous I, 2010). This horizontal entrepreneurial activity dominated the type of indigenous companies being established over the more recent period of 2007 to 2016 (see Figure 1).

A clear specialization in vascular-related medicine (cardiovascular and endovascular) emerged in the ecosystem. As demonstrated in Figure 2, about 30% of newly established foreign-owned and indigenous firms in each time period were primarily involved in producing devices, components or systems to meet needs in vascular medicine. However, whereas the specialism persisted and under-pinned the entrepreneurial ecosystem, early signs of increasing diversity and variation in new domains are evident. Patent data from 2009 shows that of the thirty-one medical-technology-related patents identified as filed from the region, just over half were directly related to vascular devices, stents or stenting procedures, while the other patents extended outside this area of activity. Many were in related branch technology. For example, by 2006 pulmonology-vascular activities were identified as being undertaken (see Figure 2) related to the cardiovascular activities that existed prior to 1996. In particular, indigenous companies founded between 1996 to 2006 were operating in more varied areas of medicine as is illustrated in Figure 2.

4.2 Evolution of a strong entrepreneurial ecosystem: heterogeneity and resilience

In the period 2007 to 2016, newly established indigenous and foreign-owned companies were involved in areas of medicine that had not been served by companies in previous decades, such as neurology and connected healthcare (see Figure 2). Patent data up to 2017 also show that the knowledge base underpinning the growing entrepreneurial ecosystem has followed multiple

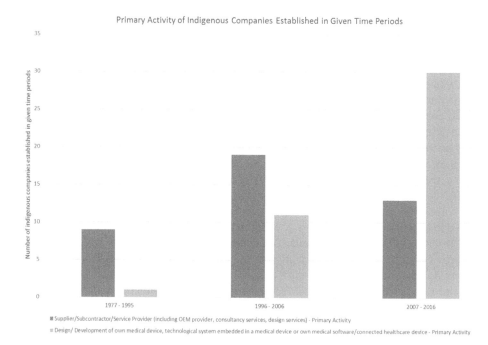

Figure 1. Indigenous activity in galway, medical technology sector.

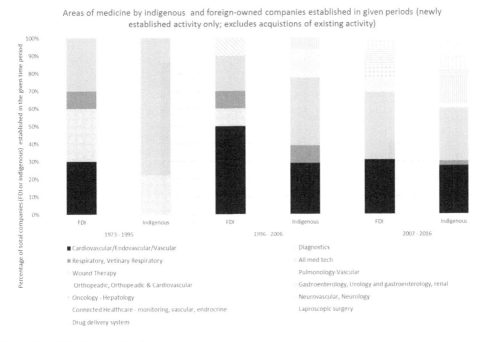

Figure 2. Specializations and diversity in the ecosystem.

innovation trajectories. Patent classification allowed us to categorize distinct innovation paths based on the typology of new technologies. Medtronic and Boston Scientific increased the number of different technological classes in which they successfully applied for a patent from 7 to 12 and from 9 to 22, respectively, between 1980 and 2017. However, innovation in unrelated domains, which eventually led to new category products such as connected healthcare, intelligent biopsy systems and nebulizers, has been mostly developed by indigenous new ventures established as spin offs of multinational corporation subsidiaries. By 2017 indigenous firms were involved in unrelated technological areas, such as medical software and connected healthcare for drug delivery. For example, companies have merged IT with medical devices to produce monitoring and reporting devices for the early detection of medical problems; this is illustrated by Bluedrop Medical that has developed an internet of things device to detect ulcers that result from diabetes. This company is an example of activity shifting towards applying IT solutions to medical problems. Another example is CompanionQMS, a recently established company that has designed a software platform specifically for medical technology companies to achieve and maintain regulatory certification for quality management. The founder of this company, who had been a Product and Quality Engineer in two local MNCs, identified an entrepreneurial opportunity that is predominantly in software development – a different technological domain.

Evidence from our longitudinal analysis shows that the vast majority of entrepreneurs who founded their own ventures across multiple technologies had spent many years working in the R&D labs of the Galway-based branches of MNEs, particularly Medtronic and Boston Scientific (Figure 3). The critical 'eureka' moment that triggered their exit to start their own business was the recognition of market opportunities in technological domains outside their employer's core business. These were spotted whilst working in the MNE R&D lab and had either been missed, ignored or deemed outside of the mandate of the MNE subsidiary. For example, one of the first indigenous companies in the region that developed their own device was Mednova, established in 1996 by three ex-employees of CR Bard (currently Medtronic). With this first endeavour these entrepreneurs identified an opportunity for producing a cardiovascular device (a filter) in

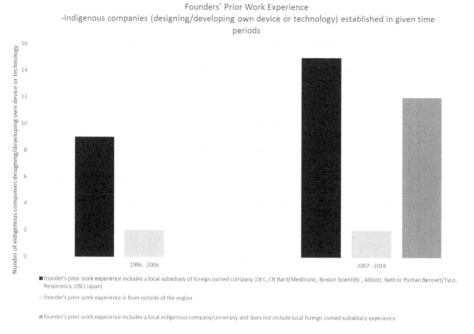

Figure 3. Prior work experience of entrepreneurs.

angioplasty procedures which was related to the activity of the MNC subsidiary. After Mednova was acquired by Abbott in 2005, two of these entrepreneurs established a new enterprise that focused on producing a bio-convertible filter device to prevent blood clots reaching the lungs during surgery, representing a move into pulmonology-cardiovascular and thereby adding further diversity to the ecosystem.

Interviews with the founders of these new companies in the entrepreneurial ecosystem demonstrate that they had built up significant international connections over the course of their careers working in local MNE subsidiaries. This international connectivity afforded by the MNE subsidiary provided the founders with critical international contacts, alongside wider market, business model, clinical and regulatory:

'When we were all in these multinationals, we built up relationships and you get to know people and you get to know the market, I know I can approach these people and I know I have some ideas and I know this doctor and he can get involved with me to check out the idea' (Founder, Indigenous B, 2010).

'Quite frankly it's [MNE subsidiary] the only place to get a grounding in the business because it's very international ….understanding markets, links in with clinicians – and it's a very relevant part of building the knowledge base to take flight in this business'. (Founder, Indigenous Firm K, 2010)

'… they [MNE subsidiaries] are almost like a university for the people who go in there, they are so well trained in the worldwide regulatory requirements … so they learn a huge amount about the market, the products, where all businesses are going … Some smart guy in there spots it and says I'm going to set up a company and do that … we know what to do, we know what has to be done, we know the people to hire and they come out of there with a lot of credibility when you go to investors' (Founder, Indigenous Firm C, 2010).

Whether in related or unrelated technological and market domains, innovation in the Galway entrepreneurial ecosystem was strategically sustained by private-public cooperation. Specifically, the local university – NUI Galway – has played a central role in the evolution of the entrepreneurial ecosystem. It responded to the needs of the emerging and growing knowledge network (both indigenous and foreign-owned) by building the local research infrastructure and specialized training resources and focusing on supporting nascent entrepreneurs through infrastructural support and mentoring (see Table 1). The university also responded to the growing activity around medical technology, and beyond into ICT, by establishing medical technology research centres that were mainly formed through industry-academic partnerships. The university established the first medical technology research centre in Ireland in 1999, called the National Centre for Biomedical Engineering Science (NCBES). Through public and private funding it established three other research centres: REMEDI (2003), ICCM (2014) and CURAM (2014) (see Table 1). REMEDI has both indigenous and foreign-owned companies (including Medtronic) as its industrial partners. Its establishment expanded the entrepreneurial ecosystem's technology base into regenerative medicine therapies such as stem cell biology and manufacturing, gene therapy, orthobiologies and immunology as well as cardiovascular areas (REMEDI, 2010). Furthermore, as knowledge was gained locally on advancements in technology the University responded with the establishment of the National Centre for Biomedical Engineering Science (NCBES), which was, at the time (1999), the first research centre in the country in the area of medical technology. The NCBES was set up to bring together scientists, engineers and clinicians to develop diagnostic and therapeutic devices and to engage in research-related projects on cardiovascular, musculoskeletal, rehabilitation and neural bioelectronics research. From the outset, CR Bard/Medtronic became an official research partner of the NCBES and began to engage in joint research-based projects with academics and researchers in the Centre. Boston Scientific joined soon after as a partner for technology development particularly in unrelated branches.

The university also established a targeted entrepreneur and new venture development programme called Bioinnovate. This programme was funded by the Government agency, Enterprise Ireland, and mentored by Stanford University which had originated the programme successfully in the USA. The programme enrolled and brought together clinicians, business people, biomedical engineers, regulatory and legal experts to form diverse new product development teams. These teams search for entrepreneurial opportunities and develop new product ideas, with the most promising ones taken from an exploratory to development level. Commercialisable ideas with high-growth potential are then funded by Enterprise Ireland for further concept development and then opened up to external funding. This initiative has proven successful resulting in the further proliferation of entrepreneurial activity in the region.

The CURAM research centre is especially notable as it merged knowledge on medical devices with ICT applications to diversify the knowledge base of the region. This was a policy endeavour to move

Table 1. Teaching and research activity in the local university targeted at medical technology.

Year established	Activity	Details of activity
1980	Mechanical Engineering Department	Skills and academic interest
1998	Biomedical Engineering Degree	Skills development specific to Medical Technology industry
1999	National Centre for Biomedical Engineering Science (NCBES) established	First research centre in Ireland in the field of medical technology.
2003	Regenerative Medicine Institute established (REMEDI)	Research institute in stem cell and gene therapy
2009	Specialist Postgraduate Diploma in Medical Device Science	Graduate skills development specific to medical technology sector
2010	Bioinnovate Ireland training programme initiated.	Training programme aimed at generating medical device start-ups
2013	Masters Programme in Biomedical Engineering	Graduate skills development specific to medical technology sector
2014	Irish Centre for Cell Manufacturing Ireland (ICCM)	The only approved centre in Ireland to engage in IN stem cell manufacturing
2014	Centre for Research in Medical Devices (CURAM)	Researching and developing implantable 'smart' medical devices.

beyond core medical device technologies into broader medical applications and thereby further broaden the knowledge base for entrepreneurial activity.

In the period 2007 to 2016, the entrepreneurial ecosystem evolved and strengthened through increased heterogeneity. After the initial period of co-specialism, many pioneer entrepreneurs successfully exited but went on to form further new ventures or act as mentors or financiers to prospective and nascent entrepreneurs. Other pioneering entrepreneurs grew their firms and in turn became incubators of the next generation of entrepreneurs. This created a virtuous cycle of development of the entrepreneurial ecosystem. Figure 3 illustrates the emergence of indigenous firms whose founders had prior experience either in local indigenous companies or the local university.

There is an evident shift in the impact of MNEs on emergent entrepreneurship from their vital early incubation role. When asked in the 2005 round of interviews what would be the impact if Boston Scientific or Medtronic were to leave the local region the response from entrepreneurs was forthright and unequivocal. One entrepreneur stated that 'it would be a significant blow to the local economy if one of these foreign subsidiaries were to leave Galway' (Indigenous firm, 2005). The same question asked in 2017 of founders provides evidence of the evolution of a strong local entrepreneurial ecosystem as follows:

'Of course it may not be ideal if one these corporations were to completely leave Galway, but there has been such a growth in med tech entrepreneurship that it certainly would not be the end of Med Tech here; if anything one of these leaving would spur all those engineers and managers currently working in these to set up their own companies – we have seen this happen already over the years' (Indigenous firm, 2017).

5. Discussion and conclusions

This paper has investigated how MNEs can give rise to the genesis of an entrepreneurial ecosystem in terms of the technology trajectories it takes and the incubation of spinout entrepreneurship in related and unrelated technology branches. In doing so, we contribute to the literature on entrepreneurial ecosystems in a number of ways. First, we contribute to the literature that seeks to explain the link between cluster theory and the concept of an entrepreneurial ecosystem (Spigel and Harrison 2018; Autio et al. 2018; Malecki 2018) by showing how a transition from a cluster (Autio et al. 2018) to an ecosystem can occur. The longitudinal case study that is presented shows how the MNE subsidiaries initially anchored and guided the entrepreneurial ecosystem into a specialism around cardiovascular device activity. Over time, these dominant MNEs (in partnership with local university research centres and supported by Government enterprise agencies), and the spinout indigenous enterprises founded by ex-employees of the subsidiaries that emerged in both related and unrelated technological areas to this specialization, enabled diversity to occur simultaneously with the original specialism. Through recent examples of the establishment of indigenous enterprises, we see that there was a gradual evolution of the ecosystem from a cluster of activity centred on medical device technology that converged with pharmaceuticals into more diverse technological areas in which the core competencies lie beyond pure medical device technology. In the case of some connected health-care companies established by founders with biomedical-mechanical engineering backgrounds, embedded software systems is the more significant capability than medical technology. This process of evolution blurs sectoral boundaries and makes industry distinctions less relevant. It has also reduced, although not eliminated, the dependence on a specific industry technology – in this case cardiovascular devices – which is the focus of an industrial cluster (Spigel and Harrison 2018; Autio et al. 2018). Ongoing coherence around a narrow specialism can make an entrepreneurial ecosystem vulnerable to decline (Mack and Mayer 2016) resulting from technological lock-in and an incapability to adapt quickly to technological disruptions. Over time, the entrepreneurial ecosystem, which in our case has its genesis in MNE activity, develops multiple trajectories to ensure its heterogeneity (Malecki 2018) and thereby strengthening its resilience (Roundy, Brockman, and Bradshaw 2017) while still maintaining the original specialism.

In a further illustration of the transition from industrial cluster to entrepreneurial ecosystem, our case shows how the firms created by the original spinout entrepreneurs from the MNEs in turn become incubators of a new generation of entrepreneurs or following a successful exit have nurtured new entrepreneurial activity with advice and capital. Therefore, the generation of architectural knowledge of 'what works' by pioneering entrepreneurs (Autio et al. 2018, 83) in terms of business modelling and how to pursue entrepreneurial opportunities has been important for fostering new ventures. The production not just of market and technical knowledge in related and unrelated products but also entrepreneurial knowledge in the region has resulted in a broader range of new ventures, a key characteristic of an entrepreneurial ecosystem that differentiates it from an industrial cluster (Spigel and Harrison 2018).

The paper also makes a contribution to theory by combining the international business and entrepreneurial ecosystem literature and thereby adding to the sparse, and mixed evidence on the MNE as an actor in an entrepreneurial ecosystem (Bhawe and Zahra 2019). Whereas Bhawe and Zhara (2019) point to the benefits of MNE entry to a host region for incumbent local firms with high absorptive capacity we show that MNE entry can also be the genesis for the development of a strong entrepreneurial ecosystem and explain the role of MNEs in the formation and strengthening of an entrepreneurial ecosystem. More specifically, we found that MNE subsidiaries, as conduits of 'global pipelines' (Bathelt, Malmberg, and Maskell 2004) into and out of the entrepreneurial ecosystem, can result in them shaping the technological trajectory of new entrepreneurial ecosystems and underpin their evolution over time. The MNE can both instigate an entrepreneurial ecosystem and also promote its development through spillovers and spinouts. There is an important 'connector' role to global entrepreneurial ecosystems that the MNE subsidiary can play. MNE employees develop global connections, particularly with customers, that provides a source of innovation and places them in a position to later exploit entrepreneurial opportunities in establishing their own globally oriented hi-tech start-ups. These international connections can also enable the employees of MNEs to identify new business opportunities in untapped global market niches.

Our study is also of significance for policy. First, it provides policymakers with insights into the dynamics sustaining the competitive advantage and innovation capabilities of geographically bounded entrepreneurial ecosystems. If attracting foreign investments is often seen as the one best ways to foster local economic development, ensuring that a local entrepreneurial ecosystem is established and thrives over time should be regarded as the second necessary condition for sustaining a regional economy. Secondly, policy-makers coping with the volatility and the centrifugal forces of globalization would benefit from understanding how entrepreneurship is nurtured and developed and the dynamics underpinning it in a local milieu. Reflecting on the empirical analysis discussed in this paper, we contend that the evolution of an entrepreneurial ecosystem relies on two critical factors: i) the initial accumulation of a distinctive stock of knowledge locally; ii) the continuous improvement of such a stock of knowledge through the exploration of new trajectories of specialization. In the case of the Galway entrepreneurial ecosystem, while the first condition was enabled by the establishment of the global subsidiaries of MNEs, the exploration of new knowledge frontiers occurred as former employees identified and exploited market opportunities. The close interdependence existing between global subsidiaries, local entrepreneurs and regional institutions, notably universities, facilitated the integration of these two necessary conditions enabling the transition from the accumulation of distinctive knowledge to the exploration of new trajectories.

As the formation of an entrepreneurial ecosystem occurs over time rather than at a single point in time, the MNE can be considered a wellspring that gives rise to the ecosystem from a cluster (Autio et al. 2018). At the same time, while an entrepreneurial ecosystem can evolve in this manner, the linkages to clustering are seen to persist for an elongated period of time. The significance of having coherency around specialisms as well as heterogeneity for a resilient entrepreneurial ecosystem (Roundy, Brockman, and Bradshaw 2017) is such that reaching an 'ideal' state is an idiosyncratic evolutionary process. Consequently, the contention that an entrepreneurial ecosystem must become industry and technology agnostic to be a 'true' form (Spigel and Harrison 2018; Malecki 2018; Autio et al. 2018) may ultimately be overly idealistic for practice.

Acknowledgments

The authors would like to sincerely thank the editorial team and two anonymous reviewers for their most helpful insights and welcome suggestions for improvement of our manuscript. We acknowledge and are grateful for the research assistance of Daniel Cho. Dieter F. Kogler would like to acknowledge funding from the Science Foundation Ireland (SFI) under the SFI Science Policy Research Program, Project: Science-Technology Space (grant agreement No 17/SPR/5324, SciTechSpace).

Disclosure Statement

No potential conflict of interest was reported by the authors.

References

Acs, Z. J., E. Autio, and L. Szerb. 2014. "National Systems of Entrepreneurship: Measurement Issues and Policy Implications." *Research Policy* 43 (3): 476–494. doi:10.1016/j.respol.2013.08.016.

Acs, Z. J., E. Stam, D. B. Audretsch, and A. O'Connor. 2017. "The Lineages of the Entrepreneurial Ecosystem Approach." *Small Business Economics* 49 (1): 1–10. doi:10.1007/s11187-017-9864-8.

Alvedalen, J., and R. Boschma. 2017. "A Critical Review of Entrepreneurial Ecosystems Research: Towards A Future Research Agenda." *European Planning Studies* 25 (6): 887–903. doi:10.1080/09654313.2017.1299694.

Audretsch, D. B., and M. Belitski. 2017. "Entrepreneurial Ecosystems in Cities: Establishing the Framework Conditions." *Journal of Technology Transfer* 42 (5): 1030–1051. doi:10.1007/s10961-016-9473-8.

Audretsch, D. B., and M. Keilbach. 2008. "Resolving the Knowledge Paradox: Knowledge-spillover Entrepreneurship and Economic Growth." *Research Policy* 37 (10): 1697–1705. doi:10.1016/j.respol.2008.08.008.

Auerswald, P. 2015. "Enabling Entrepreneurial Ecosystems." In *The Oxford Handbook of Local Competitiveness*, edited by D. Audretsch, A. Link, and M. L. Walsok, 54–83. Oxford: Oxford University Press.

Auerswald, P. E., and L. Dani. 2017. "The Adaptive Life Cycle of Entrepreneurial Ecosystems: The Biotechnology Cluster." *Small Business Economics* 49 (1): 97–117. doi:10.1007/s11187-017-9869-3.

Autio, E., M. Kenney, P. Mustar, D. Siegel, and M. Wright. 2014. "Entrepreneurial Innovation: The Importance of Context." *Research Policy* 43 (7): 1097–1108. doi:10.1016/j.respol.2014.01.015.

Autio, E., S. Nambisan, L. D. Thomas, and M. Wright. 2018. "Digital Affordances, Spatial Affordances, and the Genesis of Entrepreneurial Ecosystems." *Strategic Entrepreneurship Journal* 12 (1): 72–95. doi:10.1002/sej.1266.

Baron, T., and A. Harima. 2019. "The Role of Diaspora Entrepreneurs in Start-up Ecosystem Development-a Berlin Case Study." *International Journal of Entrepreneurship and Small Business* 36 (1/2): 74–102. doi:10.1504/IJESB.2019.096968.

Bathelt, H., A. Malmberg, and P. Maskell. 2004. "Clusters and Knowledge: Local Buzz, Global Pipelines and the Process of Knowledge Creation." *Progress in Human Geography* 28 (1): 31–56. doi:10.1191/0309132504ph469oa.

Berends, H., and F. Deken. 2019. "Composing Qualitative Process Research." *Strategic Organization*: 1–13.

Berrill, J., M. O'Hagan-Luff, and A. van Stel. 2018. "The Moderating Role of Education in the Relationship between FDI and Entrepreneurial Activity." *Small Business Economics*: 1–19.

Bhawe, N., and S. A. Zahra. 2019. "Inducing Heterogeneity in Local Entrepreneurial Ecosystems: The Role of MNEs." *Small Business Economics* 52 (2): 437–454. doi:10.1007/s11187-017-9954-7.

Boschma, R. 2015. "Towards an Evolutionary Perspective on Regional Resilience." *Regional Studies* 49 (5): 733–751. doi:10.1080/00343404.2014.959481.

Boschma, R., and D. Forndahl. 2011. "Cluster Evolution and a Roadmap for Future Research." *Regional Studies* 45 (10): 1295–1298. doi:10.1080/00343404.2011.633253.

Boschma, R., and K. Frenken. 2006. "Why Is Economic Geography Not an Evolutionary Science? Towards an Evolutionary Economic Geography." *Journal of Economic Geography* 6 (3): 273–302. doi:10.1093/jeg/lbi022.

Boschma, R., and K. Frenken. 2011. "Technological Relatedness and Regional Branching." In *Beyond Territory—Dynamic Geographies of Knowledge Creation, Diffusion and Innovation*, edited by H. Bathelt, M. P. Feldman, and D. F. Kogler, 64–81. London: Routledge.

Breznitz, D., and G. Buciuni. 2015. "Keeping up in an Era of Global Specialization. Semi-public Goods and the Competitiveness of Integrated Manufacturing Districts." In *The Oxford Handbook of Local Competitiveness*, edited by D. Audretsch, A. Link, and M. Walshok, 102–124. Oxford: Oxford University Press.

Brown, R., and C. Mason. 2017. "Looking inside the Spiky Bits: A Critical Review and Conceptualisation of Entrepreneurial Ecosystems." *Small Business Economics* 49 (11): 1–30. doi:10.1007/s11187-017-9865-7.

Buciuni, G., and G. Pisano. 2018. "Knowledge Integrators and the Survival of Manufacturing Clusters." *Journal of Economic Geography* 18 (5): 1069–1089. doi:10.1093/jeg/lby035.

Cantwell, J., and R. Mudambi. 2005. "MNE Competence-creating Subsidiary Mandates." *Strategic Management Journal* 26 (12): 1109–1128. doi:10.1002/()1097-0266.

Cantwell, J. A., and R. Mudambi. 2011. "Physical Attraction and the Geography of Knowledge Sourcing in Multinational Enterprises." *Global Strategy Journal* 1 (3–4): 206–232. doi:10.1002/gsj.v1.3/4.

Christopherson, S., R. Martin, P. Sunley, and P. Tyler. 2014. "Reindustrialising Regions: Rebuilding the Manufacturing Economy?" *Cambridge Journal of Regions, Economy and Society* 7 (3): 351–358. doi:10.1093/cjres/rsu023.

Clarysse, B., M. Wright, J. Bruneel, and A. Mahajan. 2014. "Creating Value in Ecosystems: Crossing the Chasm between Knowledge and Business Ecosystems." *Research Policy* 43 (7): 1164–1176. doi:10.1016/j.respol.2014.04.014.

Cohen, B. 2006. "Sustainable Valley Entrepreneurial Ecosystems." *Business Strategy and the Environment* 15 (1): 1–14. doi:10.1002/()1099-0836.

Colombelli, A., E. Paolucci, and E. Ughetto. 2019. "Hierarchical and Relational Governance and the Life Cycle of Entrepreneurial Ecosystems." *Small Business Economics* 52 (2): 505–521. doi:10.1007/s11187-017-9957-4.

Colombo, M. G., G. B. Dagnino, E. E. Lehmann, and M. Salmador. 2019. "The Governance of Entrepreneurial Ecosystems." *Small Business Economics* 52 (2): 419–428. doi:10.1007/s11187-017-9952-9.

Cuervo-Cazurra, A., U. Andersson, M. Y. Brannen, B. Nielsen, and B. Reuber. 2016. "Can I Trust Your Findings? Ruling Out Alternative Explanations in International Business Research." *Journal of International Business Studies* 47 (8): 881–897. doi:10.1057/s41267-016-0005-4.

Cunningham, J., M. Menter, and K. Wirsching. 2019. "Entrepreneurial Ecosystem Governance: A Principal Investigator-centered Governance Framework." *Small Business Economics* 52 (2): 545–562. doi:10.1007/s11187-017-9959-2.

De Backer, K., and L. Sleuwaegen. 2003. "Does Foreign Direct Investment Crowd Out Domestic Entrepreneurship?" *Review of Industrial Organisation* 22 (1): 67–84. doi:10.1023/A:1022180317898.

Delany, E. 2000. "Strategic Development of the Multinational Subsidiary through Subsidiary Initiative-taking." *Long Range Planning* 33 (2): 220–244. doi:10.1016/S0024-6301(00)00029-7.

Delgado, M., M. E. Porter, and S. Stern. 2010. "Clusters and Entrepreneurship." *Journal of Economic Geography* 10 (4): 495–518. doi:10.1093/jeg/lbq010.

Dunning, J. H., and S. M. Lundan. 2008. *Multinational Enterprises and the Global Economy*. 2nd ed. Cheltenham: Edward Elgar.

Eisenhardt, K. 1989. "Building Theories from Case Study Research." *Academy of Management Review* 14 (4): 532–550. doi:10.5465/amr.1989.4308385.

Eisenhardt, K., and M. E. Graebner. 2007. "Theory Building from Cases: Opportunities and Challenges." *Academy of Management Journal* 50 (1): 25–32. doi:10.5465/amj.2007.24160888.

Feldman, M. 2003. "The Locational Dynamics of the US Biotech Industry: Knowledge Externalities and the Anchor Hypothesis." *Industry and Innovation* 10 (3): 311–328. doi:10.1080/1366271032000141661.

Feldman, M., J. Francis, and J. Bercovitz. 2005. "Creating a Cluster while Building a Firm: Entrepreneurs and the Formation of Industrial Clusters." *Regional Studies* 39 (1): 129–141. doi:10.1080/0034340052000320888.

Feldman, M., and D. F. Kogler. 2010. "Stylized Facts in the Geography of Innovation." In *Handbook of the Economics of Innovation*, edited by H. Bronwyn and N. Rosenberg, 381–410. Oxford: Elsevier.

Frost, T. 2001. "The Geographic Sources of Foreign Subsidiaries' Innovations." *Strategic Management Journal* 22 (2): 101–123. doi:10.1002/()1097-0266.

Frost, T., J. Birkinshaw, and P. Ensign. 2002. "Centers of Excellence in Multinational Corporations." *Strategic Management Journal* 23 (11): 997–1018. doi:10.1002/()1097-0266.

Fuerlinger, G., U. Fandl, and T. Funke. 2015. "The Role of the State in the Entrepreneurship Ecosystem: Insights from Germany." *Triple Helix* 2 (1): 1–26. doi:10.1186/s40604-014-0015-9.

Giblin, M., and P. Ryan. 2012. "Tight Clusters or Loose Networks? The Critical Role of Inward Foreign Direct Investment in Cluster Creation." *Regional Studies* 46: 245–258. doi:10.1080/00343404.2010.497137.

Gupta, A. K., and V. Govindarajan. 1991. "Knowledge Flows and the Structure of Control within Multinational Corporations." *Academy of Management Review* 16: 768–792. doi:10.5465/amr.1991.4279628.

Hassink, R., and S. Dong-Ho. 2005. "The Restructuring of Old Industrial Areas in Europe and Asia." *Environment and Planning A* 37: 571–580. doi:10.1068/a36273.

Hochberg, Y. V. 2016. "Accelerating Entrepreneurs and Ecosystems: The Seed Accelerator Model." *Innovation Policy and the Economy* 16 (1): 25–51. doi:10.1086/684985.

Holm, U., and T. Pedersen. 2000. *The Emergence and Impact of MNE Centres of Excellence*. London: McMillan.

Isenberg, D. J. 2010. "How to Start an Entrepreneurial Revolution." *Harvard Business Review* 88 (6): 41–50.

Isenberg, D. J. 2011. *The Entrepreneurship Ecosystem Strategy as a New Paradigm for Economic Policy: Principles for Cultivating Entrepreneurship, the Babson Entrepreneurship Ecosystem Project*. Wellesley, MA: Babson College.

Karatas-Özkan, M., A. R. Anderson, A. Fayolle, J. Howells, and R. Condor. 2014. "Understanding Entrepreneurship: Challenging Dominant Perspectives and Theorising Entrepreneurship through New Post Positivist Epistemologies." *Journal of Small Business Management* 52 (4): 589–593. doi:10.1111/jsbm.12124.

Kedron, P., S. Rocchetta, and D. F. Kogler. 2019. *Mind the Gap: Advancing Evolutionary Approaches to Regional Development with Progressive Empirical Strategies.* Geography Compass. forthcoming.

Klepper, S. 2010. "The Origin and Growth of Industry Clusters: The Making of Silicon Valley and Detroit." *Journal of Urban Economics* 67: 15–32. doi:10.1016/j.jue.2009.09.004.

Kogler, D. F. 2015. "Editorial: Evolutionary Economic Geography – Theoretical and Empirical Progress." *Regional Studies* 49 (5): 705–711. doi:10.1080/00343404.2015.1033178.

Kogler, D. F. 2017. "Relatedness as Driver of Regional Diversification: A Research Agenda – A Commentary." *Regional Studies* 51 (3): 365–369. doi:10.1080/00343404.2016.1276282.

Langley, A., C. Smallman, H. Tsoukas, and A. Van de Ven. 2013. "Process Studies of Change in Organization and Management: Unveiling Temporality, Activity, and Flow." *Academy of Management Journal* 56 (1): 1–13. doi:10.5465/amj.2013.4001.

Liguori, E., J. Bendickson, S. Solomon, and W. McDowell. 2019. "Development of a Multi-dimensional Measure for Assessing Entrepreneurial Ecosystems." *Entrepreneurship & Regional Development* 31 (1–2): 7–21. doi:10.1080/08985626.2018.1537144.

Mack, E., and H. Mayer. 2016. "The Evolutionary Dynamics of Entrepreneurial Ecosystems." *Urban Studies* 53 (10): 2118–2133. doi:10.1177/0042098015586547.

Malecki, E. 2018. "Entrepreneurship and Entrepreneurship Ecosystems." *Geography Compass* 12 (3): 1–21. doi:10.1111/gec3.12359.

Manning, S. 2008. "Customizing Clusters: On the Role of Western Multinational Corporations in the Formation of Science and Engineering Clusters in Emerging Economies." *Economic Development Quarterly* 22: 316–332. doi:10.1177/0891242408325585.

Martin, R., and P. Sunley. 2011. "Conceptualizing Cluster Evolution." *Beyond the Life Cycle Model?" Regional Studies* 45: 1299–1318.

Martin, R., and P. Sunley. 2015. "Towards a Developmental Turn in Evolutionary Economic Geography?" *Regional Studies* 49: 712–732. doi:10.1080/00343404.2014.899431.

Mason, C., and R. Brown. 2013. "Creating Good Public Policy to Support High-growth Firms." *Small Business Economics* 40 (2): 211–225. doi:10.1007/s11187-011-9369-9.

Mason, C., and R. Brown. 2014. "Entrepreneurial Ecosystems and Growth Oriented Entrepreneurship." In *Background paper prepared for the workshop organised by the OECD LEED Programme and the Dutch Ministry of Economic Affairs on Entrepreneurial Ecosystems and Growth Oriented Entrepreneurship.* The Hague, Netherlands. https://www.oecd.org/cfe/leed/Entrepreneurial-ecosystems.pdf

Menzel, M., and D. Forndahl. 2009. "Cluster Life Cycles – Dimensions and Rationales of Cluster Evolution." *Industrial & Corporate Change* 19: 205–238. doi:10.1093/icc/dtp036.

Michailova, S., and Z. Mustaffa. 2012. "Subsidiary Knowledge Flows in Multinational Corporations: Research Accomplishments, Gaps and Opportunities." *Journal of World Business* 47: 383–396. doi:10.1016/j.jwb.2011.05.006.

Miller, D., and Z. Acs. 2017. "The Campus as Entrepreneurial Ecosystem: The University of Chicago." *Small Business Economics* 49 (1): 75–95. doi:10.1007/s11187-017-9868-4.

Mudambi, R., and T. Swift. 2012. "Multinational Enterprises and the Geographical Clustering of Innovation." *Industry & Innovation* 19: 1–21. doi:10.1080/13662716.2012.649058.

Narula, R. 2002. "Innovation Systems and 'Inertia' in R&D Location: Norwegian Firms and the Role of Systemic Lock-in." *Research Policy* 31: 795–816. doi:10.1016/S0048-7333(01)00148-2.

Neck, H., D. Meyer, B. Cohen, and A. Corbett. 2004. "An Entrepreneurial System View of New Venture Creation." *Journal of Small Business Management* 42 (2): 190–208. doi:10.1111/j.1540-627X.2004.00105.x.

O'Connor, A., E. Stam, F. Sussan, and D. B. Audretsch. 2018. *Entrepreneurial Ecosystems: Place-based Transformations and Transitions.* Switzerland: Springer.

Pettigrew, A. M. 1990. "Longitudinal Field Research on Change: Theory and Practice." *Organization Science* 1 (3): 267–292. doi:10.1287/orsc.1.3.267.

Rocha, H. O., and R. Sternberg. 2005. "Entrepreneurship: The Role of Clusters Theoretical Perspectives and Empirical Evidence from Germany." *Small Business Economics* 24 (3): 267–292. doi:10.1007/s11187-005-1993-9.

Roundy, P. T., B. K. Brockman, and M. Bradshaw. 2017. "The Resilience of Entrepreneurial Ecosystems." *Journal of Business Venturing Insights* 8: 99–104. doi:10.1016/j.jbvi.2017.08.002.

Ryan, G., and H. Bernard. 2000. "Data Management and Analysis Methods." In *Handbook of Qualitative Research*, edited by K. Denzin and S. Lincoln, 769–802. 2nd ed. Thousand Oaks, CA: Sage.

Ryan, P., M. Giblin, U. Andersson, and J. Clancy. 2018. "Subsidiary Knowledge Creation in Co-evolving Contexts." *International Business Review* 7 (5): 915–932. doi:10.1016/j.ibusrev.2018.02.003.

Silverman, D. 2000. *Doing Qualitative Research: A Practice Handbook.* London, UK: Sage.

Sobh, R., and C. Perry. 2006. "Research Design and Data Analysis in Realism Research." *European Journal of Marketing* 40 (11): 1194–1209. doi:10.1108/03090560610702777.

Spigel, B. 2017. "The Relational Organization of Entrepreneurial Ecosystems." *Entrepreneurship Theory and Practice* 41 (1): 49–72. doi:10.1111/etap.12167.

Spigel, B., and R. Harrison. 2018. "Toward a Process Theory of Entrepreneurial Ecosystems." *Strategic Entrepreneurship Journal* 12 (1): 151–168. doi:10.1002/sej.2018.12.issue-1.

Stam, E. 2015. "Entrepreneurial Ecosystems and Regional Policy: A Sympathetic Critique." *European Planning Studies* 23 (9): 1759–1769. doi:10.1080/09654313.2015.1061484.

Stam, E., and B. Spigel. 2017. "Entrepreneurial Ecosystems." In *The SAGE Handbook of Small Business and Entrepreneurship*, edited by R. Blackburn, D. De Clercq, J. Heinonen, and Z. Wang, 407-420. London: SAGE.

Welch, C., and E. Paavilainen-Mantymaki. 2014. "Putting Process (Back) In: Research on the Internationalization Process of the Firm." *International Journal of Management Reviews* 16 (1): 2–23. doi:10.1111/ijmr.2014.16.issue-1.

Welch, C., R. Piekkari, E. Plakoyiannaki, and E. Paavilainen-Mantymaki. 2011. "Theorising from Case Studies: Towards a Pluralist Future for International Business Research." *Journal of International Business Studies* 42: 740–762. doi:10.1057/jibs.2010.55.

Williams, N., and T. Vorley. 2014. "Economic Resilience and Entrepreneurship: Lessons from the Sheffield City Region." *Entrepreneurship and Regional Development* 26 (3–4): 257–281. doi:10.1080/08985626.2014.894129.

Yin, R. 2003. *Case Study Research: Design and Methods*. 3rd ed. Newbury Park, CA: Sage.

Zahra, S. A., and M. Wright. 2011. "Entrepreneurship's Next Act." *Academy of Management Perspectives* 25 (4): 67–83. doi:10.5465/amp.2010.0149.

Meeting its Waterloo? Recycling in entrepreneurial ecosystems after anchor firm collapse

Ben Spigel(iD) and Tara Vinodrai(iD)

ABSTRACT

The 'recycling' of people, capital, and ideas within an entrepreneurial eco-system is a key process driving high-growth entrepreneurship. Skilled work-ers who leave firms after successful exits or firm collapse bring knowledge and insights that they can use to start new ventures or work at existing scale-up firms. This makes large anchor firms important actors in attracting workers who may subsequently recycle into the local ecosystem. However, there is limited empirical research on recycling into an ecosystem after the loss of an anchor firm. This paper develops a novel methodology using career history data to track recycling into ecosystems. The paper develops a study of Waterloo, Ontario, home to the smartphone manufacturer Blackberry, whose decline in 2008 represented a significant shock to the local entrepreneurial ecosystem. We find that alumni of this firm engaged in very little high-growth entrepreneurship, instead entering the ecosystem as technology employees at high-growth scale-up firms. This was aided by the region's increased institutional capacity to match skilled workers with new ventures, ensuring the continued success of the ecosystem over time. These findings provide a more nuanced understanding of the role of anchor firms in entrepreneurial ecosystems and how recycling affects the dynamics of entrepreneurial ecosystems.

1. Introduction

Entrepreneurial recycling is the flow of resources such as skilled workers, capital, and ideas from successful or unsuccessful firms into the surrounding region (Mason and Harrison 2006). This is seen as a key process underlying the impact of ecosystems – the social, economic, cultural, and political contexts that support high-growth entrepreneurship in a region (Spigel and Harrison 2018). Work on ecosystems has consistently emphasized the importance of highly skilled employees who can help entrepreneurs develop, build, and sell highly innovative new products and services (Malecki 2018; Stam 2015; Mack and Mayer 2016; Mason and Brown 2014). The innovative potential of such workers increases the competitiveness of their employers, allowing these firms to compete in global markets for high-end products and services. This means that the ability of regions to produce, attract, and most importantly, retain highly skilled workers through recycling is a key component of building a sustainable entrepreneurial ecosystem.

Large private or public employers, commonly known as 'anchors', are key actors in this process. Anchors act as talent magnets, drawing in highly skilled workers by offering career opportunities and embedding these workers in the region as they establish local social and professional connections. They may subsequently recycle into the broader ecosystem as founders or employees of new, innovative start-up and scale-up firms (Bahrami and Evans 1995; Mason and Harrison 2006). Indeed, the ability of a region recycle these workers after an economic shock such as the loss of an anchor firm has been seen as an important criterion of a region's overall resilience (Martin and Sunley 2015). But while the migration patterns of highly skilled workers has been well studied in the literature (Kerr 2018), there is little empirical evidence about how workers who leave anchor firms recycle within their local economy. In particular, little is known about their propensity to enter the entrepreneurial ecosystem either by becoming entrepreneurs or working at local scale-up firms. This is a critical research gap as regions turn to high-growth entrepreneurship as a way to build resilient economies. The lack of sustained engagement with questions surrounding the dynamics of recycling within ecosystems represents a major research gap in the literature.

A challenge in studying intra-regional employment mobility and entrepreneurial recycling comes from the paucity of data on the workers' career histories. Such data is difficult to come by, either generated through detailed, qualitative interviews (Vinodrai 2006) or longitudinal microdata, such as that is only available in data rich Nordic countries (Dahl and Sorenson 2012). Outside of these examples, most literature on this topic uses census data, which do not provide sufficient detail to examine the effects of local shocks such as the collapse of an anchor firm. To address this issue, we develop a novel methodology to collect data on individual career trajectories from employment-based social media sources. These data are used to explore the consequences of the decline of smartphone manufacturer Blackberry (formerly Research in Motion or RIM) on the entrepreneurial ecosystem in Waterloo (Canada), where the firm was founded and remains headquartered. Waterloo is one of North America's strongest entrepreneurial ecosystems due in no small part to the Blackberry's ability to attract highly skilled workers to the region and the firm's support of local entrepreneurial institutions such as university programmes and local economic development organizations. The data suggest that recycling, like other ecosystem processes, are temporally dynamic, meaning that their nature and intensity changes over time in response to broader institutional developments in the region.

In this paper, we focus on entrepreneurial recycling as the transition of workers at large firms in a region to either being growth-oriented entrepreneurs or workers at a high-growth venture after a critical exit moment such as a large layoff event. In doing so, this paper makes three contributions to the growing literature on entrepreneurial ecosystems. First, it provides some of the first empirical evidence on the dynamics of entrepreneurial recycling, giving a baseline for comparison with other regions that experience exit events. Second, it explores the relationship between local institutions and recycling by showing how the recycling of skilled workers into the local ecosystem changes over time in response to local institutional developments. Finally, this paper responds to calls for using more fine-grained data sources to understand the flow of people and resources within entrepreneurial ecosystems (Feldman and Lowe 2015) by developing a novel method and dataset to track employee career trajectories within ecosystems. Both the dataset and the insights it offers on the recycling process provide new perspectives on questions about the evolution of entrepreneurial ecosystems and the foundations of regional resiliency.

The paper proceeds as follows. In the next section, we discuss the nascent literature on entrepreneurial ecosystems and recycling, connecting this with work on anchor firms and economic shocks. Following from this discussion, we provide background information and details on the case study firm (Blackberry) and region (Waterloo, Canada). We also describe the dataset employed in this paper and the methodology used to collect and process it. Section four uses this dataset to explore the recycling of tech-based talent into Waterloo's ecosystem after the decline of Blackberry. Section five contextualizes these data by showing the impact of local institutional factors on the recycling process. The paper concludes by discussing what this tells us about the dynamic processes underlying entrepreneurial ecosystems and identifies avenues for future research.

2. Entrepreneurial ecosystems, recycling and anchor firms

Entrepreneurial ecosystems are a region's 'actors and factors' (Stam 2015, 1765) that contribute to the increased creation and survival of high-growth new ventures. Though the term 'entrepreneurial ecosystem' dates back more than three decades (Malecki 2018), its recent ascendance can be attributed to work in the popular business sphere by Dan Isenberg (2010) and Brad Feld (2012). Both argue that a regional 'ecosystem' of entrepreneurs, investors, and public officials, in addition to a supportive local culture and dense interpersonal networks, is needed to support the ongoing creation of high-growth entrepreneurial firms. Researchers have identified several key localized resources or attributes that promote high-growth entrepreneurship. These include individuals such as ambitious entrepreneurs, knowledgeable investors, local 'dealmakers' with large social networks, as well as broader regional attributes like favourable public policies, strong research universities, and a culture that promotes risk-taking and collaboration (Stam and Spigel 2018; Nicotra et al. 2017). These create an environment that promotes entrepreneurial ambition and provides critical resources like financing, entrepreneurial know-how and skills required to successfully develop new products and business models, thus enabling firm growth. The presence of skilled workers has been consistently identified in the literature as a critical factor (Dubini 1989; Van de Ven 1993; Spigel 2017). Skilled workers are important for new ventures to develop innovative new products and sell them to global markets (Eckardt, Skaggs, and Lepak 2018).

While sharing similarities with previous concepts such as clusters and industrial districts, entrepreneurial ecosystem research is distinct in at least three ways. First, ecosystems maintain a specific focus on high-growth startups and scale-ups. These high-growth firms are responsible for the bulk of new job creation and regional economic growth (Brown, Mason, and Mawson 2014; Mason and Brown 2014). Definitions of high-growth firms differ, but generally refer to companies that are growing by at least 20% in terms of revenues or sales per year or have the potential to reach this state. This differs from previous entrepreneurship policy research, which instead looked at how to increase overall firm formation or self-employment rates (Autio et al. 2017). High-growth firms require different support environments than startups in lower growth areas such as retail, consumer services, or consulting, leading to the need for new policy approaches (Brown, Mawson, and Mason 2017). Entrepreneurial ecosystems research represents a new direction in the entrepreneurship policy literature due its distinct focus on this small subset of new ventures.

Second, entrepreneurial ecosystem research has emphasized the role of entrepreneurs themselves in creating a strong entrepreneurial community rather than state or other large organizational actors. Research on ecosystems has highlighted the importance of entrepreneurs as regional leaders who identify the issues that need to be addressed and create the organizations and institutions that drive changes within the ecosystem (Stam 2015). Successful entrepreneurs often emerge as ecosystem leaders, working with other stakeholders to build new organizations and institutions to support entrepreneurial endeavours (Lowe and Feldman 2017). While the ecosystem framework acknowledges entrepreneurs as critical agents, it is important to recognize that these ecosystems remain influenced by multiple actors, including governments, universities, industry associations, philanthropic groups and other local and regional actors (Hayter 2016).

Finally, entrepreneurial ecosystem research has emphasized the interconnections between different elements of a region's entrepreneurial environment and economy (Spigel 2017). For example, a growing stream of research has pointed to the importance of interactions between entrepreneurship support programmes that create a cohesive environment supporting entrepreneurial growth (Motoyama and Knowlton 2016). Entrepreneurial ecosystems are more than regions with high rates of start-up creation; they are defined by the self-reinforcing relationships between various attributes that reproduce and transform the ecosystem over time, creating durable environments and cultural outlooks that catalyse high growth entrepreneurship. Thus, entrepreneurial ecosystems are just as much about regionally-specific institutional structures and collective beliefs about entrepreneurship as they are about particular regional policy configurations or firm structures (Roundy 2016).

Entrepreneurial ecosystems are therefore distinct from concepts such as clusters or innovation systems (Spigel and Harrison 2018). Unlike clusters, entrepreneurial ecosystems are primarily comprised of entrepreneurial start-ups and scale-ups that are actively developing new products and entering new markets. These ventures draw on their regional economy in very different ways than larger, established firms. Entrepreneurial ventures are more dependent on local resources and are more influenced by their local contexts (Fritsch and Storey 2014). In particular, they are much more dependent on the local labour market and other local resources because they lack the capacity to open up branch offices until late in the firm growth process (Wapshott and Mallett 2016). More traditional cluster or innovation systems perspectives often miss how entrepreneurial firms differ in how they use and are affected by their regional context (Ylinepää 2009).

2.1. Recycling in entrepreneurial ecosystems

While the entrepreneurial ecosystems concept has been critiqued for being static (Alvedalen and Boschma 2017; Auserwald and Dani 2017), previous work has explicitly examined how entrepreneurial ecosystems form and change over time (Mack and Mayer 2016; Thompson, Purdy, and Ventresca 2017). One of the key evolutionary processes of ecosystems is *recycling*: the 'fluidity' of resources like people, skills, knowledge, and capital that move between different firms within an ecosystem (Mason and Harrison 2006; Spigel and Harrison 2018). Recycling occurs when the resources created or attracted by existing firms, often large corporations or local ventures that have scaled up, flow to new startups and scaleups in a region, who leverage these resources to enhance their innovation and growth potential. Such flows are often triggered by particular events, such as a successful firm exit through merger or acquisition or an unsuccessful firm exit like bankruptcy. These events reduce the opportunity costs associated with starting a new firm, encouraging entrepreneurship (Frederiksen, Wennberg, and Balachandran 2016). While people leaving a failing firm are often forced to due to layoffs, even a successful exit can lead to an exodus because of disagreements with new management or windfall profits from stock options.

Recycling highlights that the resources in an ecosystem are not bound to the firm that created them, but can move throughout the ecosystem. Actions like employees leaving firms to start their own firm or founders stepping back from their firms to mentor entrepreneurs or invest in other firms spread entrepreneurial resources within the ecosystem. In turn, this helps entrepreneurs access the resources they need for firm growth and enables the ecosystem to reproduce itself over time.

As illustrated in Figure 1, three types of resources can recycle back into an ecosystem after an exit event: business know-how, financial capital, and skills embodied in workers. However, it is also possible that these resources will fail to flow into the ecosystem, as talent and capital leave the region or because people take jobs at larger, corporate employers outside of the local ecosystem. Some forms of entrepreneurial and business know-how are ephemeral and non-rivalrous, meaning that they can be provided to many different people at once. They are produced from business experience and shared through social networks and interpersonal interactions. Other resources like investment capital are more footloose, able to circulate within or leave the entrepreneurial ecosystem quickly.

But other resources are fundamentally people-based, such as workers and the skills they possess. Their networks and abilities are inseparable from themselves (Corce et al 2016). Indeed, the recycling of people is perhaps the most important form of recycling: while capital and advice can be acquired from outside the region, skilled workers are amongst the most crucial resources a firm needs in order to grow and prosper and generally must be found locally or attracted at great expense (Gjerlov-Juel and Guenther 2018; Saurmann 2017). Recycling ensures a steady pool of skilled workers that entrepreneurial ventures can draw on as well as a pool of new entrepreneurs to found new innovative ventures. Such people bring with them the skills and insights they developed in their previous jobs along with knowledge of organizational routines and market opportunities, making them particularly valuable as founders or early-stage workers (Toft-Kehler, Wennberg, and Kim 2014).

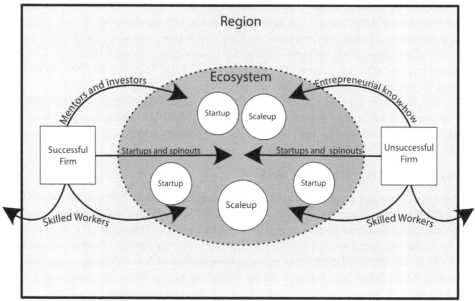

Figure 1. Recycling within entrepreneurial ecosystems.
Source: Authors' conceptualization based on the literature

Former founders and workers at exited firms can recycle back into the ecosystem by creating new spinout firms or taking jobs at existing scale-up firms. Entrepreneurs often start with unique insights about opportunities that their former employer did not pursue, giving them an early advantage for achieving product/market fit (Klepper 2007). Serial entrepreneurs who leave the firm they founded often generate useful entrepreneurial know-how and legitimacy, even if the firm ultimately failed (Zhang 2011). They can spread this knowledge both by creating new firms and by mentoring other entrepreneurs using their experiences. Spinout-based recycling allows for the Darwinian evolution of an ecosystem because the leaving founders can take what they feel are the most effective elements of the parent organization while leaving behind what they feel are needless or inferior elements (Klepper and Sleeper 2005).

The movement of workers between firms is also an important source of recycling within ecosystems. Employees bring with them insights and skills they developed at their previous employer as they move to new firms (Wu, Jin, and Hitt 2017). Working at innovative firms helps employees build their own technical and entrepreneurial skills, which they bring with them to their subsequent employers, making them more productive (Tambe and Hitt 2014). These actors bring with them technical and business insights, market knowledge, ties to customers and suppliers, and knowledge of organizational routines they acquired at their former employers (Feldman, Ozcan, and Reichstein 2019).

Recycling is triggered by particular events that affect firms and individuals. When a firm is acquired or goes public, its founders and early employees are able to 'cash out' and may choose to recycle into the ecosystem. For example, after a firm is acquired by an outside company, its successful founders can return to the local entrepreneurial ecosystem as both serial entrepreneurs and as knowledgeable angel investors or mentors, helping to support further entrepreneurship within the ecosystem (DeTienne 2010). Their experience allows them to have unique insights into market dynamics that help them identify new entrepreneurial opportunities (Zahra 2008). Workers at that firm might use profits from stock options as seed capital for new ventures, or take what they have learned from the firm as they assume management or technical positions at other local firms.

But firm failure also triggers a release of resources back into the entrepreneurial ecosystem where they can be used by other local firms. The loss of a job decreases the opportunity cost of entrepreneurship (Frederiksen, Wennberg, and Balachandran 2016), allowing laid off workers to draw on the insights and ideas they had at their former job to identify new opportunities. These workers bring with them potentially valuable know-how and insights that can be used by others. Similarly the founders of these failed firms can learn from their experience, increasing their chances of succeeding in subsequent ventures.

These different ways of recycling are affected by a region's social and economic institutions. Some institutional configurations make a place 'sticky', keeping resources locally and making them available to local entrepreneurs in the ecosystem. For example, the ability of entrepreneurs and workers from failed ventures to recycle back into the ecosystem depends on the presence of a local culture that is tolerant of failure and setbacks. As Bahrami and Evans (1995, 81) argue: 'the process of "flexible recycling" is enhanced in the absence of the typical stigma associated with organisational failure.' Other cultural structures may make it difficult for anyone associated with a firm failure to recycle back into the ecosystem. This may lead to brain drain where skilled workers leave the region for better economic or social prospects.

On the other hand, certain economic and institutional configurations may make recycling more common, such as regional economies dominated by secure civil service or health-related jobs; in such places workers who are laid off cannot easily relocate because of their partners' careers and instead they must seek other local jobs or create their new ventures in order to stay in the region (Harrison, Cooper, and Mason 2004). Similarly, high levels of amenities and deep social ties to a place will encourage founders and workers to stay after a successful exit. Recycling is therefore a contextual phenomenon that depends on place-specific institutions and cultures.

2.2. The role of anchor firms in entrepreneurial ecosystems

Large firms are often important players in building a supportive ecosystem for innovative new ventures (Brown and Mason 2017; Spigel 2017). The headquarters of large multinational corporations, research universities, public research labs and hospitals have long been viewed as anchors for regional development (Agrawal and Cockburn 2003). Their relative size gives them outsized importance within regional economies, often through their influence on localized production networks and informal institutional norms that often provide the foundation for entrepreneurial ecosystems (Colombelli, Paolucci, and Ughetto 2017). As such, they are critical players in how entrepreneurial ecosystems develop and ultimately help high-growth entrepreneurs. While both public and private sector organizations can act as anchors, we focus our discussion here on large corporate firms and their role as anchors in the entrepreneurial ecosystem.

Table 1 presents a framework for understanding the contributions of anchor firms to entrepreneurial ecosystems. First, anchor firms assist in the development of *talent*. Employment opportunities at anchor firms attract highly skilled workers to the region, some of whom may become future entrepreneurs (Wolfe and Gertler 2004). This 'magnet' function is often critical to the creation of a strong ecosystem. In addition to attracting global talent, anchors play a leading role in skills upgrading and training in the local labour market, through the provision of in-house training and on-the-job experience or through partnerships with local universities (Croce et al. 2016).

Second, anchor firms have wider *entrepreneurial effects*. New ventures can spin out of anchors, from either strategic corporate entrepreneurship activities or new ventures created by former employees without the permission of the parent firm (Klepper 2007). In either cases, these spinouts inherit technical and market knowledge, as well as organizational routines from the parent, providing them with an early source of competitive advantage. Founders of spinoffs often have superior knowledge of the marketplace, allowing them to more easily identify market opportunities and gain market legitimacy necessary to make early sales. Furthermore, the literature suggests that anchor firms can are a source of knowledge spillovers to nearby firms, through direct partnerships,

Table 1. The contributions of anchor firms to entrepreneurial ecosystems.

Talent	Global talent attraction	Highly skilled global workers attracted to region to work at anchor firm
	Local labour upskilled	Anchor firm increases skills of local workers through either in-house training or supporting programmes at local universities
Entrepreneurial effects	Spinoff creation	Workers at anchor firms form their own new ventures that take advantage of their unique skillset
	Worker mobility & knowledge spillovers	Workers attracted to anchor firm leave to work at local firms, bringing with them unique technological and market insights
Formal institutional capacity	Business leadership	Founders and senior managers of local anchor firms help build regional industry associations and formal organizations to support entrepreneurship and innovation
	Dealmaking	Founders and senior managers help build local networks and connect entrepreneurs with supporters
	Corporate venture capital & angel investing	Anchor firms and their founders provide early stage equity investment in new ventures
Informal institution building	Entrepreneurial culture	Anchor firm leaders normalize risk taking and entrepreneurial behaviours
	Role models	Anchor firm leaders provide inspiration to potential entrepreneurs

Source: Authors' conceptualization based on the literature

observation or worker mobility (Lucas, Sands, and Wolfe 2009). Under the right conditions, local firms can integrate knowledge related to technical innovations and innovative practices into their own products, services and organizational routines (Gertler 2010). Informal knowledge flows through social and professional connections, frequently made when an employee works at an anchor firm before leaving to work at a nearby firm, are a crucial conduit for these knowledge spillovers (Whittington, Owen-Smith, and Powell 2009).

Third, anchor firms contribute to the creation of *formal institutional capacity* that supports the ecosystem. This capacity can be developed in several ways. For instance, the rapid growth and scaling up of a local venture creates a new pool of skilled angel investors who can support new rounds of high-growth entrepreneurship. Large firms will engage politically with local policymakers to create a more business-friendly environment. Anchors, particularly those founded by local entrepreneurs, have political power that can be used to lobby for the creation of new local programmes or policies that strengthen the local economy. This might include investments in university programmes, training programmes, new infrastructure, and quality of life improvements such as parks and schools to attract and retain skilled workers to the region (Katz and Nowak 2018). However, this is not an automatic or deterministic process: ecosystem actors must take purposeful steps to help build a stronger entrepreneurial community. This is often achieved through civic engagement by leading members of the business and entrepreneurial community, who contribute their own time, energy, and civic capital to cultivate strong entrepreneurial communities (Feldman and Zoller 2012). Such 'dealmakers' or 'ecosystem coordinators' can help develop formal institutions, such as policies that fund and train local entrepreneurs or accelerators that help incubate them, as well as informal institutions such as supportive cultures, that help encourage and assist high-growth entrepreneurs.

Finally, anchor firms play a role in *building informal institutions*, specifically related to developing an entrepreneurial culture and acting as role models for potential entrepreneurs. The growth of a locally founded firm into a globally competitive anchor firm helps create a local cultural confidence in entrepreneurship, which can encourage other entrepreneurs to make their own similar journeys. The founders of such firms become local role models, directly and informally aiding other entrepreneurs in the community (Spigel 2013). They might inspire others to become entrepreneurs, angel investors or mentors. In this way a few dedicated entrepreneurs can help create a broader community that sustains an entrepreneurial culture and coordinates the flow of key resources throughout the ecosystem.

These activities contribute to the health of the entrepreneurial ecosystem, improving its capacity to support high-growth firms. Anchors' size gives them the resources and legitimacy to take on major ecosystem roles, such as sponsoring new support programmes or acceleration programmes.

Their local supply chains create markets that entrepreneurs in the ecosystem can use to introduce new products and the alumni of anchors often become important local investors, mentors, or dealmakers.

But while one of the most important contributions anchor firms make to an entrepreneurial ecosystem is attracting highly skilled workers, we cannot assume that these workers will easily enter the ecosystem. Not all employees are willing to work in new ventures or scaling firms, which are often characterized by low levels of hierarchy, fuzzy job roles, and less job security than larger corporate or public employers (Stam 2013). Workers at start-ups tend to be younger, and more risk-oriented than their peers at larger employers and are often attracted by the prospect of having a more direct impact on a firm's development, as well as a 'cooler' firm culture (Ouimet and Zarutskie 2014).

Recycling from anchor firms is therefore not automatic; if workers leave an anchor employer they may prefer working for another large corporate employer in the region rather than a riskier new venture. The extent to which workers are willing to take on the risks of working at an entrepreneurial venture depends on context of their ecosystem. A supportive local culture helps employees develop the forms of entrepreneurial orientation and skills that ensures that they are willing to work at entrepreneurial firms (Roach and Sauermann 2015). This may include normalizing high job insecurity, frequent job changes, and accepting risky stock options in exchange for lower wages (Neff 2012). However, these cultural effects are not homogenous: even within very strong entrepreneurial ecosystems there are skilled workers who are more comfortable working at larger employers rather than smaller and riskier ones.

Thus, there is a tension in the potential effects of anchor firms on the surrounding entrepreneurial ecosystem. On one hand, anchors play a key role in attracting highly skilled workers to a region and increasing the entrepreneurial potential of the region through knowledge spillovers, institutional development, and local value chain creation. On the other hand, there is no reason to assume that the workers attracted to anchor firms have entrepreneurial mindsets or a desire to start or work at new ventures. Indeed, high wages at anchor firms increase the opportunity cost of spinout activities. An anchor firm whose organizational culture supports entrepreneurship is likely to attract workers with an entrepreneurial mindset, which in turn helps create and reproduce a region's entrepreneurial culture. Anchor firms that lack an entrepreneurial culture may not attract entrepreneurial workers and might actively prevent spinouts, hurting a region's entrepreneurial culture and ecosystem.

2.3. Anchor firm collapse, recycling and the evolution of ecosystems

Entrepreneurial ecosystems are inherently temporally dynamic, with their future development paths enabled and constrained by local economic and social histories (Spigel and Harrison 2018). The success of both scale-ups and anchor firms attracts new entrepreneurial resources to the ecosystem such as skilled workers and investment capital, which can then recycle through the ecosystem, allowing newer rounds of entrepreneurs to benefit from them and over time pressing forward the ecosystem's evolution. This strengthens the ecosystem over time, allowing it to support new generations of startups and scale-ups and reproducing the support systems enabling growth.

The decline or loss of an anchor firm will therefore have a significant impact on an ecosystem. This may lead to the ecosystem and the broader regional economy declining as people and financial capital leave for more prosperous regions, which in turn will damage local institutions and support infrastructure for entrepreneurship. But the loss of an anchor firm might also catalyse ecosystem development, creating new opportunities and enriching the resource pool that entrepreneurs can draw on. The most obvious effect is the release of large numbers of skilled technical and managerial workers into the regional labour market. Some of these workers may become entrepreneurs themselves or go to work at local startups. In the most positive cases, newly unemployed workers may have severance packages that can serve as seed capital for new firms where they can pursue new entrepreneurial or technological opportunities their previous employer overlooked. However, these laid off workers might not recycle into the ecosystem, either because they took jobs at nearby large corporations or because they left the region for opportunities elsewhere. Finally, skilled workers laid off from an anchor firm might turn to necessity entrepreneurship and open small low-productivity consultancies with few growth prospects. The loss of an anchor firms may also mean the loss of a critical ecosystem actor, making it harder for support organizations to coordinate their activities. Finally, an anchor firm's decline might have a negative impact on a region's cultural confidence in entrepreneurship. These outcomes will contribute to an overall reduction of the ecosystem's capacity to support high-growth entrepreneurship.

In other words, there are two potential pathways that an ecosystem can follow after a shock, such as the decline or collapse of a regional anchor organization. As Figure 2 shows, the ability of an ecosystem to recover or even benefit from the loss of an anchor depends on the ability of resources released from the collapse of the anchor to recycle back into the ecosystem, either in the form of spinouts and entrepreneurship or the movement of highly skilled workers into local startups. At time t (Figure 2(a)), the anchor firm attracts skilled workers and new resources such as financial capital, some of which recycles through the rest of the ecosystem, supporting new venture creation and growth. The anchor firm contributes to the development of new formal institutions such as industry associations or startup support groups, which in turn can provide additional support to the ecosystem. After a crisis, the resources built up in the anchor firm can either recycle into the ecosystem (Figure 2(b)) or leave the region (Figure 2(c)). In the former case, this creates a stronger ecosystem because new and growing ventures benefit from access to a high calibre workforce, as well as from the support they receive from the institutions and organizations seeded by the anchor firm. This in turn ensures that external resources, such as inbound investment, continue to flow into the regional economy. In the latter case, large-scale out-migration occurs as employees move elsewhere to find new career opportunities. This can contribute to a decline in the regional economy, with fewer

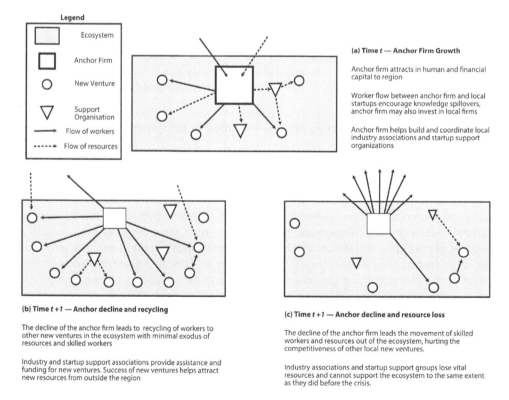

(b) Time $t+1$ — Anchor decline and recycling

The decline of the anchor firm leads to recycling of workers to other new ventures in the ecosystem with minimal exodus of resources and skilled workers

Industry and startup support associations provide assistance and funding for new ventures. Success of new ventures helps attract new resources from outside the region

(c) Time $t+1$ — Anchor decline and resource loss

The decline of the anchor firm leads the movement of skilled workers and resources out of the ecosystem, hurting the competitiveness of other local new ventures.

Industry associations and startup support groups lose vital resources and cannot support the ecosystem to the same extent as they did before the crisis.

Figure 2. Entrepreneurial ecosystem pathways after anchor collapse.
Source: Authors' conceptualization based on the literature

resources available for new ventures and reducing the ability of local support organizations to contribute to the ecosystem.

How an ecosystem responds to a shock and more broadly how it develops over time depends on the extent to which entrepreneurial resources are recycle into the ecosystem after an exit. Recycling can be seen as a form of entrepreneurial resilience that enables regions to respond to a shock by recirculating important resources towards new aims rather than losing them completely. This can support to the renewal of the regional economy along a different trajectory than it had when the anchor was still dominant (Martin 2011). Smaller, more dynamic startup firms may be able to weather a shock better than larger firms and the shock may even create more opportunities for them, which in turn allows them to absorb more resources coming out of other firms in the regional economy (Williams and Vorley 2015).

But while recycling has an intuitive logic and there are ample examples of spinouts from an anchor firm helping to establish strong ecosystems, there is only limited empirical evidence of whether or not recycling occurs within ecosystems, particularly after a shock, and how this process unfolds. There are substantial gaps in our knowledge about the dynamics of entrepreneurial ecosystems. This paper seeks to address these gaps in our knowledge by asking the following questions. Do workers at a failed anchor firm recycle back into their entrepreneurial ecosystem? And, do the processes of recycling change over time as the region and its institutions adapt to the loss of an anchor firm? Answering these questions provides greater insight into how recycling occurs in entrepreneurial ecosystems and the extent to which this recycling can help compensate for the loss of an anchor firm in a regional economy.

3. Methods

3.1. Case study context

To address these issues we conducted an in-depth study of Waterloo, Canada to understand the dynamics of worker recycling within entrepreneurial ecosystems after the decline of a major anchor firm. Waterloo is a city-region of about 500,000 people about 100 kilometres west of Toronto. It is well known for its strengths in digital technology, wireless communications, and quantum comput-ing (Vinodrai 2016). The region is ranked as one of the world's top entrepreneurial ecosystems (Startup Genome 2018) and is frequently held up in the literature as an example of a region characterized by technological innovation and entrepreneurship (Bramwell and Wolfe 2008). The city is characterized by a supportive entrepreneurial culture, which has generated high levels of trust and cooperation between entrepreneurs and community leaders. This culture is enhanced and reproduced by the presence of several highly effective local entrepreneurial support agencies, incubators, and accelerators. One agency in particular, Communitech, has taken the lead in coordi-nating the ecosystem by offering training, financing, programming and spaces for entrepreneurs to learn from each other.

Waterloo's ecosystem is based around two key anchors: the University of Waterloo (UW) and the smartphone company Blackberry (formerly Research in Motion or RIM). UW is well-known as an entrepreneurial university due to its permissive IP policy, which encourages research-based spinouts; its internal entrepreneurial culture, which attracts students and faculty interested in commercializing new technological advances; and a co-op educational programme that sees students work directly for local and global firms as part of their degree. Blackberry was founded locally in 1984 as a pager manufacturer and went public in 1998 after pioneering the email enabled cellphone (McQueen 2010). Though not a direct university spinout, it drew on the technical expertise of UW researchers and the skills of its co-op students and alumni as it grew to become a leader in the global cellphone market. However, Blackberry's fortunes shifted in 2008 as the company was unable to adapt to changes in the smartphone market, including the emergence of new competitors such as Apple's iPhone and Google's Android platform (McNish and Silcoff 2015).

As a result, the company's global workforce dropped from a high of over 17,500 in 2011 to fewer than 6,200 in 2015. This decline represented a profound shock to Waterloo's entrepreneurial ecosystem and the broader regional economy. While the company did not report employment by location or the number of jobs shed by region, newspaper reports suggest that at least 2,200 workers were laid off from the Waterloo headquarters alone. Local leaders expressed a fear of losing top talent from Blackberry to nearby Toronto as well as global technology clusters like Silicon Valley or Seattle. Losing this talent would weaken the region's economic strength and could ultimately lead to further losses as employers attracted to the region's strong technology labour pool followed the emigrating workers, potentially precipitating a broader downturn in the regional economy.

3.2. Data and methodology

Existing census data and other administrative data sources do not provide sufficient detail to examine the career trajectories of former Blackberry employees and their propensity to recycle into Waterloo's ecosystem. Indeed, the paucity of data on employee mobility and entrepreneurial endeavours is one of the chief challenges in studying entrepreneurial ecosystems. As Feldman and Lowe (2015, 1785) argue: 'insufficient micro-level data has inhibited understanding of the underlying dynamic processes within regions that lead to and sustain, innovation and entrepreneurship.' In response to these challenges, there has been a call for the use of alternative data sources that can capture new dynamics of entrepreneurial ecosystems and other phenomena (Strangler and Bell-Masterson 2015).

Data drawn from career-based social media platforms are increasingly popular way of studying large-scale trends in employment because they offer highly detailed data at the individual level. For example, Avnimelech and Feldman (2010) examine the role of anchor firms in creating new pools of entrepreneurs, Chen and Thompson (2015) look at skill balance and entrepreneurship, and Jiang, Wang, and Philip Wang (2017) examine the career trajectories of credit analysts. Career-based social media platforms feature structured job histories uploaded by users along with other information such as their education, job location, job duties, and dates of employment. Users are incented to maintain up-to-date and accurate profiles because these platforms are used to find new jobs and connect with potential clients or partners.

We acquired employment data from one career-based social media platform on former Blackberry employees who listed their job functions as either engineering or information technology. By restricting job function, we were able to focus wholly on workers with technical skills, rather than managers or administrators. This provides clearer insight into the recycling of valuable technology workers in an ecosystem. While the data is highly structured (meaning fields such as job title and employer are delineated), user-entered fields such as job title, job duration, and location are very inconsistent. A manual cleaning process was necessary to resolve confusing or unclear entries. For example, Blackberry was referred to as Blackberry, RIM, Research in Motion, or by the name of a subsidiary. In some cases, users did not include complete data about their jobs, such as dates of employment or location.

Figure 3 illustrates the data selection and reduction process used to identify former Blackberry workers in Waterloo. In 2016, a total of 30,024 former Blackberry workers are listed on the platform, including 5,292 former Blackberry workers who classified themselves as either engineering and IT workers. While this does not likely capture the entire population of former Blackberry technology workers, we see no evidence of systematic bias in the dataset. We further narrowed our selection to the 1,082 individuals in engineering and IT roles who reported that at least one of their former jobs was located at Blackberry's headquarters in Waterloo. We then limited our analysis of recycling in Waterloo's entrepreneurial ecosystem to the 782 workers who left their jobs after Blackberry's decline began in 2008 to focus on the impact of anchor firm collapse on the local entrepreneurial ecosystem. While not exhaustive, we believe that this method captures a high proportion of the technical talent housed at Blackberry's headquarters and believe that the utility of career-based

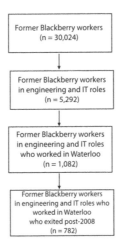

Figure 3. Data selection process.

Source: Authors' calculations.

social media platforms would be similar for all highly skilled tech workers regardless of whether they pursued employment or entrepreneurship related pathways.

For each individual we coded variables relating to their current and former employers and their personal characteristics. First, we coded the characteristics of their past five employers (including their current employer). These characteristics include: 1) firm size, classified as micro (1 to 5 employees), small (6 to 50 employees), medium (51 to 500 employees) and large (more than 500 employees) as recorded by their employer's public profile on the platform; 2) the firm's primary sector, classified as technology, finance/insurance, health/medical, or other based on an analysis of the firm's operations; and 3) whether or not the firm was a member of Waterloo's entrepreneurial ecosystem. Ecosystem membership was determined using three criteria: A) if the firm was founded in the Waterloo region; B) if the firm was less than ten years old; and C) if the firm had a profile on Crunchbase. Crunchbase is a user-maintained database of firms that are actively seeking venture financing or that have otherwise scaled significantly; it is a popular data source for researchers due to its scope and the relative quality of its data. More than 90 research papers have already drawn on Crunchbase because it is one of the largest publicly available data sources for early stage entrepreneurial ventures (Dalle, Besten, den, and Menon 2017). While not complete, its coverage of smaller firms makes it a superior source for this study than traditional business data sources such as Dunn and Bradstreet.

Second, individual characteristics were coded. These included: 1) job tenure at Blackberry; 2) whether or not an individual had received undergraduate or graduate degrees in Waterloo; 3) whether or not an individual was currently employed in a firm in Waterloo's entrepreneurial ecosystem; and 4) whether or not the individual had experience as an entrepreneur, defined as having listed a job title such as CEO, president, founder, co-founder, or owner. This allowed us to characterize individuals' post-Blackberry employment and entrepreneurial activities and examine how this related to their prior experience at Blackberry.

4. Recycling and labour market transitions in Waterloo

4.1. Descriptive results

While Blackberry's decline in the smartphone market began in 2008, Figure 4 shows that the exodus of technical workers from its Waterloo headquarters began in 2010 and reached its peak in 2014. The figure

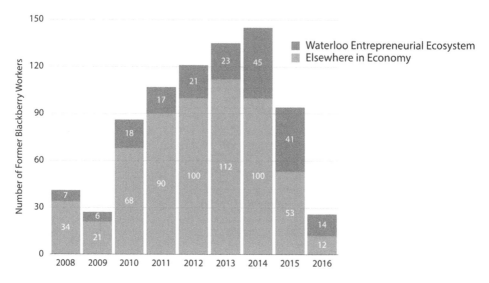

Figure 4. Last year of employment at Blackberry.
Source: Authors' calculations

also shows the proportion working in the entrepreneurial ecosystem, a discussion we return to below. Table 2 summarizes some of the key characteristics of former Blackberry employees included in our analysis. The majority of those who left Blackberry from 2008 onwards were new to the company, 526 workers in the sample (67.3%) had less than five years of experience in the firm before leaving. Of these, 18.7% of the overall sample had less than a year of experience at the firm and had attended the University of Waterloo, suggesting that they had been at the firm as part of a temporary co-op work placement. Less than a third of the sample (226 people) had been at Blackberry for more than five years before leaving. This suggests that Blackberry shed younger workers and attempted to retain their more experienced employees. Former Blackberry workers have largely remained in the technology sector. More than three-quarters of the sample (77.9%) were still employed by technology firms in 2016. Importantly, slightly more than half

Table 2. Key characteristics of former Blackberry employees.

Key characteristics	Count (%)
Years of experience at Blackberry	
Co-op term	146 (18.7)
New to firm (< 2 years)	253 (32.4)
Some firm experience (2 to 5 years)	127 (16.2)
Established in firm (5 to 10 years)	171 (21.9)
Embedded in firm (> 10 years)	55 (7.3)
Unknown/not specified	30 (3.8)
Sector of current employer	
Financial services	42 (5.4)
Healthcare/medical services	18 (2.3)
Technology	609 (77.9)
Other	87 (11.1)
Unknown/not specified	26 (3.3)
Size of current employer	
Micro (> 5 employees)	27 (3.5)
Small (6 to 50 employees)	123 (15.7)
Medium (51 to 500 employees)	166 (21.2)
Large (< 500 employees)	439 (56.1)
Unknown/not specified	27 (3.5)
TOTAL	**782 (100)**

Source: Authors' calculations

(56.1%) of these former Blackberry employees were still working a large firm (500+ employees). This suggests that many of Blackberry employees prefer to work at larger corporate firms, due to familiar management structures, the presumably higher wages, and/or the likelihood of improved job security often associated with larger organizations. This makes them less likely to recycle into the ecosystem. This confirms that recycling should not be viewed as an automatic process: even within entrepreneurial places, workers at larger firms are likely to try to find employment at other large firms.

4.2. Worker mobility and entrepreneurship

The majority of former Blackberry workers (54.6%) remained in the Waterloo region, with another 14.3% finding a job in nearby Toronto. Moreover, there was relatively limited migration to other North American technology centres like Silicon Valley (8.8% of the sample) or Seattle (1.3%). This suggests that, contrary to the expectations of local officials, there was not a substantial out-migration of talent due to Blackberry's decline. Table 3 breaks this down further looking at current location by amount of experience at Blackberry. It shows that the longer workers had been employed at Blackberry (and therefore, the longer their likely tenure in Waterloo), the more likely they were to stay in the region even if their skills and experience may have allowed them to move elsewhere for employment. Despite their more developed skills, these more experienced workers were less footloose than their newer colleagues.

Former Blackberry workers exhibited minimal entrepreneurial activity. This is not unexpected given that many went to work for large firms after leaving Blackberry. Only 6.8% (53) of the sample had job titles that indicated that they were founders. Moreover, only 12 of these new ventures (22.6% of all new ventures formed, or 1.5% of the total sample) could be described as high growth firms in Waterloo's entrepreneurial ecosystem. The majority of new ventures in the sample are best characterized as small technology consultancies, service firms or retail shops with few growth prospects. This contradicts early predictions by local policymakers that the decline of Blackberry would be a boon to high-growth entrepreneurship, but instead reflects the reality that Blackberry's organizational culture discouraged entrepreneurship amongst its employees, and the anchor did not attract many technology workers with entrepreneurial ambitions.

Notably, the majority of former Blackberry workers who became entrepreneurs left early in the firm's decline, with 20 (37%) of the total entrepreneurs leaving the firm in 2011 (Figure 5). As shown in Figure 5, the number of entrepreneurial ventures formed by ex-Blackberry employees declined year-on-year after 2011. And, the majority of new ventures (36 or 67.9%) were located in Waterloo (25) or the neighbouring Toronto region (11), confirming earlier work that suggests that entrepreneurs prefer to start their ventures in the regions where they already live (Stam 2007).

Table 3. Current worker location by experience at Blackberry.

Location	<1 year	1 to 3 years	3 to 5 years	5 to 10 years	10+ years	Unknown	Total
Waterloo	69 (47.3%)	125 (49.4%)	73 (57.5%)	102 (59.6%)	38 (69.1%)	20 (66.7%)	**427 (54.6%)**
Toronto	26 (17.8%)	41 (16.2%)	16 (12.6%)	20 (11.7%)	5 (9.1%)	3 (10%)	**111 (14.2%)**
Rest of Canada	14 (9.6%)	45 (17.8%)	24 (18.9%)	19 (11.1%)	5 (9.1%)	4 (13.3%)	**111 (14.2%)**
Silicon Valley	23 (15.8%)	19 (7.5%)	8 (6.3%)	13 (7.6%)	3 (5.5%)	3 (10%)	**69 (8.8%)**
Seattle	2 (1.4%)	4 (1.6%)	3 (2.4%)	1 (0.6%)	–	–	**10 (1.3%)**
Rest of United States	11 (7.5%)	18 (7.1%)	3 (2.4%)	13 (7.6%)	4 (7.3%)	–	**49 (6.3%)**
Rest of World	–	1 (0.4%)	–	3 (1.8%)	–	–	**4 (0.5%)**
Unknown	1 (0.7%)	–	–	–	–	–	**1 (0.1%)**
Total	**146 (100%)**	**253 (100%)**	**127 (100%)**	**171 (100%)**	**55 (100%)**	**30 (100%)**	**782 (100%)**

Source: authors' calculations

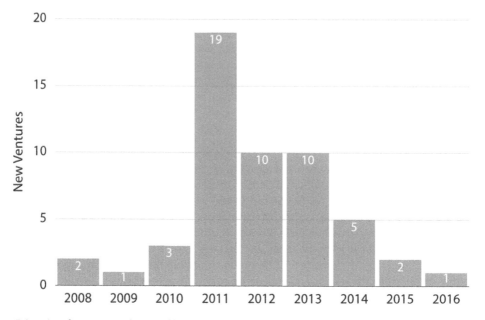

Figure 5. Location of new ventures by year of last employment at Blackberry.

Source: Authors' calculations

4.3. Recycling into the entrepreneurial ecosystem

Spinoffs were not the only way in which recycling from a declining anchor firm can influence the entrepreneurial ecosystem. The movement of skilled workers from an anchor firm to start-ups and scale-ups is also an important outcome. As shown earlier in Figure 4, there was a growing number of former Blackberry workers who entered Waterloo's wider entrepreneurial ecosystem after 2008. Overall, almost a quarter of the sample (192 of 782) worked in the entrepreneurial ecosystem, meaning they took at a job at a high-growth firm based in Waterloo. Of the 517 workers leaving between 2008 and 2013, 17.8% worked in the entrepreneurial ecosystem. By contrast, amongst the 265 workers departing in subsequent years, 37.7% worked in the entrepreneurial ecosystem. Overall, this demonstrates a robust level of recycling, with substantial levels of technical talent from Blackberry in local high-growth ventures. Moreover, the growing proportion of workers entering the ecosystem over time suggests that the capacity of the ecosystem to absorb these workers and the willingness by former Blackberry workers to work at startups in the ecosystem grew over this period. This shows that recycling is not static, but changes over time as the nature of local employment opportunities and the social value of working in the ecosystem shift.

Table 4 breaks down participation in Waterloo's entrepreneurial ecosystem based on years of experience at Blackberry. Interestingly, workers with more experience at Blackberry (5 to 10 years or more than 10 years) were the most likely to recycle into the local ecosystem as opposed to younger workers with less work experience. This suggests that new ventures in the ecosystem seek top technical talent with substantial experience in mobile technology rather than less experienced and less expensive junior developers.

Several interlinked trends are responsible for the increased capacity of the ecosystem. First, since 2008, there has been an increase in the flow of venture capital into the Waterloo ecosystem. Figure 6 shows that venture capital investments reached a peak of 368 USD million (USD) in 2016, including a 168 USD million investment in Thalmic Labs (now North), a wearable technology company that took on at least seven former Blackberry technology workers. Other high-growth firms in Waterloo received substantial venture capital investment. The steady increase in venture capital flows allowed

Table 4. Ecosystem Membership by Blackberry Experience.

Years of experience	Entrepreneurial ecosystem	Elsewhere in the economy	Total
Co-op term	26 (17.8%)	120 (82.2%)	146
New to firm (< 2 years)	55 (21.7%)	198 (78.3%)	253
Some firm experience (2 to 5 years)	27 (21.3%)	100 (78.7%)	127
Established in firm (5 to 10 years)	55 (32.2%)	116 (67.8%)	171
Embedded in firm (> 10 years)	23 (41.8%)	32 (58.2%)	55
Unknown/not specified	6 (20.0%)	24 (80.0%)	30
TOTAL	**192 (24.6%)**	**590 (75.4%)**	**792**

Source: authors' calculations

local firms to expand coincident with when increasing number of former Blackberry workers were available.

Second, entrepreneurial organizations throughout the region increased their efforts to link former Blackberry workers with local firms. Organizations such as Communitech, established in 1997 by the former founders of Blackberry along with other local business leaders, developed a series of programmes linking start-ups looking for skilled technical workers with former Blackberry technical employees. Many of these programmes included other partners, including the provincial government and the Canadian Digital Media Network. A 2013 news article appropriately titled 'RIM Refugees,' details initiatives such as workshops, job boards, and employment fairs designed to encourage entrepreneurship amongst laid off Blackberry workers, connect them with the local ecosystem, and encourage local firms to expand their operations in order to take advantage of available talent (Sher 2013).

Finally, Communitech, the region's main ecosystem support organization, invested heavily in expanding the spaces and programming that supported the creation of a new generation of tech-based start-ups firms and convince tech companies in places like Silicon Valley to open offices in Waterloo to take advantage of local talent. These new firms offered a new source of demand for skilled workers, especially seasoned workers who could provide a depth of experience and knowledge to these fledgling firms. For example, it opened the Communitech Hub (Vinodrai 2016) to

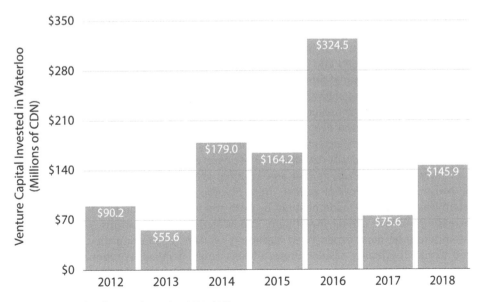

Figure 6. Venture capital in the Waterloo region, 2012–2018.

Source: Innovation Policy Lab Database; Authors' calculations

house the start-up programmes run by the local universities; Communitech also developed programming to assist start-ups and link large corporate clients with the local startup ecosystem.

5. Discussion

Blackberry's decline was the result of a new disruptive technology – the iPhone – and the failure of its management to recognize shifts in the smartphone market. The job losses that occurred from 2008 onwards represented a profound economic and cultural shock to the Waterloo region. As the company's decline intensified, there were concerns that this would damage the 'Waterloo miracle' that allowed a highly innovative technology economy to thrive in a relatively small region. However, this economy has grown as Blackberry declined, driven largely through the development of an increasingly dynamic entrepreneurial ecosystem. Part of this growth is due to the recycling of workers from Blackberry into the local ecosystem instead of them leaving the region to take up jobs elsewhere. This mitigated the effects of Blackberry's decline and helped avoid a shock that could have ruptured the regional economy. Waterloo's experience resembles the 'anchor decline and recycling' case in Figure 2(b) above. The institutional structure of the ecosystem enabled recycling of skilled workers to local high-growth firms rather than them leaving the ecosystem by either migrating out of the region or turning to lower-growth firms in the region.

Our data reveal substantial levels of recycling into Waterloo's entrepreneurial ecosystem. Approximately one-quarter of technology workers who left the firm are now working in high-growth startups in the ecosystem as opposed to migrating to other regions or working for lower-growth firms in the region. However, the nature of recycling differs from the implicit assumptions made in the literature about how recycling works. We found very low levels of *direct* entrepreneurial activity by the skilled technologists and engineers who left Blackberry. Only 1.5% of those who left Blackberry during the study period went on to found high-growth technology ventures in Waterloo. This counters the expectation that large technology firms should seed numerous spinouts. While some large global technology firms such as Google or Hewlett-Packard have historically encouraged spinouts, other large anchors develop corporate cultures that discourage spinouts both through the direct threat of lawsuits but also by attracting less entrepreneurial employees. Thus, the loss of a large anchor firm will not necessarily lead to dynamic start-up activity by former workers, even in very strong entrepreneurial ecosystems. The entrepreneurial efforts of Blackberry's former employees were primarily related to lifestyle entrepreneurship: laid off workers replacing their lost wages with low-growth firms of limited potential.

However, our data show that most recycling occurred through the movement of workers away from declining firms and into innovative start-up and scale-up firms in the local ecosystem. Employment in entrepreneurial firms, rather than entrepreneurship itself, was the most important form of recycling associated with Blackberry's decline. The skilled workers from Blackberry did not create their own companies but many appeared willing to work at high-growth new ventures. This trend increased over time, with the proportion of workers who left Blackberry to enter Waterloo's ecosystem increasing in the later years of the study. As argued above, this suggests that region's capacity to absorb these workers into the entrepreneurial ecosystem increased over time, driven by formal and informal institutional forces and increased venture capital investments. The flow of workers from Blackberry to firms in the local entrepreneurial ecosystem was – in part – made possible by both the increasing number of new ventures and the increasing venture capital investment into Waterloo-based startups. Firms in Waterloo's ecosystem hired the most experienced Blackberry workers, suggesting they had the resources required to pay the higher salaries these workers could demand. Without significant venture investment into Waterloo's ecosystem, these employment opportunities would either not exist or not be remunerative enough to keep them in the region.

Waterloo's institutional structure helped coordinate connections between new firms who needed skilled labour and the skilled workers leaving Blackberry. Organizations like Communitech worked to build the region's global presence to attract new investment, while at the same time working to create stronger local networks within the business and technology community. As Blackberry's decline worsened, Communitech and other local organizations created both entrepreneurship training programmes for former Blackberry employees (which did not appear to be effective) as well as networking events and other programmes to connect these workers with start-ups and scale-ups who needed top technical talent.

Communitech's capacity to mediate this crisis was not an accident. The organization received substantial support from Blackberry throughout its history. This allowed Communitech to build a reputation as an intermediary between the entrepreneurial community, major anchor firms like Blackberry, and local and provincial governments. Communitech's local reputation as an organization responsive to the needs of entrepreneurs allowed it to achieve the necessary buy-in to address the crisis. The organization's ability to help facilitate recycling from the declining Blackberry to the more dynamic local entrepreneurial ecosystem was ironically made possible by Blackberry's engagement with the organization over the previous decades, which helped Communitech establish itself as a key player within the ecosystem.

Overall, these results suggest that entrepreneurial recycling is not a 'natural' part of ecosystems. Rather, it is temporally dynamic, evolutionary process linked to a place's pre-existing institutional, economic, and cultural structures. As the economic and social institutions of a place change, so does the quantity of people recycling into the ecosystem. The ability of workers from declining anchor firms to recycle back into the ecosystem depends on a region's culture (if it is accepting or intolerant of people associated with a failure and if the culture promotes entrepreneurialism), its formal institutions or organizations (who can link employees with new ventures who need highly skilled workers) and economic systems (if the new firms have the financial resources to afford the wages of those leaving anchor firms). Recycling from Blackberry was not inevitable: it depended on the existence of local organizations such as Communitech to create pathways to channel highly skilled technical workers between the anchor and the ecosystem. In this case, Waterloo's ecosystem was 'sticky', creating pathways not only to retain workers in the region but to move them into the start-up and scale-up firms that needed their expertise.

6. Conclusion

Entrepreneurial ecosystems are not static collections of actors and factors: they are dynamic social and economic systems that provide the resources required for innovative new ventures to form and grow. Skilled workers are one of the most important resources for entrepreneurial growth. The ability of regions to attract or produce these workers and ensure that entrepreneurial ventures are able to benefit from this talent pool is a crucial component of successful entrepreneurial ecosystems. Anchor firms are key players in building this talent pool – they attract skilled workers globally through their global recruitment activities and work to build it up locally through partnerships with local universities and colleges. However, there is almost no empirical evidence of the recycling of talent from anchor firms to the surrounding local or regional ecosystem. This is a major research gap in the literature, especially since this is identified as a significant process through which ecosystems reproduce and change over time.

By examining the labour mobility of anchor firm employees after a shock, this paper provides new empirical evidence for how entrepreneurial recycling works within the dynamics of entrepreneurial ecosystems. Employing a novel methodology to gather data on the career paths of former Blackberry workers, the paper finds surprisingly little evidence of entrepreneurial activity being undertaken by these highly skilled workers. Only a small proportion of technical workers who left Blackberry after its decline started new ventures and even fewer of these were high-growth firms. Rather, former anchor firm employees were more likely to find employment in the local ecosystem and the likelihood of this pattern increased over time. Notably, those who had worked at Blackberry the longest were the most likely to recycle into the ecosystem, which reflects both their embeddedness in the region, as well as the importance placed on technical experience by fast-growing firms.

Because of the active recycling into the ecosystem through labour mobility, Waterloo's ecosystem avoided an economic trajectory characterized by resource loss, outmigration, and reduced entrepreneurial ambitions. Unlike other regions that have lost an anchor firm, such as Nortel (Ottawa) in the early 2000 s, the decline of Blackberry did not dampen activity in the local entrepreneurial ecosystem. Instead, local organizations like Communitech were central in creating formal and informal institutions that connected departing Blackberry employees with local scale-up firms. This encouraged recycling, as evidenced by the increased flow of workers from Blackberry to the ecosystem as the anchor's decline worsened and the capacity of local entrepreneurial ventures to absorb these workers increased. Ironically, Blackberry itself had a hand in forming these institutional structures, demonstrating the importance of evolutionary conditions in the recycling process.

Overall, this paper makes three contributions to the entrepreneurial ecosystems and regional economies literature. First, it exploits new data sources and methods to track employee mobility within and between entrepreneurial ecosystems. These data provide new perspectives on labour market transitions and the role of human capital in entrepreneurial growth. Second, this paper provides some of the first empirical evidence for entrepreneurial recycling. The findings suggest that the largest impact of shocks to local anchors is the movement of skilled workers to high-growth entrepreneurial ventures, rather than spurring new waves of entrepreneurship. Third, it demonstrates the evolutionary and dynamic nature of ecosystems and the key role of local institutional structures in addressing sudden shocks to the local economy.

However, we must be aware of the limitations posed by working with alternative datasets like the one used here. The present study only looked at technical workers. It may be that managerial workers, for instance those in operations, marketing, or sales, are more likely to either leave the region or take up jobs in other large firms. While technology firms obviously prize technology skills, the business skills these managerial workers bring are important to firm growth. Similarly, we cannot show that firms that hired these recycling workers performed better than their peers that didn't or otherwise assign causality between taking advantage of the recycled skills and improved firm outcomes. We must therefore be cautious in generalizing these findings. Secondly, career-based social media platforms present significant issues with missing data, particularly around the location of employers and the timing and duration of their work there. This limits our ability to construct detailed career histories to follow workers from job to job and link these with individual characteristics such as work experience, age, or gender. Finally, we look at only one ecosystem in this study. Further research is necessary to determine if Waterloo's experience is typical for an entrepreneurial ecosystem following the loss of a major anchor or if its institutional structure has helped insulate the economy from a more serious decline.

Acknowledgments

The authors are grateful for the helpful comments made by the editors and three anonymous reviewers, as well as feedback on previous versions of this paper presented at conferences and the Creating Digital Opportunities Partnership annual meetings. We thank John Barber, Martin Holicka and Ondrej Bohdal for research assistance. We would like to acknowledge financial support from Social Sciences and Humanities Research Council of Canada and the University of Waterloo. This paper represents the equal contributions of the authors. Any errors and omissions remain the responsibility of the authors.

Disclosure Statement

No potential conflict of interest was reported by the authors.

ORCID

Ben Spigel (iD) http://orcid.org/0000-0002-2634-6021
Tara Vinodrai (iD) http://orcid.org/0000-0002-5734-7473

References

Agrawal, A., and I. Cockburn. 2003. "The Anchor Tenant Hypothesis: Exploring the Role of Large, Local, R&D-intensive Firms in Regional Innovation Systems." *International Journal of Industrial Organization* 21: 1227–1253. doi:10.1016/S0167-7187(03)00081-X.

Alvedalen, J., and R. Boschma. 2017. "A Critical Review of Entrepreneurial Ecosystems Research: Towards A Future Research Agenda." *European Planning Studies* 25 (6): 887–903.

Auerswald, P. E., and L. Dani. 2017. "The Adaptive Life Cycle of Entrepreneurial Ecosystems: The Biotechnology Cluster." *Small Business Economics* 49 (1): 97–117.

Autio, E., S. Nambisan, L. D. W. Thomas, and M. Wright. 2017. "Digital Affordances, Spatial Affordances, and the Genesis of Entrepreneurial Ecosystems." *Strategic Entrepreneurship Journal* 12 (1): 72–95.

Avnimelech, G., and M. Feldman. 2010. "Regional Corporate Spawning and the Role of Homegrown Companies." *Review of Policy Research* 27 (4): 475–489.

Bahrami, H., and S. Evans. 1995. "Flexible Re-Cycling and High-Technology Entrepreneurship." *California Management Review* 37 (1): 62–89.

Bramwell, A., and D. A. Wolfe. 2008. "Universities and Regional Economic Development: The Entrepreneurial University of Waterloo." *Research Policy* 37: 1175–1187.

Brown, R., and C. Mason. 2017. "Looking inside the Spiky Bits: A Critical Review and Conceptualisation of Entrepreneurial Ecosystems." *Small Business Economics* 49 (1): 11–30.

Brown, R., C. Mason, and S. Mawson. 2014. *Increasing "The Vital 6 Percent": Designing Effective Public Policy to Support High Growth Firms*. London: NESTA.

Brown, R., S. Mawson, and C. Mason. 2017. "Myth-Busting and Entrepreneurship Policy: The Case of High Growth Firms." *Entrepreneurship & Regional Development* 45 (1): 1–30.

Chen, L.-W., and P. Thompson. 2015. "Skill Balance and Entrepreneurship Evidence from Online Career Histories." *Entrepreneurship Theory and Practice* 40 (2): 289–305.

Colombelli, A., E. Paolucci, and E. Ughetto. 2017. "Hierarchical and Relational Governance and the Life Cycle of Entrepreneurial Ecosystems." *Small Business Economics* 49 (1): 1–17.

Croce, G., E. Di Porto, E. Ghignoni, and A. Ricci. 2016. "Agglomeration and Workplace Training: Knowledge Spillovers versus Poaching." *Regional Studies* 51 (11): 1635–1651. doi:10.1080/00343404.2016.1230270.

Dahl, M. S., and O. Sorenson. 2012. "Home Sweet Home: Entrepreneurs' Location Choices and the Performance of Their Ventures." *Management Science* 58: 1059–1071.

Dalle, J.-M., M. Besten, den, and C. Menon. 2017. "Using Crunchbase for Economic and Managerial Research." OECD Science, Technology and Industry Working Papers. OECD: Paris.

DeTienne, D. R. 2010. "Entrepreneurial Exit as a Critical Component of the Entrepreneurial Process: Theoretical Development." *Journal of Business Venturing* 25 (2): 203–215.

Dubini, P. 1989. "The Influence of Motivations and Environment on Business Start-Ups: Some Hints for Public Policies." *Journal of Business Venturing* 4 (1): 11–26.

Eckardt, R., B. C. Skaggs, and D. P. Lepak. 2018. "An Examination of the Firm-Level Performance Impact of Cluster Hiring in Knowledge-Intensive Firms." *Academy of Management Journal* 61 (3): 919–944. doi:10.5465/amj.2016.0601.

Feld, B. 2012. *Startup Communities: Building an Entrepreneurial Ecosystem in Your City*. Hoboken, NJ: Wiley.

Feldman, M., and N. Lowe. 2015. "Triangulating Regional Economies: Realizing the Promise of Digital Data." *Research Policy* 44 (9): 1785–1793.

Feldman, M., and T. D. Zoller. 2012. "Dealmakers in Place: Social Capital Connections in Regional Entrepreneurial Economies." *Regional Studies* 46 (1): 23–37.

Feldman, M. P., S. Ozcan, and T. Reichstein. 2019. "Falling Not Far from the Tree: Entrepreneurs and Organizational Heritage." *Organization Science* 30 (2): 337–360.

Frederiksen, L., K. Wennberg, and C. Balachandran. 2016. "Mobility and Entrepreneurship: Evaluating the Scope of Knowledge-Based Theories of Entrepreneurship." *Entrepreneurship Theory and Practice* 40 (2): 359–380.

Fritsch, M., and D. J. Storey. 2014. "Entrepreneurship in a Regional Context: Historical Roots, Recent Developments and Future Challenges." *Regional Studies* 48 (6): 939–954.

Genome, S. 2018. *Global Startup Ecosystem Report 2018: Succeding in the New Era of Technology*. San Francisco.

Gertler, M. S. 2010. "Rules of the Game: The Place of Institutions in Regional Economic Change." *Regional Studies* 44: 1–15.

Gjerløv-Juel, P., and C. Guenther. 2018. "Early Employment Expansion and Long-run Survival Examining Employee Turnover as a Context Factor." *Journal of Business Venturing* 34 (1): 80–102.

Harrison, R. T., S. Y. Cooper, and C. M. Mason. 2004. "Entrepreneurial Activity and Dynamics of Technology-Based Cluster Development: The Case of Ottawa." *Urban Studies* 41: 1045–1070.

Hayter, C. S. 2016. "A Trajectory of Early-Stage Spinoff Success: The Role of Knowledge Intermediaries within an Entrepreneurial University Ecosystem." *Small Business Economics* 47 (3): 633–656.

Isenberg, D. J. 2010. "The Big Idea: How to Start an Entrepreneurial Revolution." *Harvard Business Review* 88: 40–50.

Jiang, J. X., I. Y. Wang, and K. Philip Wang. 2017. "Revolving Rating Analysts and Ratings of MBS and ABS: Evidence from LinkedIn." *Management Science* 64 (12): 5832–5854.

Katz, B., and J. Nowak. 2018. *The New Localism: How Cities Can Thrive in the Age of Populism*. Washington D.C: Brookings Institution Press.

Kerr, W. R. 2018. *The Gift of Global Talent: How Migration Shapes Business, Economy & Society*. Stanford: Stanford Business Books.

Klepper, S. 2007. "Disagreements, Spinoffs, and the Evolution of Detroit as the Capital of the U.S. Automobile Industry." *Management Science* 53 (4): 616–631. doi:10.1287/mnsc.1060.0683.

Klepper, S., and S. Sleeper. 2005. "Entry by Spinoffs." *Management Science* 51 (8): 1291–1306.

Lowe, N. J., and M. P. Feldman. 2017. "Institutional Life within an Entrepreneurial Region." *Geography Compass* 11 (3): e12306–10.

Lucas, M., A. Sands, and D. A. Wolfe. 2009. "Regional Clusters in a Global Industry: ICT Clusters in Canada." *European Planning Studies* 17 (2): 189–209.

Mack, E., and H. Mayer. 2016. "The Evolutionary Dynamics of Entrepreneurial Ecosystems." *Urban Studies* 53 (10): 2118–2133.

Malecki, E. J. 2018. "Entrepreneurship and Entrepreneurial Ecosystems." *Geography Compass*. 2018-01-08. e12359. doi:10.1111/gec3.12359.

Martin, R. 2011. "Regional Economic Resilience, Hysteresis and Recessionary Shocks." *Journal of Economic Geography* 12 (1): 1–32.

Martin, R., and P. Sunley. 2015. "On the Notion of Regional Economic Resilience: Conceptualization and Explanation." *Journal of Economic Geography* 15 (1): 1–42.

Mason, C. M., and R. Brown. 2014. *Entrepreneurial Ecosystems and Growth Oriented Entrepreneurship*. The Hague: OECD.

Mason, C. M., and R. T. Harrison. 2006. "After the Exit: Acquisitions, Entrepreneurial Recycling and Regional Economic Development." *Regional Studies* 40 (1): 55–73.

McNish, J., and S. Silcoff. 2015. *Losing the Signal: The Untold Story behind the Extraordinary Rise and Spectacular Fall of Blackberry*. New York: Flatiron Books.

McQueen, R. 2010. *Blackberry: The Inside Story of Research in Motion*. Toronto, ON: Key Porter Books.

Motoyama, Y., and K. Knowlton. 2016. "From Resource Munificence to Ecosystem Integration: The Case of Government Sponsorship in St. Louis." *Entrepreneurship & Regional Development* 28 (5–6): 448–470.

Neff, G. 2012. *Venture Labor: Work and the Burden of Risk in Innovative Industries*. Cambridge, MA: MIT Press.

Nicotra, M., M. Romano, M. Del Giudice, and C. E. Schillaci. 2017. "The Causal Relation between Entrepreneurial Ecosystem and Productive Entrepreneurship: A Measurement Framework." *The Journal of Technology Transfer* 29 (1): 19–34.

Ouimet, P., and R. Zarutskie. 2014. "Who Works for Startups? the Relation between Firm Age, Employee Age, and Growth." *Journal of Financial Economics* 112 (3): 386–407.

Roach, M., and H. Sauermann. 2015. "Founder or Joiner? the Role of Preferences and Context in Shaping Different Entrepreneurial Interests." *Management Science* 61 (9): 2160–2184.

Roundy, P. T. 2016. "Start-Up Community Narratives: The Discursive Construction of Entrepreneurial Ecosystems." *The Journal of Entrepreneurship* 25 (2): 232–248.

Sauermann, H. 2017. "Fire in the Belly? Employee Motives and Innovative Performance in Start-ups versus Established Firms." *Strategic Entrepreneurship Journal* 12 (4): 423–454.

Sher, J. 2013. "Rim Refugees." *The London Free Press* 12 (October): A2.

Spigel, B. 2013. "Bourdieuian Approaches to the Geography of Entrepreneurial Cultures." *Entrepreneurship & Regional Development* 25: 804–818.

Spigel, B. 2017. "The Relational Organization of Entrepreneurial Ecosystems." *Entrepreneurship Theory and Practice* 41 (1): 49–72.

Spigel, B., and R. T. Harrison. 2018. "Towards a Process Theory of Entrepreneurial Ecosystems." *Strategic Entrepreneurship Journal* 12 (1): 151–168.

Stam, E. 2007. "Why Butterflies Don't Leave: Locational Behavior Of Entrepreneurial Firms." *Economic Geography* 83 (1): 27–50. doi:10.1111/ecge.2007.83.issue-1.

Stam, E. 2013. "Knowledge and Entrepreneurial Employees: A Country-Level Analysis." *Small Business Economics* 41 (4): 887–898. doi:10.1007/s11187-013-9511-y.

Stam, E. 2015. "Entrepreneurial Ecosystems and Regional Policy: A Sympathetic Critique." *European Planning Studies* 23 (9): 1759–1769.

Stam, E., and B. Spigel. 2018. "Entrepreneurial Ecosystems." In *The SAGE Handbook of Small Business and Entrepreneurship*, edited by R. Blackburn, D. de Clercq, and H. Heinonen. London: SAGE Publications Ltd.

Strangler, D., and J. Bell-Masterson. 2015. *Measuring an Entrepreneurial Ecosystem*. Kansas City: Kauffman Foundation.

Tambe, P., and L. M. Hitt. 2014. "Job Hopping, Information Technology Spillovers, and Productivity Growth." *Management Science* 60 (2): 338–355. doi:10.1287/mnsc.2013.1764.

Thompson, T., J. Purdy, and M. J. Ventresca. 2017. "How Entrepreneurial Ecosystems Take Form: Evidence from Social Impact Initiatives in Seattle." *Strategic Entrepreneurship Journal*. 2017-11-24. doi:10.1002/sej.1285.

Toft-Kehler, R., K. Wennberg, and P. H. Kim. 2014. "Practice Makes Perfect: Entrepreneurial-experience Curves and Venture Performance." *Journal of Business Venturing* 29 (4): 453–470.

Van de Ven, A. 1993. "The Development of an Infrastructure for Entrepreneurship." *Journal of Business Venturing* 8: 211–230.

Vinodrai, T. 2006. "Reproducing Toronto's Design Ecology: Career Paths, Intermediaries, and Local Labor Markets." *Economic Geography* 82 (3): 237–263.

Vinodrai, T. 2016. "A City of Two Tales: Innovation, Talent Attraction and Governance in Canada's Technology Triangle." In *Growing Urban Economies: Innovation, Creativity, and Governance in 21st Century Canadian City-Regions*, edited by D. A. Wolfe and M. S. Gertler. Toronto: University of Toronto Press.

Wapshott, R., and O. Mallett. 2016. *Managing Human Resources in Small and Medium-Sized Enterprises*. New York: Routledge.

Whittington, K. B., J. Owen-Smith, and W. Powell. 2009. "Networks, Propinquity, and Innovation in Knowledge-Intensive Industries." *Administrative Science Quarterly* 54 (1): 90–122. doi:10.2189/asqu.2009.54.1.90.

Williams, N., and T. Vorley. 2015. "The Impact of Institutional Change on Entrepreneurship in a Crisis-hit Economy: The Case of Greece." *Entrepreneurship & Regional Development* 27 (1–2): 28–49. doi:10.1080/08985626.2014.995723.

Wolfe, D. A., and M. S. Gertler. 2004. "Clusters from the Inside and Out: Local Dynamics and Global Linkages." *Urban Studies* 41: 1071–1093.

Wu, L., F. Jin, and L. M. Hitt. 2017. "Are All Spillovers Created Equal? a Network Perspective on Information Technology Labor Movements." *Management Science* 64 (7). July. mnsc.2017.2778.

Ylinenpää, H. 2009. "Entrepreneurship and Innovation Systems: Towards a Development of the ERIS/IRIS Concept." *European Planning Studies* 17 (8): 1153–1170.

Zahra, S. A. 2008. "The Virtuous Cycle of Discovery and Creation of Entrepreneurial Opportunities." *Strategic Entrepreneurship Journal* 2 (3): 243–257.

Zhang, J. 2011. "The Advantage of Experienced Start-Up Founders in Venture Capital Acquisition: Evidence from Serial Entrepreneurs." *Small Business Economics* 36 (2): 187–208. doi:10.1007/s11187-009-9216-4.

Degrees of integration: how a fragmented entrepreneurial ecosystem promotes different types of entrepreneurs

Katharina Scheidgen

ABSTRACT

Entrepreneurial Ecosystems (EEs) are expected to support high growth entrepreneurship. Yet, little is known about how they actually promote entrepreneurial activities. Based on Giddens' structuration theory, this paper takes the entrepreneurs' perspective to understand how they actually use the resources provided by an EE. Based on semi-structured interviews with entrepreneurs and other relevant actors in the Berlin EE along with participant observation at entrepreneurship events, this case study focuses on the resourcing practices of different types of entrepreneurs. It shows that the Berlin EE comprises two distinct subsystems. On the basis of this evidence it is proposed that EEs can have different degrees of integration and that this characteristic strongly impacts how entrepreneurs can actually acquire resources from the EE and thus how specific EEs promote different types of entrepreneurs. Heterogeneous structures therefore do not only exist between EEs but also within EEs. This heterogeneity needs to be recognized in order to understand how EEs function, enhance the comparability of research results, and design suitable political instruments to promote entrepreneurship effectively.

1. Introduction

Over the past two decades, researchers have increasingly begun to recognize the importance of analysing the context of entrepreneurship (Welter 2011; Garud, Gehman, and Giuliani 2014; Autio et al. 2014; Ozgen and Baron 2007). In this line of research, *entrepreneurial ecosystems* (EEs) have emerged as one of the key concepts (Alvedalen and Boschma 2017; Malecki 2017). The central question of this research strand is: *Which elements promote successful entrepreneurship in a region?* Several elements that support entrepreneurship have been identified, such as risk capital, universities, policies, support organizations, worker talent and a supportive culture (Spigel 2017; Alvedalen and Boschma 2017; Isenberg 2011). Across regions, we find heterogeneous entrepreneurial ecosystem (EE) configurations (Brown and Mason 2017), but we still do not fully understand how these different configurations promote entrepreneurs specifically.

Although the question of how EEs influence entrepreneurship is highly relevant, two major gaps persist that hinder a full understanding of how different configurations of EEs actually promote entrepreneurs. First, the concept of EE lacks a strong theoretical foundation and a theory of how the elements of EEs interact (Spigel and Harrison 2018; Malecki 2017; Alvedalen and Boschma 2017). Second, we know little about how entrepreneurs actually make use of EEs (Motoyama and Knowlton 2017). How they do so might vary between different types of entrepreneurs since different types may need different resources – start-up entrepreneurs may, for instance, require a different set of resources than university spin-off entrepreneurs (Elfring and Hulsink 2007; Powell and Sandholtz

2012; Rasmussen, Mosey, and Wright 2015). If this is true, different types of entrepreneurs might benefit from different elements of EEs, and different substructures of EEs might promote different types of entrepreneurs. To develop a more differentiated understanding of the co-existence of different types of entrepreneurs and heterogeneous substructures within a single EE, the question of this paper is the following: *How do EEs promote different types of entrepreneurs?*

To develop a more precise understanding of how EEs promote entrepreneurship – and, more specifically, how different configurations of EEs promote entrepreneurship in certain ways – we do not only need to know which elements are necessary and how these elements interact with each other (Spigel 2017; Stam and Spigel 2016) but also – and most importantly – how entrepreneurs actually make use of them (Motoyama and Knowlton 2017). It is necessary to take account of action and structure—and Giddens' (1984) structuration theory does exactly that (Sarason, Dean, and Dillard 2006). It enables us to explain how the structure of an EE enables and constrains the actions of entrepreneurs, and how entrepreneurs (re-)produce the structure of the EE through their actions.

This embedded single case study (Yin 1994) of the Berlin EE compares the resourcing practices of three types of entrepreneurs: (i) start-up entrepreneurs, (ii) university spin-off entrepreneurs, and (iii) entrepreneurs funded through the Federal Ministry of Economic Affairs and Energy's Exist pro- gramme. While the resourcing practices of university spin-off and Exist entrepreneurs show a considerable number of similarities, the resourcing practices of start-up entrepreneurs are rather different. Start-up entrepreneurs predominantly acquire entrepreneurial knowledge and financial capital from or via the entrepreneurial community. University spin-off and Exist entrepreneurs rely foremost on public funding programmes and public investors as well as on the university's incu- bator, its events, and recommended coaches. It becomes apparent that the different types of entrepreneurs are embedded in two distinct subsystems, pointing to the *fragmentation* of the Berlin EE. These findings indicate that heterogeneous structures might not only exist between but also within EEs.

The insights from this empirical study and previous research on EEs in other regions suggests introducing a new theoretical construct, namely, the *integration* of EEs. It is argued that the integration of an EE strongly impacts how EEs support entrepreneurship. EEs can exhibit different degrees of integration and can thus be either highly integrated or fragmented into subsystems accordingly. The fragmentation of the Berlin EE into two subsystems (re-)produces different resour- cing trajectories for different types of entrepreneurs and conversely, their different resourcing practices reproduce these subsystems. Consequently, the actors in the Berlin EE promote distinctive types of entrepreneurs.

In section two, this paper conceptualizes EEs from a structurationist perspective. Section three outlines the design of the qualitative case study. Section four compares the identified resourcing practices, elaborates on the relationship of the two subsystems within the Berlin EE, and develops the new theoretical construct of a *fragmentation* of EEs. Section five discusses these findings with respect to previous research, indicating that EEs do not necessarily have to be fragmented but might show varying *degrees of integration*, and develops propositions about the causes and consequences of different degrees of integration. These might inspire and guide future research. The final section draws conclusions for future research.

2. Conceptualizing entrepreneurial ecosystems from a structurationist perspective

To develop a more comprehensive understanding of how EEs actually promote different types of entrepreneurs, we (1) need a theoretically grounded conceptualization of EEs and (2) more closely investigate how entrepreneurs actually acquire resources from their EE. Giddens (1984) theory of structuration offers an approach to deal with these requirements. Structuration theory emphasizes that actors and social systems co-evolve, as illustrated in Figure 1. Thus, it offers huge potential to explore the link between the actions of entrepreneurs and the EE in which they are embedded (Jack and Anderson 2002). Entrepreneurial action is guided by structure, and structure is created by

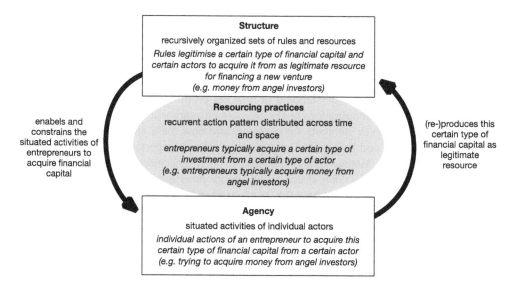

Figure 1. Resourcing activities, resourcing practices, and structure of the EE.

entrepreneurial action (Chiasson and Saunders 2005). The actions of the entrepreneurs are as much enabled and constrained by the structures of the EE as they (re-)produce them (Sarason, Dean, and Dillard 2006). Although this approach has long been established in management studies (e.g., Barley and Tolbert 1997; Sydow and Windeler 1998; Whittington 2010), it is only rarely considered in EE discourse.

In the following, EEs will be conceptualized from a structurationist perspective along three implicit, more or less critical assumptions made by previous EE research: an EE is a specific environment for entrepreneurs that (1) comprises several elements whose sheer presence promotes entrepreneurship, (2) is regionally bounded, and (3) is homogenous in that it promotes all kinds of entrepreneurs equally. But how does an EE actually promote entrepreneurs? This paper argues that this question is best answered by focusing on the resourcing practices of entrepreneurs.

2.1. Defining entrepreneurial ecosystems as social systems

Driven by political efforts to promote innovative, high-growth entrepreneurship in certain regions (Isenberg 2010; Mason and Brown 2014), EE discourse has predominantly focused on identifying success factors, often based on successful EEs and best practices (Isenberg 2011; Stam 2015). A broad consensus can be identified regarding the supportive effect of investment capital, research universities, entrepreneurial knowledge, an entrepreneurial community, and a conducive culture (Spigel 2017; Isenberg 2011).

The vast majority of previous studies and conceptual frameworks more or less implicitly assume that an EE will be successful as long as certain actors and factors (Spigel 2017; Stam and Spigel 2016), domains (Isenberg 2011), and components (Alvedalen and Boschma 2017) are present. The great diversity in terminology in itself points to a lack of theoretical foundation and cohesion. It remains unclear which elements entail which consequences (Stam 2015; Motoyama and Knowlton 2017) and what happens if some elements are missing (Mack and Mayer 2016). By focusing on 'the essential ingredients' (Malecki 2017, 5) and writing 'laundry lists' (Spigel and Harrison 2018, 158), this discourse has widely neglected any reasoning on cause and effect and the interplay of these elements, or, as Malecki (2017) puts it, on the 'recipes' for their combination.

Understanding the impact and interplay of certain elements requires analytically distinguishing different types of elements. Previous studies have predominantly analysed which actors, rules, and resources are involved in a specific EE without analytically distinguishing between actors, rules, and resources. Structuration theory does exactly that. By distinguishing actors who interact in a social system and rules and resources as the structure of the social system, it offers a theoretically well-grounded conceptualization of EEs.

The EE is a social system and as such comprises the *'reproduced relations between actors or collectivities, organized as regular social practices'* (Giddens 1984, 25) aimed at providing *'resources specific to the entrepreneurship process'* (Spigel 2017, 52). This definition sharpens our view for different actors providing similar resources or a single actor providing more than one resource. In different EEs, different actors might provide comparable resources. EEs thus do not only vary according to the resources they provide but also with respect to the actors through which entrepreneurs can access them. If resources are available but some actors are not, the resources might be accessed through other actors, leading to functional equivalents and equifinal resourcing practices (Hallen and Eisenhardt 2012).

Resources cannot be conceptualized apart from rules (Giddens 1984). How entrepreneurs evaluate resources, and whom they see as suitable actors to acquire them from, is influenced by normative aspects and socially constructed criteria that might vary between EEs. As Figure 1 shows, the rules of one EE might constitute financial capital as a necessary resource for the founding process and define angel investors as suitable actors to acquire it from. By contrast, the rules of another EE might legitimize a public funding programme. These rules and resources are reproduced in social practices, that is, in action patterns distributed in time and space. Consequently, to understand how EEs promote entrepreneurship, the focus shifts from the question of *which actors and factors are important* to *which resources are legitimized by the rules of the EE and how and from whom can entrepreneurs acquire them.*

2.2. Boundaries of entrepreneurial ecosystems

Although there is no agreement on the scope of an EE (Audretsch 2015; Autio et al. 2018; Acs et al. 2017), the majority of research focuses on regionally bounded environments, often cities or metropolitan areas (Audretsch and Belitski 2017; Ferrary and Granovetter 2009). In addition to the flourishing and prominent example of Silicon Valley (Saxenian 1996; Bahrami and Evans 1995), other regions such as the area around Route 128 in Boston (Saxenian 1996) and the Washington metropolitan area (Feldman 2001) have also been analysed. Other authors have focused on cities, such as Waterloo and Calgary (Spigel 2017), Victoria, Canada (Cohen 2006), or St. Louis (Motoyama and Knowlton 2017), Boulder (Neck et al. 2004), and Phoenix (Mack and Mayer 2016), USA.

According to a structurationist approach, actors are only part of an EE if entrepreneurs (and other actors) recognize them as such and refer to them in their practices. Rules and resources only exist to the extent that they are actualized in social practices. Consequently, the boundaries of an EE have to be defined empirically. Only those actors, rules, and resources are included in the analysis of an EE that are actually recognized as important by entrepreneurs and other relevant actors. If the boundaries are set from an outside perspective, the researcher might identify certain actors as important, but the actors involved in the EE might not share that assumption. Empirically identifying the actors and resources that entrepreneurs actually refer to in their practices also enables us to identify heterogeneous substructures within an EE.

2.3. Heterogeneity between and within entrepreneurial ecosystems

Although previous research has predominantly portrayed EEs as homogenous environments, their heterogeneity has been implicitly addressed in three ways. First and foremost, EE research has emphasized heterogeneity across regions yet implicitly treated each EE as a homogenous environment for entrepreneurship within a region. Second, a few studies have focused on a specific EE that has emerged around one type of entrepreneur, implicitly raising, yet failing to address, the question whether there are also other types in the same region who operate within the context of their own EEs, and how these might relate to each other. Third, network research has emphasized the differences between different types of entrepreneurs yet has neglected the causes and effects at the EE level.

(1) One of the key findings of EE research is that EEs in different regions have their particularities (Spigel 2017; Feldman 2001; Saxenian 1996). Entrepreneurship is often shaped by these particular exogenous factors (Feldman 2001; Audretsch and Belitski 2017). Consequently, these reactions vary, resulting in different EE designs. Cultural peculiarities in a region (Saxenian 1996) or the presence of a very strong industry (Spigel 2017) can lead to different configurations and modes of functioning of EEs. Despite this strong emphasis on regional differences, the EE in a specific region is mostly treated as a homogenous environment for all types of entrepreneurs there. A few recent studies, however, have argued that entrepreneurs in the same region might engage differently with the EE. Brush et al. (2018), for instance, found that it is more challenging for women than for men to acquire resources from an EE, which suggests that entrepreneurs with different characteristics might not have the same access to resources. Similarly, Qin, Wright, and Gao (2019) show heterogeneity within a single accelerator and emphasize that various entrepreneurs pursue different strategies of making use of this accelerator programme. Interestingly, both studies nevertheless conceptualize the EE as a homogeneous environment for all entrepreneurs; what varies is their abilities or strategies to make use of it.

(2) Other studies focus on one type of entrepreneur and the EE that has evolved around that one type – for example, technology entrepreneurs (Spigel 2016), entrepreneurs involved with sustainability (Cohen 2006), social entrepreneurs (Thompson, Purdy, and Ventresca 2018; McCarthy 2012), or university-related entrepreneurs (Schaeffer and Matt 2016; Youtie and Shapira 2008; Kenney, Nelson, and Patton 2009). Thompson, Purdy, and Ventresca (2018), for instance, focus on the emergence of a social entrepreneurship EE in Seattle. Although it is not their issue of concern, their study suggests that commercial entrepreneurship might have its own subsystem alongside social entrepreneurship. The same applies to Schaeffer and Matt's (2016) study of the university's role in the emergence of the Strasbourg EE. They show the strong impact of the university as a hub organization and argue that the EE matured around that university. Since their research question and data focused on the role of this university in the emergence of the EE, there could also be other subsystems in parallel to the EE that they identified. On the basis of these findings, it can be argued that different subsystems within a single EE might promote different types of entrepreneurs and that these subsystems might co-exist, overlap, or influence each other within one region.

(3) Another strand of research – namely, on networks and entrepreneurship – emphasizes the different resource needs of different types of entrepreneurs or new ventures (Elfring and Hulsink 2007; Lockett and Wright 2005; Partanen, Chetty, and Rajala 2014) and in different founding stages (Hite and Hesterly 2001; Larson and Starr 1993; Butler and Hansen 1991). Special emphasis is given to the distinct resource needs of university spin-offs (Wright et al. 2006; Lockett and Wright 2005). These spin-offs originate in the scientific context of a university, where entrepreneurial knowledge is generally not as present and easily available as it is for start-up entrepreneurs in a business environment (Rasmussen, Mosey, and Wright 2015; Vohora, Wright, and Locket 2004). Like any other entrepreneur, spin-off entrepreneurs need to acquire resources from their EE but are often not that familiar with this context in advance (Maurer and Ebers 2006; Keating, Geiger, and McLoughlin 2014). The initial founding conditions – that is, whether the new ventures spin out of a university, an incubator, or start independently – impact resource acquisition (Elfring and Hulsink 2007). These findings suggest that different types of entrepreneurs – for example, start-up and university spin-off entrepreneurs – might engage differently with the EE, and thus a specific EE might promote different types of entrepreneurs in distinct ways, or – as reasoned above – different subsystems might promote different types of entrepreneurs. To analyse empirically how a specific EE promotes

different types of entrepreneurs, we need to understand how these different types of entrepreneurs actually acquire resources from these differently shaped EEs.

2.4. Resourcing entrepreneurial knowledge and financial capital

Mobilizing resources from external actors is one of the most elementary activities that defines the entrepreneurship process (Clough et al. 2019; Macpherson, Herbane, and Jones 2015; Dubini and Aldrich 1991). The fact that these actors and resources are only part of the EE if entrepreneurs actually incorporate them into their resourcing practices moves these resourcing practices to the centre of attention. The entrepreneur is not necessarily the most powerful actor in an EE but, by its definition, the concept of EE moves the entrepreneur and his or her entrepreneurial activities to the centre of attention (Spigel 2016; Motoyama and Knowlton 2017). While other elements might have functional equivalents, entrepreneurs are indispensable; without entrepreneurs, the supportive infrastructure has no one to support. This paper focuses on two critically important resourcing practices of entrepreneurs: resourcing (1) entrepreneurial knowledge and (2) financial capital.

To start a new venture, knowledge about how to found a business (Aldrich and Yang 2013; Vissa and Chacar 2009; Ruef 2005) and other entrepreneurial knowledge is an essential resource (Isenberg 2011; Spigel and Harrison 2018). Often, entrepreneurial knowledge is exchanged through informal communication between entrepreneurs (Feldman 2001; Aldrich and Yang 2012), which makes other entrepreneurs and mentors crucial actors (Thompson, Purdy, and Ventresca 2018; Motoyama and Knowlton 2017). Successful entrepreneurs often remain part of the ecosystem as serial entrepreneurs, angel investors, or mentors, providing their money and knowledge to the EE, which results in resources circulating in a process of entrepreneurial recycling (Spigel and Harrison 2018; Mason and Harrison 2006; Bahrami and Evans 1995).

Financial capital is often acquired from external actors, for instance, from angel investors or venture capitalists (VCs). Yet the sheer presence of financial capital in an EE might not be enough, as several failed government-backed venture capital and venture support programmes have demonstrated (Brown, Mawson, and Mason 2017; Spigel and Harrison 2018). Promoting the wrong entrepreneurs on account of public funding programmes applying mistaken evaluation criteria might even harm the ecosystem because of unsuccessful ventures staying in the EE for too long (Isenberg 2011).

Focusing on the resourcing practices of entrepreneurs sheds light on how an EE actually promotes entrepreneurship. Analysing different types of entrepreneurs promises valuable insights into heterogeneous structures within EEs. There is reason to believe that distinct subsystems might evolve around different types of entrepreneurs. Yet we do not know much about the co-existence and interplay of substructures within EEs.

3. Methods

Given the limited theory and evidence on how an EE promotes different types of entrepreneurs, an embedded single case study promises high potential to generate theoretical insights that might guide future research (Yin 1994). The Berlin EE serves as an exemplary case to theorize about how EEs might promote different types of entrepreneurs. One characteristic of EEs that particularly stands out when focusing on the resourcing practices of entrepreneurs is the *degree of integration*, or the *fragmentation* of an EE as one possible form that this can take.

3.1. Case selection

The present research applied Yin's (1994) embedded single case study design. The cases are at two levels. First, the Berlin EE was treated as a single case and the focus of this analysis. Second, the study looked at multiple entrepreneurs who are embedded in that single case to analyse how the Berlin EE supports different types of entrepreneurs. This was done by focusing on the resourcing practices of entrepreneurs who are embedded in the Berlin EE. Berlin is a very interesting case to analyse how an EE supports different types of entrepreneurs because of its intense political promotion of entrepreneurship and the parallel emergence of an independent entrepreneurial community after Germany's reunion.

Until 1990, the city was divided in East and West Berlin. After the reunion, there were an abundance of opportunities for young, creative people to establish a dynamic culture. Today, Berlin is ranked one of the top three entrepreneurial ecosystems in Europe. For examples, it ranks 3rd behind London and Paris in terms of the number of deals closed with VC firms and ranks 2nd, behind London with respect to the amount of capital invested (Ernst and Young 2019). It is a metropolitan area with plenty of well-educated, often international young people, has four universities, and boasts affordable, albeit increasing, costs of living. Most of the entrepreneurial activity, especially of innovative, independent start-ups, is locally clustered around two neighbouring districts in the heart of Berlin (Mitte and Friedrichshain-Kreuzberg) (BSM 2018).

Since the late 1990s, the German government made strong efforts to promote entrepreneurship at universities, not only in the form of spin-offs that transfer IP from the university but also in the form of non-IP-based businesses started by students or alumni (Heumann 2010; Kulicke 2014, 2017). As part of that strategy, the Federal Ministry for Economic Affairs and Energy launched a funding programme to support university spin-offs.[1] It comprises two funding lines: *Exist Forschungstransfer* (Exist FT) and *Exist Gründerstipendium* (Exist GS). Exist FT focuses on the commercialization of IP and finances teams of up to four entrepreneurs for one and a half years; Exist GS awards scholarships for one year to teams of up to three entrepreneurs that do not transfer IP. A third pillar of this governmental strategy is establishing incubator programmes at universities.

The case study of the Berlin EE comprised 29 embedded entrepreneurs. They were theoretically sampled (Eisenhardt 1989; Glaser and Strauss 1967) to cover three types of entrepreneurs, namely, *start-up entrepreneurs, university spin-off entrepreneurs*, and *Exist entrepreneurs*. As argued in Section 2.4, start-up and university spin-off entrepreneurs might be expected to engage differently with the EE because of their different resource needs and founding backgrounds. The same applies to entrepreneurs who received public funding from the Exist programme.

In contrast to start-ups or spin-offs from companies, university spin-offs transfer IP from a university or research institute to commercialize research results (Vanaelst et al. 2006; Wright et al. 2006; Lockett and Wright 2005). For simplicity, this group will henceforth be called *spin-off entrepreneurs*.

Exist entrepreneurs, the third type of entrepreneur in the Berlin EE, are closely associated with the Exist GS funding line. Their technologies show similar characteristics to the ones start-up entrepreneurs typically develop, but their founding background resembles more that of spin-off entrepreneurs. As a result, their resource needs are comparable to start-up entrepreneurs, but at the outset they face a funding and support infrastructure similar to spin-off entrepreneurs. Hence, this support infrastructure might have a potential imprinting effect on them even though their resource needs are different from spin-off entrepreneurs.

3.2. Data collection

Since the focus of this study is to analyse the supporting role of an EE through the resourcing practices of entrepreneurs, the primary data source was semi-structured interviews with entrepreneurs. Thirteen start-up entrepreneurs, thirteen spin-off entrepreneurs, and three Exist entrepreneurs were theoretically sampled to participate in this study. This data was triangulated with two other sources – interviews with other relevant actors of the EE and observations of entrepreneurship events – to bolster confidence in the accuracy of the emergent theory.[2]

Thirty-four interviews were conducted with 29 entrepreneurs[3] (see Table 1).[4] The interviews were conducted in German[5] and lasted about one hour on average. All interviews were recorded,

Table 1. Data.

Entrepreneur	Previous career	IP/no IP	Industry	Position	Age of new venture	Interview number
SU-A	Employee/start-up	no IP	Consumer Electronics	CMO	1 year	i-1
					2 years	i-2
SU-B	Employee/corporate	no IP	Online platform	CEO	1 year	i-3
					2 years	i-4
SU-C	Employee/start-up	no IP	Online platform	CTO	1 year	i-5
SU-D	Student	no IP	Online platform	CEO	2 years	i-6
SU-E	Entrepreneur	no IP	SaaS	CEO	1.5 years	i-7
					2.5 years	i-8
SU-F	Entrepreneur	no IP	SaaS	COO	1.5 years	i-9
SU-G	Employee/corporate	no IP	SaaS	CTO	1.5 years	i-10
SU-H	Employee/start-up	no IP	e-commerce	CEO	2 years	i-11
SU-I	Entrepreneur	no IP	e-commerce	CEO	1.5 years	i-12
SU-J	Entrepreneur	no IP	Fintech	CTO	2 years	i-13
					3 years	i-14
SU-K	Entrepreneur	IP	SaaS	CEO	1.5 years	i-15
SU-L	Employee/start-up	no IP	e-commerce	CEO	6 years	i-16
SU-M	Employee/start-up	no IP	e-commerce	CEO	5 years	i-17
SO-N	Student	IP	Consumer Electronics	CTO	1 year	i-18
SO-O	Student	IP	SaaS	CEO	1 year	i-19
SO-P	Employee/corporate	IP	Fintech	CEO	2 years	i-20
SO-Q	Researcher	IP	Physics	CEO	2 years	i-21
SO-R	Researcher	IP	SaaS	CTO	1.5 years	i-22
SO-S	Researcher	IP	Physics	CTO	1 year	i-23
SO-T	Researcher	IP	Physics	CEO	1 year	i-24
SO-U	Employee/corporate	IP	Physics	CEO	2 years	i-25
SO-V	Researcher	IP	App	CEO	2 years	i-26
SO-W	Researcher	IP	Agriculture	CTO	3 years	i-27
SO-X	Researcher	IP	SaaS	CEO	4 years	i-28
SO-Y	Researcher	IP	Physics	CEO	5 years	i-29
SO-Z	Researcher	IP	Chemistry	CTO	5 years	i-30
EX-1	Student	no IP	Consumer Electronics		1 year	i-31
					2 years	i-32
EX-2	Student	no IP	Agriculture		1.5 years	i-33
EX-3	Student	no IP	App		6 years	i-34

34 interviews with 29 entrepreneurs (total of 33 hours and 51 minutes).
Interviews with other actors: 9 (total of 6 hours and 16 minutes).
(angel investors, head of accelerator, public and semi-public investors, coaches).
Total number of Interviews: 43 Interviews (40 hours and 7 minutes).

transcribed, and entered into the MaxQDA software package, which is specifically designed for qualitative data analysis. The interviews focused on which resources entrepreneurs perceive as important for the founding process and on how and from whom they (tried to) acquire them. All interviews were based on the same interview schedule to ensure that differences in the stated resourcing activities were not simply the result of asking different questions. However, to also utilize the advantages of qualitative research – namely, to adapt data collection to new insights – two questions were carefully added after the first few interviews. It became apparent that start-up and spin-off entrepreneurs mentioned different actors whom they approached to acquire similar resources. To determine whether the two groups were not aware of the respective other actors or if and why they consciously decided against them, questions such as 'Did you consider to apply for Exist? Why?/Why not?' or 'Did you consider angel investors/VCs?' were added at the end. By including them at the end of the interview schedule, these additional questions could not influence the previous course of the interview.

To not only rely on the entrepreneurs' perceptions but to also gather data on and gain insight into the EE, nine relevant actors from the EE were also interviewed. The research also involved visiting and taking notes at fifteen relevant events, including those hosted by the university's incubators, big corporations and meet-ups organized by entrepreneurs. Special attention was given to who the typical participants visiting different types of events were, who the typical speakers at what type of event were, and what type of entrepreneurs typically visited which type of event.

A qualitative case study must address the issue of potential bias rooted in the mode of data collection. Several measures were taken to do so. First, it involved carefully choosing interview participants. For example, recruiting spin-off entrepreneurs only through a single incubator could have resulted in all of them identifying the same actors as highly relevant or all engaging in similar resourcing practices because of having attended the same courses, thus leading to wrong conclusions about the Berlin EE. To mitigate that risk, entrepreneurs were approached in different, well-considered ways. Although all spin-off entrepreneurs included in the analysis received funding from Exist or an equivalent programme, this was not just the outcome of a narrow case selection strategy. Potential interview partners were searched via the websites of two research institutes and the incubators of three universities and at various types of entrepreneurship events.[6] According to the collected data, only one start-up entrepreneur and one angel investor in the sample knew each other.[7] Thus, similarities in resourcing activities cannot be attributed to the interview participants' familiarity. Second, as noted above, the interview guideline was largely the same for all interviews with entrepreneurs, with only a few additional questions carefully added at the end of some interviews. Third, the interviews with the entrepreneurs were triangulated with interviews with other relevant actors of the EE and with observations of different types of entrepreneurship events. Forth, all interview partners were guaranteed anonymity, which can be expected to encourage candour.

3.3. Data analysis

The analysis began by coding the data. Following Miles, Huberman, and Saldana (2014), this involved two coding cycles to determine patterns across individual resourcing activities (as illustrated in Figure 2). The first cycle consisted of inductive process coding to identify the diverse individual resourcing activities of all interviewed entrepreneurs (e.g., whether they applied for or received Exist or EU funding). The second coding cycle served to discover patterns across entrepreneurs. Similar resourcing activities were grouped into a smaller number of resourcing practices in a process of pattern coding (e.g., 'resourcing financial capital from Exist (or equivalent)'). Similar practices were

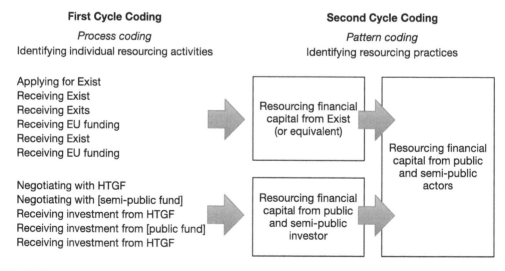

Figure 2. Coding process.

again grouped into more general practices (e.g., *'resourcing financial capital from Exist (or equivalent)'* and *'resourcing financial capital from public and semi-public investor'* were grouped into *'resourcing financial capital from public and semi-public actors'*).

The second step in the analysis involved searching for patterns across all types of entrepreneurs, not just among each type, to be able to identify similar practices across different types. Cross-case analysis mitigates the risk of overemphasizing differences between the pre-defined types of entrepreneurs. Yet despite these efforts to allow for similarity between the three types of entrepreneurs, this analysis identified major differences between start-up and spin-off entrepreneurs, and surprisingly many similarities between spin-off entrepreneurs and Exist entrepreneurs.

The third step was devoted to developing theoretical constructs from the data by contrasting and comparing resourcing practices. Developing the idea of the *fragmentation* of the Berlin EE resulted in a 'conceptual leap' (Klag and Langley 2013). How well or poorly this emergent frame of fragmentation fits with the data was assessed in a highly iterative process (Eisenhardt 1989). For example, as the concept of *fragmentation* took shape, special attention was paid to the three Exist entrepreneurs. The goal was to analyse to what extent their resourcing activities show more similarities to start-up or spin-off entrepreneurs, and why. One way to do this was to pair two entrepreneurs – one start-up and one Exist entrepreneur (SU-A and EX-1) – whose products feature especially similar characteristics and compare their resourcing activities in depth (Eisenhardt 1989). This comparison revealed stronger similarities between Exist and spin-off entrepreneurs, even though the resource needs of Exist entrepreneurs are very similar to start-up entrepreneurs. The *degree of integration*, and *fragmentation* as one example of a low degree of integration, emerged as a new theoretical construct.

4. Findings

How does an EE promote different types of entrepreneurs? Or, to put it differently, how can different types of entrepreneurs acquire resources from the EE? In Berlin, the practices for resourcing entrepreneurial knowledge and financial capital differ between start-up entrepreneurs and spin-off entrepreneurs but not so much between spin-off and Exist entrepreneurs. The fragmentation of the Berlin EE becomes especially apparent when we analyse the resourcing practices of entrepreneurs; it is through these different practices that renders the fragmentation of the Berlin EE visible.

4.1. Resourcing entrepreneurial knowledge

The analysis identified six practices for resourcing entrepreneurial knowledge. Some are more relevant than others, but not all entrepreneurs engage in all practices, nor do they do so randomly. Rather, they show patterns, as Table 2 illustrates.[8]

Start-up entrepreneurs largely gain entrepreneurial knowledge through *informal exchange within the entrepreneurial community* or extensive interaction with a small group of mentors *(gaining entrepreneurial knowledge from mentors)*. As Table 2 shows, eleven of the interviewed start-up entrepreneurs have or had a mentor, and only entrepreneur SU-J explicitly said that he does not learn much from the entrepreneurial community, except for the exchange with his mentor, who is also a member of this community. This underscores that the entrepreneurial community is a very important source of business advice and mutual education. Five of the interviewed start-up entrepreneurs also worked in a start-up before founding their own one. As one of them explains, he did so precisely to learn about the entrepreneurship process:

> For me it was extremely helpful to have the experience before founding my first start-up. Not to be one hundred percent responsible but to be able to co-decide and experience how to build a company in order to apply this knowledge to my own company. (SU-H, i-11)

All spin-off and Exist entrepreneurs participated in a university's incubator or comparable incubator programme. These programmes strongly shape how and from whom spin-off and Exist

Table 2. Practices for resourcing entrepreneurial knowledge and financial capital.

| | | Resourced Entrepreneurial Knowledge … | | | | | | Resourced financial capital from … | | | | | |
| | | From Informal Exchange | | From | | By learning in | | Private investors | | Public and semi-public actors | | | |
Group	Entrepreneur	Within the EC	With a few other entrepreneurs	Mentors	Coaches	Accelerators	Incubators	Angel investors	VCs	Exist (or equivalent)	Others	Strategic investors	Via personal network/EC
Start-up entrepreneurs	SU-L	✓		✓									✓
	SU-G	✓							✓				✓
	SU-F	✓		✓					✓				✓
	SU-E	✓		✓ (had one)					✓				
	SU-J			✓				✓	O				✓
	SU-M			✓				✓	✓				✓
	SU-C			✓				✓	O				✓
	SU-H			✓				✓					✓
	SU-A			✓				✓					✓
	SU-I			✓		✓		O					
	SU-D			✓		✓	O	O					
	SU-B			✓	O	✓	O	✓	O				✓
	SU-K			✓	✓			✓	✓				✓
Exist	EX-3	✓	✓		✓			O	O	✓	✓		
	EX-1		✓		✓		O	✓		✓			
	EX-2		✓		✓					✓			
University spin-off entrepreneurs	SO-P		✓	✓	✓		O			✓	✓		✓
	SO-R		✓		✓					✓	✓		
	SO-U		✓		✓					✓	✓		
	SO-Z		✓							✓	O		
	SO-Y		✓				✓			✓	O		
	SO-V		✓				O			✓	O		
	SO-S		✓		✓					✓	O		
	SO-T		✓		✓					✓			
	SO-N		✓		✓					✓	✓		
	SO-W		✓	✓			✓			✓	✓	✓	
	SO-X		✓							✓		✓	
	SO-Q		✓		✓		✓			✓		✓	
	SO-O		✓										

✓ – entrepreneur engaged in this practice **❘** O – entrepreneur mentioned this practice, but only rarely engages in it **❘** EC – entrepreneurial community.

entrepreneurs acquire entrepreneurial knowledge. Eleven spin-off entrepreneurs and two Exist entrepreneurs engaged in *informal knowledge exchanges with other entrepreneurs* but apparently with just one or two other spin-off entrepreneurs who often participated in the same incubator programme and who were not members of the entrepreneurial community. As part of the incubator programme, spin-off entrepreneurs are encouraged to *gain entrepreneurial advice from coaches*. Coaches are quite different from mentors, as will be explained below. Exist provides financial resources specifically earmarked for consulting coaches. The university's incubator then suggests suitable coaches. As Table 2 shows, seven spin-off entrepreneurs and the three Exist entrepreneurs explicitly referred to coaches as a source of entrepreneurial knowledge, all of whom were suggested by the university's incubator. The incubator also hosts workshops and events. Although neither the workshops nor the events were considered to be very helpful, the events appear to have been the more important source of entrepreneurial knowledge, with five spin-off entrepreneurs evaluating them as somewhat relevant. Although five of the thirteen entrepreneurs expected to gain knowledge from the workshops, only three actually evaluated this knowledge as useful.

At first glance the practices of *informal exchange of entrepreneurial knowledge within the entrepreneurial community* (start-up entrepreneurs) and *with other entrepreneurs* (spin-off and Exist entrepreneurs) as well as *gaining advice from mentors* (start-up entrepreneurs) and *from coaches* (spin-off and Exist entrepreneurs) seem rather similar. But in reality they are different in highly significant ways, especially with respect to the actors of the EE who are important for each of these practices.

The informal knowledge exchange of start-up entrepreneurs is characterized by generalized reciprocity within the entrepreneurial community. This comprises informal learning while working at a start-up as well as frequent exchange with several people within that community. These are mostly other entrepreneurs with diverse levels of experience – first time founders, serial entrepreneurs, or angel investors – who work in a variety of industries. As the quote in Table 3 shows, entrepreneur SU-M mentions asking '*20 other entrepreneurs*' (i-17) about their experience in a certain area, which illustrates the wide net they cast to resource entrepreneurial knowledge. In contrast, entrepreneur SO-O points to '*one, two other spin-offs*' (i-19) with whom he communicates and who are not members of the entrepreneurial community. The interviewed spin-off entrepreneurs predominantly exchange entrepreneurial knowledge on a one-on-one basis with a few other entrepreneurs who are in the same founding stage and thus have a similar level of experience. They meet these entrepreneurs mostly in the shared office space provided by the university's incubator or at

Table 3. Informal exchange of entrepreneurial knowledge within the entrepreneurial community vs. with other entrepreneurs.

Start-up entrepreneurs	Spin-off entrepreneurs
Informal exchange of entrepreneurial knowledge within the entrepreneurial community	Informal exchange of entrepreneurial knowledge with other entrepreneurs
• With many other entrepreneurs with different levels of experience • Guided by generalized reciprocity	• Only a few other entrepreneurs with a similar level of experience • Guided by direct reciprocity
*'(After founding one successful start-up), we know all the other entrepreneurs in Berlin and were able to learn from their experiences. Let's say, we have only little experience in hiring employees who work in IT. **We would just ask 20 other people** how they hired their developers'.* (SU-M, i-17) *'You know, **we help each other**. This is a general requirement within the entrepreneurial community. You always also think about the others, make introductions, give feedback, and so on.'* (SU-D, i-6) *'**All my friends are entrepreneurs** or other people involved with entrepreneurship. So if I need to know something about product design, I just ask of my friends who are designers.'* (SU-I, i-12)	*'I have **one other spin-off, no, two other spin-offs**, with whom I communicate a lot because we know each other, and I can simply ask: "How did you do it?"'* (SO-O, i-19) *'We **shared an office** with [another spin-off] when we participated in this **incubator programme**. I still talk with them rather often. We talk about possible ways of funding, and so on.'* (SO-Q, i-21) **Exist entrepreneurs** *'Here, in this **incubator**, there are a couple of other spin-offs with whom I chat a lot. You just start chatting and ask: "How did you do that? What did you do first? What came next?"'* (EX-1, i-31)

one of the events hosted by the latter. Consequently, the university's incubator and its pre-selection of participants has a strong imprinting effect on whom spin-off entrepreneurs choose to approach for informal knowledge exchange.

A comparable imprinting effect of the university's incubator on the selection of actors can be identified with regard to resourcing entrepreneurial knowledge from coaches. The public funding programme Exist has a dedicated budget for consulting coaches, and the university's incubator recommends specific coaches from a network called B!Gründet. However, none of the interviewed start-up entrepreneurs mentioned coaches as a source of entrepreneurial knowledge. They referred to mentors instead, as Table 4 shows. Mentors are mostly more experienced entrepreneurs, who sometimes also invest as angel investors and thus have a high personal interest in the success of the start-up, as opposed to coaches, who get paid by the hour. Mentors pass on their knowledge and their experience because this is 'something you do' according to the rules emphasizing generalized reciprocity within the entrepreneurial community. As a successful start-up entrepreneur and mentor explains, his motivation is to give something back to the community. In expressing this, he highlights generalized reciprocity as a guiding rule:

> I really gained a lot from my mentor back in the day. So, I want to give back a little, to this network, this community. (SU-M, i-17)

These four practices of resourcing entrepreneurial knowledge attribute importance to very different types of actors of the EE: while the two dominant resourcing practices of start-up entrepreneurs emphasize the importance of the entrepreneurial community, the two dominant practices among spin-off and Exist entrepreneurs attribute a key role to the university's incubator.

4.2. Resourcing financial capital

As Table 2 shows, two dominant practices of resourcing financial capital can be identified: *resourcing financial capital (1) from private investors* and (2) *from public or semi-public actors*. Each practice (re-) produces certain resourcing trajectories. While start-up entrepreneurs predominantly engage in the former practice, spin-off and Exist entrepreneurs foremost engage in the latter one. Entrepreneurs can switch between the resourcing trajectories that result from each of these practices, although this comes with several challenges.

Table 4. Gaining entrepreneurial advice from mentors vs. from coaches.

Start-up entrepreneurs	Spin-off entrepreneurs
Gained entrepreneurial knowledge from mentors	Gained entrepreneurial knowledge from coaches
• More experienced entrepreneurs • Motivated to help less experienced entrepreneurs because of generalized reciprocity	• Do not necessarily have entrepreneurial experiences • Get paid
'It was really cool: our mentor founded a start-up with a similar business model two or three years before we started. So he already experienced all the things that we went through, because he dealt with the same stuff two years before we did.' (SU-M, i-17)	'Within this Exist programme, there is a network called "B! Gründet", and of course, we got some coaches from this network.' (SO-R, i-22)
'Most mentors have been entrepreneurs themselves. They made an exit, now they are VCs, or just do something, thinking about ideas, and they just like to help other entrepreneurs.' (SU-B, i-3)	'Yes, we also participated in coaching sessions. For example from "B!Gründet." We got a coach from there. You know, we had several coaches whom we paid for coaching us, and we had very mixed experiences.' (SO-W, i-27)
"He is one of our five mentors who help us just out of passion. These mentors came from my contacts, my co-founder's contacts. They help us because they are passionate about this entrepreneurial community. (SU-A, i-1)	**Exist-Entrepreneurs** 'We participated in two, three coaching sessions. We searched a coach for a certain topic via the network of the university incubator's network. Then we met with him and he explained something to us. This was okay, but I mean it should be okay, since we paid him for that.' (EX-1, i-31)

The general resourcing practice of start-up entrepreneurs' of *acquiring funding from private investors*' comprises the resourcing practices *'acquiring funding from angel investors'* and *'acquiring funding from VCs.'* Seven of the analysed start-up entrepreneurs acquired angel investments for their start-up, and two were negotiating such an investment at the time of the interview. Six start-up entrepreneurs already knew their angel investor before founding their first start-up because they were members of the entrepreneurial community beforehand, as shown in Table 2. The initial angel investor(s) connect(s) the entrepreneurs with other interested angel investors, or later on, with VCs (*finding investors via personal connections in the entrepreneurial community*). For follow-up financing, VCs become more important. Three start-up entrepreneurs already acquired VC investment for their start-ups; the founders of the other eight start-ups negotiated with VCs or planned to do so in the near future. Contacts with potential VCs are often established through angel investors or current VCs (*'contacting the second investor(s) through the first'*), as shown in Table 5. Personal connections within the entrepreneurial community are important for both practices. Consequently, the entrepreneurial community plays a key role in resourcing financial capital.

By contrast, spin-off entrepreneurs acquire financial capital predominantly from public or semi-public actors. During their early founding stages, all spin-off and Exist entrepreneurs received funding from Exist or comparable public funding programmes (*'acquiring funding from Exist'*). As a spin-off entrepreneur explains, the following is the typical path pursued:

> We did what you do with technological ideas. We tried to get it financed by Exist. (SO-Y, i-29)

During the later stages, spin-off entrepreneurs mostly acquire financial resources from public and semi-public investors. Four spin-off entrepreneurs received investments from public or semi-public investors, two received funding from a mix of semi-public and strategic investors, and five negotiated with public or semi-public investors. At this point, the networking events organized by the university's incubator have typically already introduced these actors to each other, thereby communicating the resourcing practice of *acquiring funding from public investors* and, in doing so, strengthening it. Spin-off entrepreneurs thus learn that this is the primary path for follow-up financing.

After having received funding from Exist, two of the three Exist entrepreneurs tried to move from the *public funding trajectory* to the *private investment trajectory* and acquire financial resources from private investors. The third Exist entrepreneur (EX-3) acquired funding from a public investor after being funded

Table 5. Resourcing of financial capital from private investors.

Start-up entrepreneurs: Resourcing of financial capital from private investors	
• Acquired funding from angel investors • Knew the angel investor before due to being a member of the entrepreneurial community	*'I worked at a start-up before founding my own. I knew [Tim] from there, and he became then invested as an angel in my start-up.'* (SU-M, i-17) *'One of our angels was my former boss, from when I worked at [a start-up]. And some others invested, too. They all came from my network and from introductions. Networking is key.'* (SU-H, i-11) *'I found the angels in my network. I knew [Thomas] from my previous start-up, I worked with him during that time. So when I started my new company, I just asked him.'* (SU-K, i-15) *'We worked at start-ups before. One of our angel investors had invested in this start-up, so we knew him.'* (SU-C, i-5) *'We found our angel investor via one of our mentors. Our mentor knew angels, and these angels new more angels, so some of them joined and invested with him.'* (SU-A, i-1)
• Acquiring funding from VCs • Contacting the second investor(s) through the first (or personal network)	*'We made a list with about one hundred investors that might be interesting to us. Then we checked how we could reach them. We had a look at LinkedIn if we were somehow connected, and who of our connections could make the strongest intro.'* (SU-C, i-5) *'In the first round, we already received funding from well-regarded investors with really good connections. They introduced us to potential follow-up investors, with whom we negotiated. After two months, we secured follow-up investment.'* (SU-E, i-8) *'I approach them mostly via intros from my network. For example, I asked one of our investors: "Can you introduce me to this and that VC?"'* (SU-M, i-17)

by Exist, and only afterwards switched to the private investment trajectory. While the first two failed, the later one managed to switch trajectories. Why does it seem to be rather difficult to switch?

This is where the *fragmentation* of the Berlin EE into – at least – two subsystems has an impact. Because each subsystem has different rules and resources, the resourcing practices of one subsystem cannot be readily transferred to the other subsystem. Once entrepreneurs are embedded in one of the subsystems, it becomes rather difficult for them to acquire resources from the other.

4.3. The fragmentation of the Berlin EE

The analysis of their resourcing practices showed that each type of entrepreneur chose different types of actors in the EE to acquire similar resources. As illustrated on the left side of Figure 3, the entrepreneurial community is highly important for start-up entrepreneurs, not only to acquire entrepreneurial knowledge but also for financial capital. As Tables 2 and 5 show, the key actors for acquiring financial capital – angel investors and VCs – are in most cases contacted via the entrepreneurial community. Spin-off and Exist entrepreneurs mostly gain knowledge from a few other entrepreneurs from the same incubator programme and from coaches and also – although less relevant – at events hosted by the university's incubator. For funding, the public funding programme Exist is especially relevant during the early founding stages, whereas later public and semi-public investors become more important, as the right side of Figure 3 shows. This demonstrates quite clearly that only some of the actors of the EE are relevant for each type of entrepreneur. It points to one of the defining characteristics of the Berlin EE: its *fragmentation* into two subsystems. The Berlin EE looks differently from the perspective of start-up entrepreneurs than it does from the perspective of spin-off and Exist entrepreneurs. While the different types of entrepreneurs attribute importance to different types of actors in the EE, they still recognize the others, as shown in Figure 3 and outlined below.

Entrepreneurs do not just randomly choose to approach a specific type of actor (e.g., mentors or coaches) to gain entrepreneurial knowledge, but they do so because the rules of the subsystem legitimize a specific type of actor as the appropriate one to approach for this purpose. The following comment by the head of an accelerator shows that he does not see coaches as a legitimate choice to learn about entrepreneurship:

> ... a lot of them [coaches] talk about founding like a blind man about colors, due to their lack of experience and due to a lack of incentives because they do not have any stake in this game. [...] Working for a university's incubator is very different. Nobody joins them voluntarily as a mentor. This is why they have to choose paid coaches. (Mentor and angel investor, i-36)

This emphasizes two aspects. First, the actors of each subsystem do recognize the others. Second, they do not attribute legitimacy to the same type of actor for providing similar resources.

Despite attributing far more relevance to the entrepreneurial community, to angel investors, and to VCs, start-up entrepreneurs do also recognize the actors who are relevant to spin-off entrepreneurs, but they consider them to be much less important for themselves and often only refer to them to distinguish themselves from spin-off entrepreneurs. Spin-off entrepreneurs do the same with regard to start-up entrepreneurs and actors from the start-up subsystem. This becomes especially apparent in their evaluation of the role of the entrepreneurial community, as demonstrated in Table 6. While start-up entrepreneurs attribute very high importance to the entrepreneurial community and consciously decide to rent office space in the heart of the start-up scene (around Rosenthaler Platz), spin-off entrepreneurs do not want to be involved with this environment since they do not identify themselves as the same kind of entrepreneur. As one of the spin-off entrepreneurs describes it, he does not feel as if he belongs there (SO-O, i-19, Table 6).

Both types of entrepreneurs do not only perceive the actors of the other subsystem, they also perceive them as being involved in a different subsystem and consciously refer to the fragmentation of the Berlin EE. Or in their words: *'two worlds that clash'* and the *'second Berlin start-up community,*

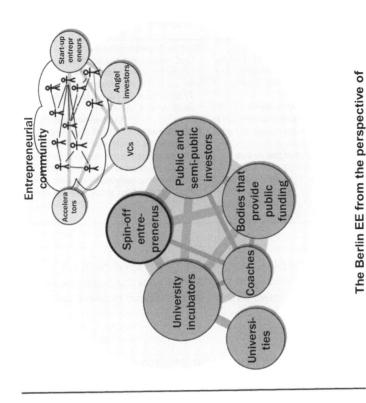

The Berlin EE from the perspective of
spin-off and Exist-entrepreneurs

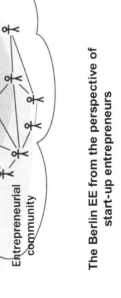

The Berlin EE from the perspective of
start-up entrepreneurs

Figure 3. The Berlin EE from different perspectives.

Table 6. The role of the entrepreneurial community.

Start-up entrepreneurs	Spin-off entrepreneurs
*'It would have been more difficult in another city, because I would not have had such a **circle of friends who are all involved in entrepreneurship** or work in Internet-related industries. And then I would not have had the **access to all these people's knowledge** that I have here.'* (SU-I, i-12)	*'These are **completely different scenes**. And to be honest, every time I get involved with this other scene, I'm mostly just annoyed. I do not like it there so much.'* (SO-Z, i-30)
*'**You should not underestimate the effect of having an office here** [in the centre of the start-up scene]. It is really cool to be able just to meet anyone spontaneously. It's just a ten-minute bike ride.'* (SU-K, i-15)	*'I stay out of this [the entrepreneurial community]. I do not feel as if I belong there. And I do not have the feeling that I would get much benefit out of it.'* (SO-O, i-19)
*'I think for fundraising it is **extremely important that we have our office here downtown.** You just coincidentally meet some investors on the street, and they say: "Yeah, right, I wanted to get in touch again!" And they actually do follow up. A lot of things happen by chance. Or you can go to some meet-up in the evening or meet someone for a quick coffee.'* (SU-C, i-5)	**Exist entrepreneurs**
	*'**All this hip start-up bla bla, this is not for me.** From the very beginning on, I could not identify with that. This is why I was also never interested in having an office space in Prenzlauer Berg [in the heart of the start-up scene]. Me and my co-founders were really happy out here [Berlin suburbs]. You easily get a parking space. That was more important for us.'* (EX-1, i-32)

the more private-sector community' (SU-K, i-15); *'here, in the real world'* (SU-B, i-4) or *'this other start-up scene'* (SO-Z, i-30). This fragmentation – and the different rules that legitimize different actors and resources as appropriate in the respective setting – make it difficult to switch trajectories and acquire resources from the other subsystem.

4.4. Switching between subsystems: how the fragemention of the EE enables and contrains resourcing practices

This fragmentation into two subsystems strongly impacts the resourcing practices of entrepreneurs and thus how the EE promotes different types of entrepreneurs. By starting in one of the two subsystems, entrepreneurs enter one of the two dominant resourcing trajectories. Switching from one trajectory to the other is inhibited by the fragmentation of the EE. The interviews testify to the difficulties of transferring the resourcing practices of one subsystem to the other.

As mentioned above, two of the three Exist entrepreneurs struggled to find follow-up financing. The typical public and semi-public investors for follow-up financing of spin-offs mostly invest in new ventures that rely on IP. Thus, they are not a very good fit for Exist entrepreneurs. Entrepreneur EX-1 tried to acquire angel investment by writing cold emails to angel investors whom he identified through lists on the Internet. This is not compatible with the dominant resourcing practice of the start-up subsystem, which is to acquire angel investment via personal connections within the entrepreneurial community. Angel investors predominantly recognize entrepreneurs via their personal network within the entrepreneurial community, and consequently they only rarely recognize entrepreneurs who are not members. Angel investors also strategically build relationships for their investments, for example, with potential VCs. They anticipate the resourcing practices of the start-up subsystem and help those entrepreneurs to acquire financial capital according to the legitimate practices of the EE. Thus, in addition to financial capital, angel investors and VCs also provide access to their network and in so doing reproduce the resourcing practices of using personal connections and finding the second investor through the first:

> We also consciously try to network very intensively with people who we don't know yet. Because it is always useful to know some people in the investment business in case one of our portfolio start-ups needs follow-up financing. So, we try to stay in touch with several VCs. (Angel investor, i-37)

This again points! to the key role of the entrepreneurial community in the start-up subsystem. Not being a member becomes a problem once spin-off or Exist entrepreneurs seek to acquire resources from the start-up subsystem. And as argued above and illustrated in Table 6, spin-off and Exist entrepreneurs consciously decide not to get involved with this community. In contrast, start-up entrepreneurs emphasize the high importance of being a member and make a considerable effort to become one. Closure of the subsystem – and thus a solidification of the resourcing trajectories – is promoted by the key role that personal relationships within the entrepreneurial community play in resourcing in this subsystem.

Furthermore, the resourcing trajectories are solidified because investors expect different quality signals in each subsystem. Receiving funding from Exist is considered a quality signal by public and semi-public investors. By contrast, the rules of the start-up subsystem legitimize investment from a successful angel investor or well-regarded VC as a quality signal – indicating that somebody with business expertise evaluated their skills, their team, and trusted them with his or her money. In that subsystem, having received Exist funding does not qualify to the same degree. To acquire Exist, entrepreneurs have to write a comprehensive application, and the decision on funding is predominantly based on this application. In the start-up subsystem, having received Exist funding only indicates the ability to write successful applications or find a university incubator that helps one to do so:

> They do not even evaluate your competencies as an entrepreneur. The only skills they evaluate are your competencies in finding a university's incubator that knows how to write Exist applications. (SU-D, i-6)

As an angel investor explains, Exist entrepreneurs are not very well regarded in the start-up subsystem. They have to convince him that they have a good idea and a good team 'even though they received Exist' (i-36). Actors from the spin-off subsystem even recognize these differing evaluation criteria of VCs:

> Many people who are not involved in public funding did see it as a malus when entrepreneurs received public funding. So we tried to mediate, for example, by cooperating with them and saying: 'Hey, it is totally okay to take public money!' (Employee of a body that provides public funding, i-38)

These different resourcing trajectories are additionally reinforced by the entrepreneurial education provided by the university's incubators. They present the bodies that provide public and semi-public investment as the first choice for acquiring follow-up funding. The start-up entrepreneur who also acquired Exist funding was wondering why the university's incubator always just invited these investors to its events:

> At these spin-off events – where you can showcase a little – they have the usual, more public-sector suspects, like the [two semi-public investors] but not so much the actual early-stage investors and angel investors. Those are in the second Berlin start-up community, in the more private-sector community. They [the organizers of the spin-off events] seem to ignore this community. (SU-K, i-15)

4.5. Other actors in the EE also refer to its fragmentation

Since this study focused on three types of entrepreneurs, there might be more than the two subsystems in the Berlin EE. Although this is conceivable, the data indicates that the two subsystems identified are the dominant ones because (1) both types of entrepreneurs refer to each other and this fragmentation, but neither to other types of entrepreneurs nor to any other types of actors in the EE and (2) the other actors of the EE also – and only – refer to the fragmentation between these two subsystems. This is further underscored by the fact that there were no indications of additional subsystems at any of the observed entrepreneurship events either.

The other actors in the EE also recognize and sometimes interact with each other but not as frequently as with the actors in their subsystems. Their practices are predominantly shaped by the rules and resources of their respective subsystem in the EE. Similar to the entrepreneurs, they also refer to the EE's fragmentation.

A mentor and angel investor strongly criticizes the German government in building up a parallel funding structure using tax money to undermine the market mechanisms in the EE. By referring to these types of actors as 'doing their parallel thing' (i-36), he makes express mention of the fragmentation of the Berlin EE. He distinguishes start-up events and private investors as *'the real events'* and *'the real investors'* (i-36) from the events hosted by the university's incubators and public funding programmes. He emphasizes that the public actors think and act in different time horizons and have different networks, pointing to the different rules within each subsystem:

> Everything takes much longer and the networks are also different ones. This holds true for both sides. Even those university people who specialize in innovation and start-ups do not have many connections with the Berlin start-up community. They don't come to our events. I don't want to say that I don't take them seriously. You don't even get the chance to take them seriously. (Mentor and angel investor, i-36)

Actors in the spin-off subsystem predominantly interact with each other. The university's incubators closely collaborate with each other and with public and semi-public investors. Since the interviewees explicitly address this division between the spin-off and the start-up community (e.g., the *'separation between private equity and public equity'* (i-38)), it becomes obvious that the actors involved with public funding are also aware of the fragmentation and even of the different evaluation criteria of VCs, as outlined above.

Actors from the spin-off subsystem increasingly try to engage with the start-up subsystem. Since this is not the main focus of their work, however, closer connections are slow to emerge. Some VCs have started to adapt their expectations or evaluation criteria in favour of Exist entrepreneurs. This might indicate an increasing intertwinement of both subsystems:

> Nowadays, the investors know: okay, money from Exist, that is not one euro for one euro. You have to discount it a bit because you can't finance certain things due to bureaucracy. (SU-K, i-15)

Since the university has begun to reach out to the start-up subsystem, joint events between these two worlds are becoming more frequent. As start-up entrepreneur SU-B notes, the university's incubators increasingly invite guest speakers from the start-up subsystem, which he considers to be very important:

> Universities try to address that, and I like it. They stage events like the one last week, where they invite private-sector people who explain how the real world works. That is a must. (SU-B, i-4)

Yet the interviewee referring to the start-up subsystem as *'the real world'* (i-4) again shows that different types of actors in the Berlin EE are aware of its fragmentation. Although some actors from the spin-off subsystem actively try to bridge this division by interacting with private actors, these efforts are only slowly reflected in the resourcing practices of the three types of entrepreneurs. Thus, the two distinct subsystems persist; they are constituted and reproduced by the different resourcing practices of the different types of entrepreneurs.

5. Discussion

To understand how different EEs promote different types of entrepreneurs, it is necessary to look at how entrepreneurs actually make use of resources and identify relevant characteristics of EEs that impact the functioning of these ecosystems. The primary contribution of this study is an emerging theoretical understanding of how a certain structural characteristic – namely the *fragmentation* of an EE – impacts how an EE promotes entrepreneurship.

5.1. The integration of EEs

This paper contributes to the research on entrepreneurial ecosystems by developing a new concept: the *integration* of an EE. The analysis of how entrepreneurs actually acquire resources from the Berlin EE revealed a defining characteristic of this EE: its *fragmentation*. With respect to previous research on EEs in different regions, it can be assumed that a fragmentation of this kind might, but does not necessarily have to, occur in other EEs. Silicon Valley, for example, seems to be characterized by a very high integration of the EE. From Silicon Valley's very early days on, Stanford University has been tightly intertwined with established corporations, new ventures, and private investors (Saxenian 1996; Gibbons 2000). Its faculty members are strongly involved in new ventures and entrepreneurship in general (Kenney and Goe 2004). VCs play a key role in connecting the entire EE (Ferrary and Granovetter 2009; Hellmann 2000; Banatao and Fong 2000). If we consider the findings from this paper in light of previous research, we can theorize that EEs can display different *degrees of integration*, that is, they can be highly integrated, fragmented, or something in between.

How and from whom an entrepreneur can acquire which resources is enabled and constrained by the extent to which certain actors share practices and refer to the same rules, and different subsystems can be characterized by different rules. In Berlin, this became apparent in how start-up entrepreneurs on the one hand and spin-off and Exist entrepreneurs on the other distinguish themselves from the respective other type. While start-up entrepreneurs actively try to become a member of the entrepreneurial community, spin-off and Exist entrepreneurs do not identify themselves as that kind of entrepreneur.

Fragmentation limits the range of actors an entrepreneur can reach with certain resourcing activities and thus has a strong impact on how an EE promotes different types of entrepreneurs. In the Berlin EE, angel investors are primarily approached via personal relationships within the entrepreneurial community. Consequently, they are largely out of the reach of spin-off and Exist entrepreneurs, who are mostly not a member of the entrepreneurial community. Due to the EE's fragmentation, angel investors primarily support only one type of entrepreneur: the start-up entrepreneur.

Proposition 1: The degree of integration impacts how an EE promotes different types of entrepreneurs. In a more integrated EE, different types of entrepreneurs can access similar resources through similar actors and consequently have easier access to more and more manifold resources of the EE.

This fragmentation might occur along different dimensions—for instance, private versus public, as in the case of the Berlin EE—or between different industries. For example, Spigel (2017) identified a strong impact of the gas and oil industry on Calgary's EE. It might be possible that a strong impact of one industry might also promote the structuration of a distinct subsystem within an existing EE, but it does not necessarily have to (Feldman 2001).

5.2. Different types of actors promote different types of entrepreneurship

Previous research has identified several actors as relevant to successful entrepreneurship (Isenberg 2011; Spigel 2017; Alvedalen and Boschma 2017). As this paper has shown, only some of these actors might be relevant for certain types of entrepreneurs. Several studies and conceptual frameworks emphasize the crucial role of universities (Saxenian 1996; Gibbons 2000; Schaeffer and Matt 2016). In Berlin, universities are foremost relevant in the spin-off subsystem. Although most start-up entrepreneurs are academics, many of them studied at universities all over Germany and have come to Berlin either to work at a start-up or to start their venture. The literature also emphasizes the importance of entrepreneurial recycling (Bahrami and Evans 1995; Mason and Harrison 2006). Cashed-out and current entrepreneurs become angel investors (Mason and Brown 2014), resources circulate in the EE, and mutual learning is key (Spigel and Harrison 2018). In Berlin, these processes can only be found in the start-up subsystem. None of the spin-off entrepreneurs founded a new venture before or mentored others, and only a few had a mentor themselves. Coaches and events hosted by the university's incubator serve as functional equivalents to mentor support. Thus, an entrepreneurial ecosystem in a specific region is not necessarily a homogenous environment for all entrepreneurs, as previous research has implicitly assumed (Audretsch and Belitski 2017; Autio et al. 2018; Mack and Mayer 2016). As a consequence, not all actors in one EE will necessarily be accessible and relevant to all kinds of entrepreneurs. If and how they can access resources depends not only on their ability and willingness to engage with the EE (Spigel and Harrison 2018; Brush et al. 2018) but also on the degree of integration of that EE and the extent to which their practices are compatible with the rules and resources of the respective (sub-)system.

Proposition 2A: The degree of integration of the EE impacts how entrepreneurs (can) acquire resources from the EE. The more fragmented the EE, the greater are the differences between the resourcing practices of different types of entrepreneurs.

Consequently, certain actors might be absent in each of the subsystems (Mack and Mayer 2016), but their function might be fulfilled by others. All three types of entrepreneurs considered in the present study manage to acquire entrepreneurial knowledge and financial capital, yet they do so by engaging with different types of actors. In Berlin, angel investors and the public funding programme Exist both provide financial capital. Thus, they act as functional equivalents in terms of providing financial capital to different types of entrepreneurs.

Proposition 2B: Different types of actors can provide comparable resources. If certain actors are missing in an EE or subsystem, functional equivalents might fulfill their functions.

To analyse the consequences of missing elements, future research might benefit from comparing how and from whom entrepreneurs acquire similar types of resources. To do so, one might compare different types of entrepreneurs within a single EE or similar types of entrepreneurs in different EEs.

5.3. *Heterogeneous resourcing practices (re-)produce the fragmentation of an EE*

Although at first glance it might appear as if the three analysed types of entrepreneurs are part of the same EE, they cannot move freely between the two subsystems since both subsystems have different resourcing practices, rules, and resources. This became especially apparent in the case of Exist entrepreneur EX-1, who was embedded in the spin-off subsystem and then tried to obtain angel investment by writing cold emails. Since access to angel investment is usually gained via pre-existing personal relationships within the entrepreneurial community and angel investors in the Berlin EE typically do not perceive Exist as a legitimate quality signal, he was not able to tap investment from the start-up subsystem.

The rules and resources of each subsystem enable and constrain the actions of each type of entrepreneur. Consequently, being embedded in one of the subsystems during the early founding stages creates paths for future resourcing. From a structurationist perspective, we can expect successful practices to be reproduced within each subsystem, thus strengthening its respective rules and resources, binding actors to one of the subsystems, and reproducing the fragmentation of the EE.

Proposition 3A: Heterogeneous resourcing practices (re-)produce fragmentation, and fragmentation (re-)produces heterogeneous resourcing trajectories. The stronger the fragmentation, the greater is the closure of each subsystem and the stronger are the trajectories. Strong resourcing trajectories hinder resource acquisition from the other subsystem(s).

As previous research on networks and entrepreneurship has emphasized, different resource needs cause different network structures (Partanen, Chetty, and Rajala 2014; Hite and Hesterly 2001; Lechner and Dowling 2003). But in this case, different resource needs do not sufficiently explain the hetero-geneity of the resourcing practices because Exist entrepreneurs show similar practices to spin-off entrepreneurs, yet they develop technologies with characteristics similar to start-up entrepreneurs.

These differences are (re-)produced by the fragmentation of the EE. Thus, the initial founding conditions appear to have a stronger impact on the resourcing practices than the resource needs.

Proposition 3B: The stronger the fragmentation of an EE, the stronger is the imprinting effect of the initial founding conditions.

5.4. The parallelism of emergence and design

In some instances, EEs are the product of top-down policies. In these cases, policy makers are typically identified as important actors in the constitution of an EE (Spigel 2016; Mason and Brown 2014; Isenberg 2011). In other cases, EEs evolve in bottom-up processes. In these instances, entrepreneurs are generally attributed greater power in shaping such EEs (Thompson, Purdy, and Ventresca 2018; Feldman 2001). If we assume this pattern to hold for structural reasons and look at the Berlin EE from this angle, we might interpret the prominence of particular groups as a sign of the nature of a subsystem.

What we observe in the Berlin case is that entrepreneurs, serial entrepreneurs, angel investors, and the entrepreneurial community play a key role in the start-up subsystem. In light of the stated pattern, it can therefore be hypothesized that this subsystem might have evolved in a bottom-up process. In the Berlin spin-off subsystem, by contrast, public actors and funding programmes implemented by policy makers play a central part, suggesting that this subsystem may have emerged in a top-down process. Seen from the vantage point of a structurationist approach, this suggests that an EE does not necessarily emerge in either a top-down or bottom-up process but that both processes can proceed in parallel, leading to the evolution of distinct subsystems. Heterogeneous and equifinal practices can thus lead to the structuration of subsystems. When a new actor enters the EE (e.g., a semi-public investor from a political initiative), he might change the rules and resources but also could establish new ones that exist in parallel to the old ones. Spigel and Harrison (2018) propose that the proper role of the state is to cultivate an entrepreneurial community and culture that will eventually help produce and reproduce the resources necessary for entrepreneurs. This paper adds to their propositions by emphasizing that, although this might be a fruitful way to support entrepreneurship, there is also a chance that such political promotion could contribute to the fragmentation of an EE and thus to the constitution of distinct subsystems, especially if the political efforts are not well integrated in the emerging entrepreneurial community (Brown, Mawson, and Mason 2017).

Proposition 4: The parallel occurrence of ecosystem emergence and design contributes to the fragmentation of an EE if political initiatives are not well integrated in the entrepreneurial community and do not adequately address the needs of entrepreneurs.

5.5. Scope conditions and research implications

Previous research has shown that there are heterogeneous structures across EEs but has so far failed to develop suitable criteria for comparing EEs other than in terms of their success. This paper proposes that EEs can have different *degrees of integration*, and the Berlin EE is an example of a fragmented one. In this case, its fragmentation occurs along the division of private and public actors. By contrast, Silicon Valley might be a good example of a highly integrated EE. More comparative research is needed to elaborate on the forms and effects of different degrees of integration. Comparing different types of entrepreneurs in an EE promises valuable insights regarding the co-existence of different subsystems within a single EE. Comparing EEs in different regions sheds light on the conditions under which certain forms of integration or fragmentation occur and how they impact the supportive effect of EEs.

More longitudinal research can be expected to contribute to a more differentiated understanding of how the relationships of distinct subsystems can change over time and how a fragmented EE can become an integrated one.

The identification of distinct subsystems within the Berlin EE also raises important questions about case selection. Searching interview partners solely through the incubator of a single university, which is quite common in entrepreneurship research (Chalmers and Shaw 2015; Forbes et al. 2006), increases the risk of overlooking subsystems that might exist in parallel.

6. Conclusions

To understand how EEs promote entrepreneurship, it is necessary to have a closer look at how entrepreneurs actually acquire resources from an EE. Adopting a structurationist approach revealed that not only the relationships and interdependencies between the actors of the EE but also shared rules enable and inhibit resource acquisition from certain actors in certain ways. While prior research has mainly taken an outside perspective and conceptualized the EE as a homogenous environment, the analysis presented here has demonstrated that future research should not only continue to analyse heterogeneity *between* EEs but also *within* EEs and pay more attention to how entrepreneurs actually (can) acquire resources from the respective – more or less integrated and thus more or less homogeneous – environment.

Notes

1. Between 2007 and 2014, Exist funded 203 new ventures in Berlin (Kulicke 2017). This is an average of 25 new ventures per year. They therefore account for a comparatively small share of entrepreneurs in Berlin.
2. Data collection started at the end of 2015 and lasted until mid 2017. Most of the data was collected in 2016.
3. Four start-up entrepreneurs and one Exist entrepreneur were interviewed twice. The second interview was conducted one year after the first one. Three of the 13 interviewed start-up entrepreneurs were involved in the same start-up; two of the 13 interviewed spin-off entrepreneurs were involved in the same spin-off.
4. All interview partners were anonymized, using the shortcuts 'SU-[letter]' for start-up entrepreneurs, 'SO-[letter]' for spin-off entrepreneurs, and 'EX-[number]' for Exist entrepreneurs.
5. German is the native language of the researcher and the interviewed entrepreneurs. All quotes in this paper were translated into English by the researcher.
6. To mitigate biases, it is important to include university spin-offs that did not receive Exist funding. I searched for those but found only very few. In the interview, it turned out that those few had also received Exist and just did not mention it on their website.
7. The three start-up entrepreneurs and two spin-off entrepreneurs who were involved in the same new venture also knew each other. In this case, including them was a conscious decision to interview two/three entrepreneurs involved in the same new venture (one of each type) in order to analyse differences in their resourcing activities according to their role in the new venture. This was also an element in the attempt to mitigate potential biases. Ultimately, it turned out that those interview partners exhibited rather similar resourcing activities in spite of their different roles within that new venture.
8. Since resourcing entrepreneurial knowledge from incubators and accelerators is much less important, this section does not elaborate on these practices. Accelerators and the university's incubators are two very different types of actors in the Berlin EE. Accelerators are mostly three-month programmes offered by private companies. The support programmes of the university's incubators last between 12 and 18 months. The university's incubators are primarily funded by public funding programmes and the university budget.

Disclosure statement

No potential conflict of interest was reported by the author.

References

Acs, Z. J., E. Stam, D. B. Audretsch, and A. O'Connor. 2017. "The Lineage of the Entrepreneurial Ecosystem Approach." *Small Business Economics* 49 (1): 1–10. doi:10.1007/s11187-017-9864-8.

Aldrich, H. E., and T. Yang. 2012. "Lost in Translation: Cultural Codes are Not Blueprints." *Strategic Entrepreneurship Journal* 6 (1): 1–17. doi:10.1002/sej.1125.

Aldrich, H. E., and T. Yang. 2013. "How Do Entrepreneurs Know What to Do? Learning and Organizing in New Ventures." *Journal of Evolutionary Economics* 24 (1): 59–82.

Alvedalen, J., and R. Boschma. 2017. "A Critical Review of Entrepreneurial Ecosystems Research: Towards A Future Research Agenda." *European Planning Studies* 25 (6): 887–903. doi:10.1080/09654313.2017.1299694.

Audretsch, D. B. 2015. *Everything in Its Place. Entrepreneurship and the Strategic Management of Cities, Regions, and States.* New York: Oxford University Press.

Audretsch, D. B., and M. Belitski. 2017. "Entrepreneurial Ecosystems in Cities: Establishing the Framework Conditions." *The Journal of Technology Transfer* 42 (5): 1030–1051. doi:10.1007/s10961-016-9473-8.

Autio, E., M. Kenney, P. Mustar, D. Siegel, and M. Wright. 2014. "Entrepreneurial Innovation: The Importance of Context." *Research Policy* 43 (7): 1097–1108. doi:10.1016/j.respol.2014.01.015.

Autio, E., S. Nambisan, L. Thomas, and M. Wright. 2018. "Digital Affordances, Spatial Affordances, and the Genesis of Entrepreneurial Ecosystems." *Strategic Entrepreneurship Journal* 12 (1): 72–95. doi:10.1002/sej.2018.12.issue-1.

Bahrami, H., and S. Evans. 1995. "Flexible Re-Cycling and High-Technology Entrepreneurship." *California Management Review* 37 (3): 62–89. doi:10.2307/41165799.

Banatao, D. P., and K. A. Fong. 2000. "The Valley of Deals: How Venture Capital Helped Shape the Region." In *The Silicon Valley Edge: A Habitat for Innovation and Entrepreneurship*, edited by C.-M. Lee, F. William, M. Miller, G. Hancock, and H. S. Rowen, 295–313. Stanford, California: Stanford University Press.

Barley, S., and P. S. Tolbert. 1997. "Institutionalization and Structuration: Studying the Links between Action and Institution." *Organization Studies* 18 (1): 93–117. doi:10.1177/017084069701800106.

Brown, R., and C. Mason. 2017. "Looking inside the Spiky Bits: A Critical Review and Conceptualisation of Entrepreneurial Ecosystems." *Small Business Economics* 49 (1): 11–30. doi:10.1007/s11187-017-9865-7.

Brown, R., S. Mawson, and C. Mason. 2017. "Myth-Busting and Entrepreneurship Policy: The Case of High Growth Firms." *Entrepreneurship and Regional Development* 29 (5–6): 414–443. doi:10.1080/08985626.2017.1291762.

Brush, C., L. F. Edelman, T. Manolova, and F. Welter. 2018. "A Gendered Look at Entrepreneurship Ecosystems." *Small Business Economics* 53 (2): 393–408.

BSM. 2018. "Berlin Startup Monitor." *Google for Entrepreneurs and Bundesverband Deutsche Startups e.V.* 1: 1-47. https://deutscherstartupmonitor.de/fileadmin/bsm/bsm_2018/Studie%20Berlin%20Startup%20Monitor%202018.pdf.

Butler, J. E., and G. S. Hansen. 1991. "Network Evolution, Entrepreneurial Success, and Regional Development." *Entrepreneurship and Regional Development* 3: 1–16. doi:10.1080/08985629100000001.

Chalmers, D., and E. Shaw. 2015. "The Endogenous Construction of Entrepreneurial Contexts: A Practice-Based Perspective." *International Small Business Journal* 33 (6): 1–21.

Chiasson, M., and C. Saunders. 2005. "Reconciling Diverse Approaches to Opportunity Research Using the Structuration Theory." *Journal of Business Venturing* 20 (6): 747–767. doi:10.1016/j.jbusvent.2004.07.004.

Clough, D. R., T. P. Fang, B. Vissa, and W. Andy. 2019. "Turning Lead into Gold: How Do Entrepreneurs Mobilize Resources to Exploit Opportunities?" *Academy of Management Annals* 13 (1): 240–271. doi:10.5465/annals.2016.0132.

Cohen, B. 2006. "Sustainable Valley Entrepreneurial Ecosystems." *Business Strategy and the Environment* 15 (1): 1–14. doi:10.1002/()1099-0836.

Dubini, P., and H. E. Aldrich. 1991. "Personal and Extended Networks are Central to the Entrepreneurial Process." *Journal of Business Venturing* 6 (5): 305–313. doi:10.1016/0883-9026(91)90021-5.

Eisenhardt, K. 1989. "Building Theories from Case Study Research." *Academy of Management Review* 14 (4): 532–550. doi:10.5465/amr.1989.4308385.

Elfring, T., and W. Hulsink. 2007. "Networking by Entrepreneurs: Patterns of Tie-Formation in Emerging Organizations." *Organization Studies* 28 (12): 1849–1872. doi:10.1177/0170840607078719.

Ernst and Young. (2019). "Start-up Barometer Europe." https://start-up-initiative.ey.com/wp-content/uploads/2019/03/EY-start-up-barometer-europa-maerz-2019-ENG.pdf

Feldman, M. P. 2001. "The Entrepreneurial Event Revisited: Firm Formation in a Regional Context." *Industrial and Corporate Change* 10 (4): 861–891. doi:10.1093/icc/10.4.861.

Ferrary, M., and M. Granovetter. 2009. "The Role of Venture Capital Firms in Silicon Valley's Complex Innovation Network." *Economy and Society* 38 (2): 326–359. doi:10.1080/03085140902786827.

Forbes, D. P., P. S. Borchert, M. E. Zellmer-Bruhn, and H. J. Sapienza. 2006. "Entrepreneurial Team Formation: An Exploration of New Member Addition." *Entrepreneurship Theory and Practice* 30 (2): 225–248. doi:10.1111/j.1540-6520.2006.00119.x.

Garud, R., J. Gehman, and A. P. Giuliani. 2014. "Contextualizing Entrepreneurial Innovation: A Narrative Perspective." *Research Policy* 43 (7): 1177–1188. doi:10.1016/j.respol.2014.04.015.

Gibbons, J. F. 2000. "The Role of Stanford University." In *The Silicon Valley Edge: A Habitat for Innovation and Entrepreneurship.*, edited by C.-M. Lee, F. William, M. Miller, G. Hancock, and H. S. Rowen, 200–217. Stanford, California: Stanford University Press.

Giddens, A. 1984. *The Constitution of Society: Outline of the Theory of Structuration.* Berkeley: University of California Press.

Glaser, B., and A. Strauss. 1967. *The Discovery of Grounded Theory: Strategies of Qualitative Research.* London: Wiedenfeld and Nicholson.

Hallen, B. L., and K. Eisenhardt. 2012. "Catalyzing Strategies and Efficient Tie Formation: How Entrepreneurial Firms Obtain Investment Ties." *Academy of Management Journal* 55 (1): 35–70. doi:10.5465/amj.2009.0620.

Hellmann, T. F. 2000. "Venture Capitalists: The Coaches of Silicon Valley." In *The Silicon Valley Edge: A Habitat for Innovation and Entrepreneurship.*, edited by C.-M. Lee, F. William, M. Miller, G. Hancock, and H. S. Rowen, 276–294. Stanford, California: Stanford University Press.

Heumann, S. 2010. "Bewegliche Ziele - Die Räumlich-Strategische Differenzierung Der Akademischen Gründungsförderung an 50 Deutschen Universitäten." *Beiträge Zur Hochschulforschung* 32: 3.

Hite, J. M., and W. S. Hesterly. 2001. "The Evolution of Firm Networks: From Emergence to Early Growth of the Firm." *Strategic Management Journal* 22: 275–286. doi:10.1002/smj.156.

Isenberg, D. J. 2010. "How to Start an Entrepreneurial Revolution." *Harvard Business Review* 88 (6): 40–50.

Isenberg, D. J. 2011. "The Entrepreneurship Ecosystem Strategy as a New Paradigm for Economic Policy: Principles for Cultivating Entrepreneurship." *Presentation at the Institute of International and European Affairs*, Dublin, Ireland.

Jack, S. L., and A. R. Anderson. 2002. "The Effects of Embeddedness on the Entrepreneurial Process." *Journal of Business Venturing* 17 (5): 467–487. doi:10.1016/S0883-9026(01)00076-3.

Keating, A., S. Geiger, and D. McLoughlin. 2014. "Riding the Practice Waves: Social Ressourcing Practices during New Venture Development." *Entrepreneurship Theory and Practice* 38 (5): 1207–1235. doi:10.1111/etap.12038.

Kenney, M., A. Nelson, and D. Patton. 2009. "The University-Centric High-Tech Cluster of Madison, United States." In OECD (2009), Clusters, Innovation and Entrepreneurship, Local Economic and Employment Development (LEED), OECD Publishing, Paris, https://doi.org/10.1787/9789264044326-en.

Kenney, M., and R. Goe. 2004. "The Role of Social Embeddedness in Professorial Entrepreneurship: A Comparison of Electrical Engineering and Computer Science at UC Berkeley and Stanford." *Research Policy* 33 (5): 691–707. doi:10.1016/j.respol.2003.11.001.

Klag, M., and A. Langley. 2013. "Approaching the Conceptual Leap in Qualitative Research." *International Journal of Management Reviews* 15 (2): 149–166. doi:10.1111/ijmr.2013.15.issue-2.

Kulicke, M. 2014. *15 Jahre EXIST Existenzgründungen Aus Der Wissenschaft - Entwicklung Des Förderprogramms von 1998 Bis 2013.* Karlsruhe: Fraunhofer ISI.

Kulicke, M. 2017. *Exist Gründerstipendium. Gründungsquote Und Entwicklung Der Neuen Unternehmen.* Karlsruhe: Fraunhofer ISI, 1–45.

Larson, A., and J. A. Starr. 1993. "A Network Model of Organization Formation." *Entrepreneurship Theory and Practice* 17 (2): 5–15. doi:10.1177/104225879301700201.

Lechner, C., and M. Dowling. 2003. "Firm Networks: External Relationships as Source for the Growth and Competitiveness of Entrepreneurial Firms." *Entrepreneurship and Regional Development* 15 (1): 1–26. doi:10.1080/08985620210159220.

Lockett, A., and M. Wright. 2005. "Resources, Capabilities, Risk Capital and the Creation of University Spin-out Companies." *Research Policy* 34 (7): 1043–1057. doi:10.1016/j.respol.2005.05.006.

Mack, E., and H. Mayer. 2016. "The Evolutionary Dynamics of Entrepreneurial Ecosystems." *Urban Studies* 53 (10): 2118–2133. doi:10.1177/0042098015586547.

Macpherson, A., B. Herbane, and O. Jones. 2015. "Developing Dynamic Capabilities through Resource Accretion: Expanding the Entrepreneurial Solution Space." *Entrepreneurship and Regional Development* 27 (5–6): 259–291. doi:10.1080/08985626.2015.1038598.

Malecki, E. J. 2017. "Entrepreneurship and Entrepreneurial Ecosystems." *Geography Compass* 12 (3): 1–21.

Mason, C., and R. Brown. 2014. "Entrepreneurial Ecosystems and Growth Oriented Entrepreneurship." *Final Report to OECD, Paris* 30 (1): 77–102.

Mason, C., and R. Harrison. 2006. "After the Exit: Acquisitions, Entrepreneurial Recycling and Regional Economic Development." *Regional Studies* 40 (1): 55–73. doi:10.1080/00343400500450059.

Maurer, I., and M. Ebers. 2006. "Dynamics of Social Capital and Their Performance Implications: Lessons from Biotechnology Start-Ups." *Administrative Science Quarterly* 51 (2): 262–292. doi:10.2189/asqu.51.2.262.

McCarthy, B. 2012. "From Fishing and Factories to Cultural Tourism: The Role of Social Entrepreneurs in the Construction of a New Institutional Field." *Entrepreneurship and Regional Development* 24 (3–4): 259–282. doi:10.1080/08985626.2012.670916.

Miles, M. B., M. Huberman, and J. Saldana. 2014. *Qualitative Data Analysis: a Methods Sourcebook.* Thousand Oaks: Sage Publications.

Motoyama, Y., and K. Knowlton. 2017. "Examining the Connections within the Startup Ecosystem: A Case Study of St. Louis." *Entrepreneurship Research Journal* 7 (1): 1–32. doi:10.1515/erj-2016-0011.

Neck, H. M., D. Meyer, B. Cohen, and A. C. Corbett. 2004. "An Entrepreneurial System View of New Venture Creation." *Journal of Small Business Management* 42 (2): 190–208. doi:10.1111/j.1540-627X.2004.00105.x.

Ozgen, E., and R. A. Baron. 2007. "Social Sources of Information in Opportunity Recognition: Effects of Mentors, Industry Networks, and Professional Forums." *Journal of Business Venturing* 22 (2): 174–192. doi:10.1016/j.jbusvent.2005.12.001.

Partanen, J., S. K. Chetty, and A. Rajala. 2014. "Innovation Types and Network Relationships." *Entrepreneurship Theory and Practice* 38 (5): 1027–1055. doi:10.1111/j.1540-6520.2011.00474.x.

Powell, W. W., and K. W. Sandholtz. 2012. "Amphibious Entrepreneurs and the Emergence of Organisational Forms." *Strategic Entrepreneurship Journal* 6 (2): 94–115. doi:10.1002/sej.1129.

Qin, F., M. Wright, and J. Gao. 2019. "Accelerators and Intra-Ecosystem Variety: How Entpreneurial Agency Influences Venture Development in a Time-Compressed Support Program." *Industrial and Corporate Change* 28 (4): 961–975. doi:10.1093/icc/dtz036.

Rasmussen, E., S. Mosey, and M. Wright. 2015. "The Transformation of Network Ties to Develop Entrepreneurial Competencies for University Spin-Offs." *Entrepreneurship and Regional Development* 27 (7–8): 430–457. doi:10.1080/08985626.2015.1070536.

Ruef, M. 2005. "Origins of Organizations: The Entrepreneurial Process." In *Entrepreneurship*, edited by Lisa A. Keister, 63–100. Research in the Sociology of Work 15. Oxford: Elsevier.

Sarason, Y., T. Dean, and J. F. Dillard. 2006. "Entrepreneurship as the Nexus of Individual and Opportunity: A Structuration View." *Journal of Business Venturing* 21 (3): 286–305. doi:10.1016/j.jbusvent.2005.02.007.

Saxenian, A. 1996. *Regional Advantage: Culture and Competition in Silicon Valley and Route 128*. Cambridge, Massachusetts: Harvard University Press.

Schaeffer, V., and M. Matt. 2016. "Development of Academic Entrepreneurship in a Non-Mature Context: The Role of the University as a Hub-Organization." *Entrepreneurship and Regional Development* 28 (9–10): 724–745. doi:10.1080/08985626.2016.1247915.

Spigel, B. 2016. "Developing and Governing Entrepreneurial Ecosystems: The Structure of Entrepreneurial Support Programs in Edinburgh, Scotland." *International Journal of Innovation and Regional Development* 7 (2): 141–160. doi:10.1504/IJIRD.2016.077889.

Spigel, B. 2017. "The Relational Organization of Entrepreneurial Ecosystems." *Entrepreneurship Theory and Practice* 41 (1): 49–72. doi:10.1111/etap.12167.

Spigel, B., and R. Harrison. 2018. "Toward a Process Theory of Entrepreneurial Ecosystems." *Strategic Entrepreneurship Journal* 12 (1): 151–168. doi:10.1002/sej.2018.12.issue-1.

Stam, E. 2015. "Entrepreneurial Ecosystems and Regional Policy: A Sympathetic Critique." *European Planning Studies* 23 (9): 1759–1769. doi:10.1080/09654313.2015.1061484.

Stam, E., and B. Spigel. 2016. "Entrepreneurial Ecosystems and Regional Policy." In *Sage Handbook for Entrepreneurship and Small Business*. U.S.E. Discussion paper series, 16 (13). SAGE.

Sydow, J., and A. Windeler. 1998. "Organizing and Evaluating Interfirm Networks: A Structurationist Perspective on Network Processes and Effectiveness." *Organization Science* 9 (3): 265–284. doi:10.1287/orsc.9.3.265.

Thompson, T. A., J. M. Purdy, and M. J. Ventresca. 2018. "How Entrepreneurial Ecosystems Take Form: Evidence from Social Impact Initiatives in Seattle." *Strategic Entrepreneurship Journal* 12 (1): 96–116. doi:10.1002/sej.1285.

Vanaelst, I., B. Clarysse, M. Wright, A. Locket, N. Moray, and R. S'Jegers. 2006. "Entrepreneurial Team Development in Academic Spinouts: An Examination of Team Heterogeneity." *Entrepreneurship Theory and Practice* 30 (2): 249–271. doi:10.1111/etap.2006.30.issue-2.

Vissa, B., and A. S. Chacar. 2009. "Leveraging Ties. The Contingent Value of Entrepreneurial Teams' External Advice Networks on Indian Software Venture Performance." *Strategic Management Journal* 30 (11): 1179–1191. doi:10.1002/smj.785.

Vohora, A., M. Wright, and A. Locket. 2004. "Critical Junctures in the Development of University High-Tech Spinout Companies." *Research Policy* 33 (1): 147–175. doi:10.1016/S0048-7333(03)00107-0.

Welter, F. 2011. "Contextualizing Entrepreneurship – Conceptual Challanges and Ways Forward." *Entrepreneurship Theory and Practice* 35 (1): 165–184. doi:10.1111/j.1540-6520.2010.00427.x.

Whittington, R. 2010. "Giddens, Structuration Theory and Strategy as Practice." In *Cambridge Handbook of Strategy as Practice*, 109–126, edited by Damon Golsorkhi, Linda Rouleau, David Seidl, and Eero Vaara. Cambridge: Cambridge University Press.

Wright, M., A. Locket, B. Clarysse, and M. Binks. 2006. "University Spin-out Companies and Venture Capital." *Research Policy* 35 (4): 481–501. doi:10.1016/j.respol.2006.01.005.

Yin, R. K. 1994. *Case Study Research: Design and Methods*. 2nd ed. Thousand Oaks: Sage Publications.

Youtie, J., and P. Shapira. 2008. "Building an Innovation Hub: A Case Study of the Transformation of University Roles in Regional Technological and Economic Development." *Research Policy* 37 (8): 1188–1204. doi:10.1016/j.respol.2008.04.012.

The injection of resources by transnational entrepreneurs: towards a model of the early evolution of an entrepreneurial ecosystem

Aki Harima(iD), Jan Harima(iD) and Jörg Freiling(iD)

ABSTRACT

Despite its rapid proliferation, the extant literature on entrepreneurial ecosystems has not paid sufficient attention to the evolutionary nature of entrepreneurial ecosystems, mainly on account of the prevailing structuralist approaches in previous research. Particularly unclear is the early evolutionary context in which a region without rich entrepreneurial resources gains momentum and transforms into a nascent entrepreneurial ecosystem. The literature overlooks ecosystem dynamics in regions with limited entrepreneurial resources, as most studies have investigated more developed entrepreneurial ecosystems. This study illuminates one means to overcome resource scarcity on a regional level: resource injection by attracting transnational entrepreneurs, who transfer unique resources from one location to another. Based on an explorative qualitative study in the Santiago entrepreneurial ecosystem in Chile, where governmental actors incentivized transnational entrepreneurs to temporarily relocate to Santiago, this article proposes a three-step model of resource injection by transnational entrepreneurs with the following components: (i) stimulation of early ecosystem evolutionary momentum, (ii) evocation of institutional changes, and (iii) establishment of a resilient ecosystem. The findings offer practical implications for policymakers in emerging countries to utilize transnational entrepreneurs' resources for developing an ecosystem in their region.

Introduction

Policymakers are showing increasing interest in learning how to build a thriving entrepreneurial ecosystem (EE) in their own regions. Research on this phenomenon has also increased, with EEs becoming one of the most popular subjects in contemporary entrepreneurship research in the second decade of the 21st century. However, extant research largely focuses on identifying common mechanisms to determine the nature and performance of EEs (Isenberg 2011; Stam 2015), comparatively neglecting evolutionary perspectives. Acknowledging the prevailing structuralist approach, which emphasizes the isomorphic (rather than idiosyncratic) nature of the phenomenon, scholars have recently begun to intensively discuss evolutionary aspects of EEs (Baron and Freiling 2019; Spigel and Harrison 2018). In this respect, several scholars have identified determinants of ecosystem evolution, such as entrepreneurial communities (Thompson, Purdy, and Ventresca 2018) and the intentionality of entrepreneurs (Roundy, Bradshaw, and Brockman 2018). Deeply rooted in regional institutional dynamics and historical contexts, such determinants are closely related to the institutional settings of an EE (Acs, Autio, and Szerb 2014).

While researchers have identified various types of drivers for ecosystem evolution, one aspect common to all of them, either directly or indirectly, is their relation to the creation, acquisition, multiplication and recycling of entrepreneurial resources on the regional level. The relative availability of rich entrepreneurial resources is a prerequisite for the emergence of EEs (Mason and Brown 2014). However, this does not mean that only regions with an abundant resource base can develop thriving EEs. Even when regions do not initially possess such resources, they can acquire them through 'resource injections' (Roundy, Bradshaw, and Brockman 2018; Spigel and Harrison 2018). One possible means for resource injections is the attraction of transnational entrepreneurs, who transfer various types of resources from one country to another by creating cross-border businesses (Drori, Honig, and Wright 2009). When transnational entrepreneurs join a foreign EE, they often contribute unique human and social capital that can enrich local environments (Baron and Harima 2019; Brown et al. 2019).

Injecting resources into the ecosystem appears to be a faster and more efficient approach than cultivating them on their own, as doing so would require a considerable amount of time and financial resources. That said, resource injection, however appealing, is an extremely dynamic process, one which requires policymakers to develop specific facilitative capacities in this regard. While scholarship is aware of the need for resource injection, little is known about *which* resources can be injected or *how* they can be intertwined with given institutional ecosystem conditions to lend momentum to EE development.

Against this background, the current study investigated how a region without rich entrepreneurial resources can use resource injection to facilitate EE dynamics by attracting transnational entrepreneurs. Accordingly, the following research questions were addressed: (1) How can a region use resource injection to facilitate EE dynamics by attracting transnational entrepreneurs? (2) How are injected entrepreneurial resources intertwined with the institutional conditions of the ecosystem? and (3) How can resource injection transform an emerging EE into a resilient EE?

To answer these questions, we conducted an explorative qualitative study in Santiago, Chile. The Santiago ecosystem is unique, as governmental actors have taken proactive political action to subsidize ecosystem actors and to attract transnational entrepreneurs with incentives to create an EE in their region (Startup Genome 2017; Gonzalez-Uribe and Leatherbee 2018). Based on the empirical evidence, we developed a conceptual model for the early evolution of the ecosystem. The model consists of three steps: (i) stimulating early evolutionary momentum, (ii) evoking institutional changes and (iii) establishing a resilient ecosystem.

This paper begins with a literature review of EEs and transnational entrepreneurship. Next, we explain our methodological approach. After that, we briefly describe the emergence of the Santiago EE and then present and explain the conceptual model. Finally, we discuss our research contributions, practical implications, limitations and future perspectives.

Conceptual background

Research status of entrepreneurial ecosystems (EEs)

EE has become an exceedingly popular concept in recent entrepreneurship research (Cavallo, Ghezzi, and Balocco 2018; Alvedalen and Boschma 2017). This alternative view on entrepreneurial activities emerged from a wide range of earlier literature streams on biological (Tansley 1935), urban (Bolund and Hunhammar 1999), educational (Crosling, Nair, and Vaithilingam 2015) and innovation ecosystems (Adner 2006). Despite some early, sporadic discussions on EEs (Valdez 1988; Bahrami and Evans 1995; Van De Ven 1993), it took more than two decades for the concept to gain acceptance among entrepreneurship scholars. In the 2000s, several researchers began paying more attention to EEs (Cohen 2006; Isenberg 2010), which in turn sparked intensive discussions in the 2010s (cf. Mason and Brown 2014; Stam 2015; Spigel 2016).

The investigation of EEs demands careful consideration from researchers for three main reasons: first, the literature has applied the term 'entrepreneurial ecosystem' to different ontological u+nits, such as national environments (Acs, Autio, and Szerb 2014; Qian, Acs, and Stough 2013), stakeholders (Bischoff, Volkmann, and Audretsch 2017), platforms (Sussan and Acs 2017; Eckhardt, Ciuchta, and Carpenter 2018), business models (Yun et al. 2017) and universities (Audretsch and Link 2019; Theodoraki, Messeghem, and Rice 2018). This study explored the most prevailing unit of EEs, namely the regional environment (Brown and Mason 2017).

Second, an EE has several conceptual antecedents. Acs et al. (2017) explained that EE research stems from two dominant approaches: strategic management and regional development. These two streams 'share common roots in ecological system thinking, focusing on the interdependence of actors in a particular community to create new value' (Acs et al. 2017, 2). Scholars also relate EEs to other conceptual antecedents, such as clusters (Gilbert, McDougall, and Audretsch 2008; Porter 2000), regional innovation systems (Asheim and Isaken 2002), business ecosystems (Adner 2017; Iansiti and Levien 2004), industrial parks (Côté and Hall 1995) and regional networks (Almeida and Kogut 1999; Saxenian 1990). While these concepts certainly bear similarities to EEs, scholars have highlighted critical differences between them. Spigel (2016) argued that a key difference between the concepts of clusters and EEs is that while both assume benefits from being in the same geographical region, clusters focus on intra-industry assets and technical synergies within a particular industry, whereas EEs primarily focus on start-up activities regardless of industry boundaries. Regional innovation systems refer to institutional networks that connect creators of knowledge, such as universities, with regional firms to facilitate spill-over effects (Asheim and Isaken 2002). Spigel and Harrison (2018) highlighted differences regarding the role of entrepreneurs: In regional innovation systems, entrepreneurs represent one of many actors involved in the creation of innovation; whereas in EEs, entrepreneurs and their activities are the focal points of the entire system.

Third, conceptually speaking, ecosystems have a 'fuzzy' nature (Brown and Mason 2017). In other words, they encompass complex phenomena with multiple interdependent dimensions and complementarities, leading to different understandings of EEs (Malecki 2018; Cavallo, Ghezzi, and Balocco 2018). While Stam (2015) stressed the interdependence of actors and factors in facilitating productive entrepreneurship within a particular territory, Acs, Autio, and Szerb (2014) highlighted 'the dynamic, institutionally embedded interaction between entrepreneurial attitudes, ability, and aspirations, by individuals, which drives the allocation of resources through the creation and operation of new ventures' (479). Further, Acs and colleagues emphasized the important role of resources and the dynamic nature and institutional embeddedness of EEs. As both aspects were essential for understanding early ecosystem evolution within a region without rich entrepreneurial resources, this study approached an EE as a *dynamic interaction between interdependent actors and other factors embedded in institutional environments of a particular region, one which drives the allocation of resources through the creation and operation of new ventures.*

Previous research on EEs employed different approaches to investigate this complex phenomenon, prominent among them being the identification and modelling of significant domains of EEs (Isenberg 2010; Stam 2015; Audretsch and Belitski 2016). Another major approach involved exploring ways to measure the output and quality of EEs based on performance indicators. Finally, an emerging approach to EEs involves creating theories inductively (Spigel 2017; Roundy 2016) and connecting them to existing theories (Roundy, Bradshaw, and Brockman 2018; O'Connor and Reed 2018).

Evolutionary perspectives of entrepreneurial ecosystems (EEs)

EEs are evolving systems – and yet, extant research tends to describe ecosystems as static phenomena, neglecting entrepreneurial dynamics and governance mechanisms relevant to EEs (Cavallo, Ghezzi, and Balocco 2018; Spigel and Harrison 2018). Recognizing this research gap, Mack and Mayer (2016) made an initial attempt to propose a framework of EE evolution comprising four life-cycle stages. Similarly, Auerswald and Dani (2017) developed a four-phase life-cycle model inspired by biodiversity. While the literature on cluster life cycles offers insights useful in the context of EEs, the clustering approach tends to incompletely investigate the evolutionary mechanisms that lead ecosystems from one stage to another.

More recently, Thompson, Purdy, and Ventresca (2018) conducted a longitudinal analysis of evolutionary EEs in Seattle, observing that EEs developed via three formative activities: community creation, legal infrastructure development, and the generation of financial support. By applying a complex adaptive system view, Roundy, Bradshaw, and Brockman (2018) conceptualized EE emergence by three forces, namely intentionality of entrepreneurs, coherence of entrepreneurial activities, and injections of resources. Mason and Brown suggested a binary typology comprising an 'embryonic ecosystem' and 'scale-up ecosystem' as two basic types of EEs (Mason and Brown 2014; Brown and Mason 2017).

Each ecosystem is idiosyncratic due to its peculiar embeddedness in context-specific institutional environments. Accordingly, the development of EEs is an outcome of social interactions between various actors and sub-ecosystems embedded in specific societal contexts (Malecki 2018). Roundy, Bradshaw, and Brockman (2018) argued that EEs are, by nature, sensitive to initial conditions and configurations, which may significantly impact their evolution. In this regard, scholars generally argue that the availability of entrepreneurial resources in a region will critically determine the initial conditions of EEs. The literature considers the possession of a rich knowledge base as a prerequisite for the emergence of EEs, as suggested by Mason and Brown (2014): '(...) the entrepreneurial ecosystems do not emerge just anywhere. They need fertile soil' (13). In reality, however, most regions for which policymakers are interested in developing an EE have not yet even reached the 'embryonic ecosystem' (Brown and Mason 2017) stage. Spigel and Harrison (2018) critically reflected on this paradoxical relationship between initial resource configuration and ecosystem evolution: 'it is tautological in that entrepreneurial ecosystems are defined as those that demonstrate successful entrepreneurship, and where successful entrepreneurship is apparent, there must be a strong entrepreneurial ecosystem' (158). This statement indicates the lack of knowledge about how an EE can emerge in a region without a critical mass of entrepreneurial resources from its inception. Thus, it is meaningful to examine how such a resource-scarce region can gain the entrepreneurial resources needed to acquire initial evolutionary momentum.

Recently, some scholars have highlighted the importance of resource injections into EEs. Spigel and Harrison (2018) conceptualized the transformation of a nascent ecosystem with few entrepreneurial resources. They argued that resource flow is decisive for such a transformation, and called for further investigation into 'the processes through which resources are created or attracted to an ecosystem and the processes by which entrepreneurs access these resources within their local ecosystem' (163). By emphasizing regional entrepreneurial resources and networks as core determinants of an ecosystem's functionality, Spigel and Harrison (2018) illustrated how a region can gain external resources and recycle them internally. Similarly, Roundy, Bradshaw, and Brockman (2018) advocated the necessity of resource injections into the ecosystem to create coherence among ecosystem actors.

While it is legitimate to argue that acquiring external resources is central to ecosystem evolution, the question of *how* such a resource injection can evoke early ecosystem mechanisms deserves serious attention. The literature has revealed that one way an EE with limited resources may acquire external resources is by involving transnational entrepreneurs (Saxenian 2001).

Transnational entrepreneurship

The literature offers some empirical evidence that transnational entrepreneurs help trigger ecosystem dynamics. For instance, immigrant entrepreneurs have played a critical role in the evolution of Silicon Valley by forming and strengthening a unique regional and global diaspora network (Saxenian 2005, 2002, 2001). More recently, Baron and Harima (2019) described how transnational entrepreneurs have influenced the development of Berlin's EE with social and human capital distinct from that of local entrepreneurs. Immigrant entrepreneurs, who have gathered entrepreneurial know-how and built a global network, inject these entrepreneurial resources into the EEs of their home countries (Saxenian 2006; Schäfer and Henn 2018). Spigel and Harrison (2018) also noted that transnational entrepreneurs can inject new capital and resources into ecosystems.

Transnational entrepreneurs play unique roles in transferring entrepreneurial resources between ecosystems. Transnational entrepreneurs are defined as 'individuals that migrate from one country to another, concurrently maintaining business-related linkages with their former country of origin, and currently adopted countries and communities' (Drori, Honig, and Wright 2009, 1001). This cross-border engagement enhances their capacity to significantly upgrade their resource base (Drori, Honig, and Wright 2009; Baltar and Icart 2013; Fraiberg 2017). Furthermore, transnational entrepreneurs acquire education, vocational experience, language proficiency and intercultural competencies in multiple institutional contexts. By experiencing different institutional environments, they develop cognitive flexibility – called 'bi-locality' (Rouse 1992; Vertovec 2004) – which allows them to judge a situation from different perspectives. By instantly, and often unintentionally, comparing multiple environments, transnational entrepreneurs identify unique entrepreneurial opportunities which have been overlooked by those without migration experience.

Migration facilitates not only human capital, but also social capital. Due to (transnational) mixed embeddedness (Bagwell 2015; Kloosterman and Rath 2001), migrants have access to networks both at home and abroad. Among such networks, researchers pay particular attention to diaspora networks (Dutia 2012; Newland and Tanaka 2010; Kuznetsov 2006). Diaspora networks can offer various forms of capital, ranging from social capital to financial capital (Newland and Tanaka 2010).

Extant research offers rich insights into the unique resources of transnational entrepreneurs, and empirical evidence positions transnational entrepreneurs as distinctive actors who can transfer these resources between EEs and across national borders. However, we still know little about how a region with limited resources mobilizes the resources of transnational entrepreneurs to initiate early ecosystem dynamics. Consequently, this article examines one EE in a regional context and analyses the injection of transnational entrepreneurs' resources into the region over time.

Methodology

Research design

This study applied an inductive qualitative research design for several reasons: first, extant studies predominantly explored successful EEs (Neck et al. 2004; Cohen 2006; Bruns et al. 2017; Nylund and Cohen 2017; Stam 2017; Thompson, Purdy, and Ventresca 2018; Spigel 2017; Goswami, Mitchell, and Bhagavatula 2018; Krishna and Bala Subrahmanya 2015) but did not explain the resource injection mechanism or nascent EEs that this study sought to investigate. Second, it is essential to understand an EE as a socially constructed and evolutionary phenomenon (Malecki 2018; Isenberg 2010). To grasp early evolutionary mechanisms on the ecosystem level, it is imperative to view a situation holistically, fully considering both entrepreneurs and different stakeholders within the ecosystem.

Data collection

We selected an EE in Santiago, Chile since the government has been extraordinarily active in national entrepreneurship policy and has allocated a considerable portion of the national budget to developing and implementing numerous policy instruments (Agosin, Grau, and Larrain 2010; Contreras and Greenlee 2018; Egusa and O'Shee 2016; Chandra and Medrano Silva 2012). Santiago is characterized by an intense demographic and economic concentration of people with access to entrepreneurial support and physical infrastructure (Amorós, Felzensztein, and Gimmon 2013). Despite intensive entrepreneurial support by the government, Santiago was 'a city until recently (…) not considered a major entrepreneurship hub' (Gonder 2012, 29). Today, however, Santiago has become one of the leading EEs in Latin America (Startup Genome 2017). Among several public instruments,

Start-Up Chile has undoubtedly received the most attention from global entrepreneurial stake-holders outside the country (Carmel and Richman 2013; Gonzalez-Uribe and Leatherbee 2018; Melo 2012). This governmental initiative offers equity-free funding and soft-landings to attract transnational entrepreneurs.

Data collection took place in 2015, 2017 and 2019. As primary data, we considered 35 interviews with different types of ecosystem stakeholders. We conducted 33 in-depth interviews ourselves and included one additional interview (from a secondary source) with Start-Up Chile's founder, as he is clearly a very influential person in the ecosystem. Additionally, we conducted an interview with an external expert in August 2019 to triangulate the findings of this study. The interview duration ranged from 40 to 130 minutes. Table 1 presents an overview of the interviewees.

We followed a snowballing strategy (without having previous contacts with ecosystem actors) while simultaneously seeking to purposefully collect data from different types of ecosystem stake-holders to grasp the 'multiple realities' (Schuetz 1945) of the Santiago EE based on critical actor types as determined by previous studies (Cohen 2006; Isenberg 2010; Feld 2012; Stam 2015). The experi-ence of entering the ecosystem as foreign researchers without contacts and with limited linguistic capacity in Spanish required a quasi-ethnographic approach to establish rapport with various ecosystem stakeholders.

Table 1. Overview of the interviewees.

ID	Type[a]	Gender	COO[b]	Role in Santiago Ecosystem	Business & Comments
TE-1	TE	Male	India	Former Start-Up Chile Participant	Robot manufacturing
TE-2	TE	Female	Romania	Start-Up Chile participant	Cooking app
TE-3	TE	Female	Columbia	Start-Up Chile participant	Healthy snack
TE-4	TE	Female	USA	Start-Up Chile participant	Market analysis software
TE-5	TE	Female	UK	Start-Up Chile participant	Online education
TE-6	TE	Female	Peru	Start-Up Chile participant	Health
TE-7	TE	Female	Brazil	Start-Up Chile participant	Nano-credit in LATAM
TE-8	TE	Female	Columbia	Start-Up Chile participant	Sales platform for start-ups
TE-9	TE	Female	USA	Start-Up Chile participant	B2B network platform
TE-10	TE	Male	USA	Start-Up Chile participant	Mentor platform
TE-11	TE	Male	Venezuela	Start-Up Chile participant	Educational toy
TE-12	TE	Male	South Africa	Start-Up Chile participant	Game technology
TE-13	TE	Female	USA	Start-Up Chile participant	Postcast Media
TE-14	TE	Male	New Zealand	Fundacion Chile start-up	App for school bus
CE-1	CE	Male	Chile	Start-Up Chile participant	Legal app
CE-2	CE	Male	Chile	Start-Up Chile participant	Fin-tech
CE-3	CE	Male	Chile	Former Start-Up Chile participant	Start-up finance
CE-4	CE	Male	Chile	Startup Weekend organizer	
EE-1	EE	Female	Chile	Start-Up Chile director	
EE-2	EE	Female	Chile	Start-Up Chile director	
EE-3	EE	Female	Germany	Start-Up Chile intern	
EE-4	EE	Male	Mexico	Start-Up Chile accelerator executive	
EE-5	EE	Male	Chile	Start-Up founder	
EE-6	EE	Male	Chile	Former Start-Up Chileemployee	Governmental accelerator in LATAM
EE-7	EE	Male	New Zealand	Former Start-Up Chile employee	Founder of co-works in Santiago
EE-8	EE	Male	Chile	Wayra Chile executive	
EE-9	EE	Female	Chile	INNOVO	
VC-1	VC	Male	Chile	Magma VC	
VC-2	VC	Male	Chile	Fundacion Chile Manager	
VC-3	VC	Male	Chile	Chile Ventures	
GV-1	GV	Male	Chile	CORFO	
GV-2	GV	Male	Chile	CORFO	
UN-1	UN	Female	Chile	Universidad Adolfo Ibáñez	Research on GEM
UN-2	UN	Male	Chile	Pontificia Universidad Católica de Chile	Research on Start-Up Chile and CORFO
EX-1	EX	Male	Argentina	Expert in Entrepreneurial Ecosystem	

aTE = Transnational Entrepreneurs; CE = Chilean Entrepreneurs; EE = Ecosystem Actors (e.g. accelerators, incubators); VC = Venture Capital; GV = Governmental Representatives; UNI = University Researchers; EX = Expert.
bCOR = Country of Origin.

Several interview partners served multiple functions within the ecosystem. For instance, CE-3 was once a participant in Start-Up Chile and now works as an academic specializing in entrepreneurial finance. EE-7 was an early employee of Start-Up Chile before founding a co-work chain in Santiago. Such multi-functional interviewees provided us with their retrospective insights from different perspectives. In addition to in-depth interviews, we conducted field observations at multiple start-up events in Santiago, at support organizations for start-ups, and at a co-working space. The observations were protocolled as observation memos and field notes. The observations allowed us to witness and analyse different types of interactions among entrepreneurs and stakeholders in natural settings.

In addition to primary data, we also collected 42 formal documents concerning the development of the Santiago EE as secondary data. These documents were particularly helpful in understanding the aims of the government's strategy and the ecosystem's historical development. Furthermore, we followed Start-Up Chile's social media activities to capture dynamics occurring on this level (Costello, McDermott, and Wallace 2017; Housley et al. 2017b, 2017a).

Data analysis

All the interviews were conducted and transcribed in English. We used MAXQDA and Microsoft Word as technical support to conduct a systematic data analysis. Both the primary and secondary data were imported into MAXQDA. We conducted a three-step analysis. In the first step, two authors paraphrased the interviews independently. Both authors each generated about 2,200 initial codes, following the methods for initial coding suggested by Charmaz (2008). In the second step, the authors collaboratively analysed all the paraphrases and classified them into two different types of emerging categories: descriptive codes and mechanism codes. While the former type was aimed at creating a descriptive overview of the information contained in the collected data, the latter addressed the changes that occurred within the ecosystem. The second step generated the final set of descriptive codes, as visualized in Figure 1. The mechanism codes, on the other hand, were emergent in nature and thus lacked a systematic and logical structure in the second stage. Finally, following the concept of theoretical coding (Charmaz 2008), two researchers conducted an intensive iterative process, contrasting emerging mechanism codes with extant literature to develop a theoretical construct of resource injection. During this iterative process, we identified three different levels of ecosystem evolution: (i) stimulating early momentum, (ii) evoking institutional changes and (iii) establishing a resilient ecosystem. Following the method of Gioia, Corley, and Hamilton (2013), we visualized mechanism codes in Figures 2 and 3. Based on the final category system, we developed the three-step model of EE evolution.

Santiago's entrepreneurial ecosystem (EE)

Presently, 40.5% of the Chilean population (17.5 million people) live in the capital, Santiago. Since the mid-1980s, Chile has successfully transformed its economy, exhibiting a consistently high growth rate (Büchi Buc 2006) thanks to the essential role played by entrepreneurship. CORFO (Corporación de Fomento de la Producción de Chile), a government agency whose primary aim is supporting small businesses and entrepreneurship, has implemented various entrepreneurship support measures. For example, the Seed Capital Programme (Capital Semilla), was implemented in 2001 to financially support business incubators (Chanra and Narczewska 2009). Another prominent policy instrument is Fundación Chile, which seeks to attract foreign direct investment in information technology (Agosin, Grau, and Larrain 2010). Such extensive political instruments appear to be successful, as indicated by their high total early-stage entrepreneurial activity rate in the Global Entrepreneurship Monitor (Global Entrepreneurship Research Association 2018).

Despite Santiago's entrepreneurship-friendly policies and high level of entrepreneurial activities, participants in this study mostly agreed that there was limited momentum in the evolution of

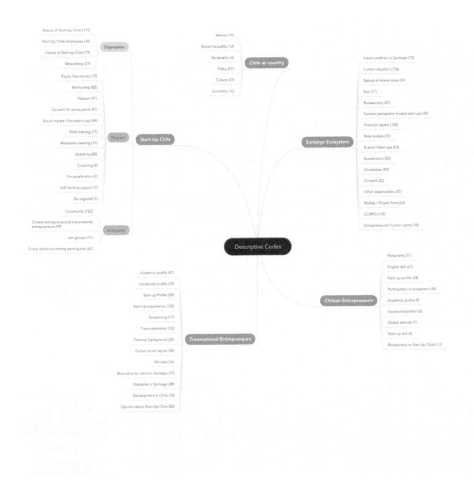

Figure 1. Overview of descriptive codes.

Santiago's EE a decade ago. Scholars have pointed to a few possible explanations, such as the lack of social capital (Klerkx, Álvarez, and Campusano 2015, Kantis, Federic, and García 2018), insufficient entrepreneurial engagement by universities (Poblete and Amorós 2013; Bernasconi 2005), immature equity funding and underdeveloped connections among investors (Romaní et al. 2013; Agosin, Grau, and Larrain 2010).

Moreover, the institutional setting of Chile as a resource-based economy (mining-centred) may explain the sluggish evolution of the Santiago ecosystem (Bas, Tomas, and Kunc 2008). Another institutional factor impeding the emergence of a vibrant EE is the Chilean culture, traditionally characterized by a strong hierarchical structure and bureaucracy which places high administrative burdens on (nascent) entrepreneurs (Schwellnus 2010). Sepúlveda and Bonilla (2014) explained that Chileans are risk-averse, tending to 'admire and greatly value anything that is foreign, particularly what comes from the Anglo-Saxon world, where they look for models of behaviours that (can) be imitated or may substitute or become their own projects' (Gómez 2001, 126). This may be attributed to Chile's geographical isolation, which creates an inward orientation among Chileans.

Acknowledging these initial environmental disadvantages, CORFO proactively attracts foreign entrepreneurs to Santiago, mainly through Start-Up Chile. This programme attracts 250–300 start-ups a year by offering equity-free investment and soft-landing support (Startup Genome 2017). Because many transnational entrepreneurs do not ultimately stay in Chile, Start-Up Chile strongly encourages them to transfer their knowledge to local communities during the programme.

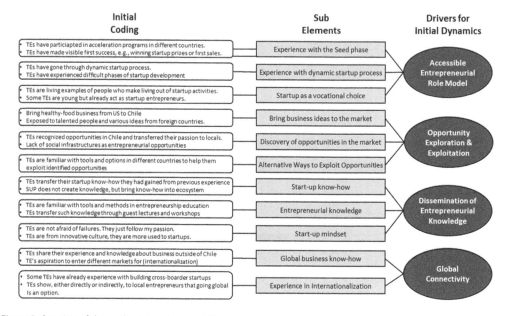

Figure 2. Overview of the mechanism codes (Level 1).

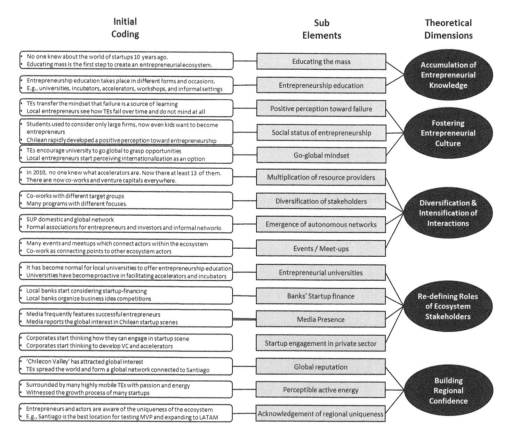

Figure 3. Overview of the mechanism codes (Level 2).

Chile's aggressive 'reverse' globalization strategy has apparently been successful within just a few years. The Santiago EE has become renowned in the global start-up community as 'Chilecon Valley' (Egusa and O'Shee 2016; Dube 2015). Despite some critical evaluations (e.g. Gonzalez-Uribe and Leatherbee 2018), Start-Up Chile has been implicated in the emergence of initial location-based dynamics by 'injecting' foreign entrepreneurial resources temporarily. The Chilean mindset and societal perception towards entrepreneurship have been changing, and the entrepreneurs' societal position has correspondingly increased.

While the emergence of the Santiago EE is undisputed, it nonetheless continues to strongly depend on governmental support and is therefore not resilient – yet. The vast majority of ecosystem actors and investors rely significantly on governmental subsidies. This is because the Santiago EE remains insufficient with regard to a large number of successful start-ups with major exits, foreign and domestic venture capital, and proactive engagement by corporate players. As such, the Santiago EE is not yet self-sustaining, even as it nears the crossroads that will determine its future.

The three-step model for ecosystem resource injection

The following model describes how a region with limited entrepreneurial resources creates initial ecosystem dynamics by gaining external resources from transnational entrepreneurs. This strategy involves three consecutive steps. In the first step, regional policy attracts transnational entrepreneurs who contribute external resources, which triggers initial dynamics. In the second step, the initial dynamics evoke institutional changes. In the final step, whether the ecosystem can evolve from dependence to independence is determined. Figure 4 presents the three-step model for resource injection for the early ecosystem evolution.

Level 1: stimulation of early evolutionary momentum

Transnational entrepreneurs trigger initial ecosystem momentum by (1) creating accessible entrepreneurial role models, (2) demonstrating how to explore and exploit entrepreneurial opportunities, (3) disseminating entrepreneurial knowledge and (4) achieving global connectivity. Table 2 compiles a list of selected quotations for each category.

First, the mass of transnational entrepreneurs created an accessible image of entrepreneurial role models. Through their attitudes towards opportunities and the actions needed to exploit opportunities creatively, transnational entrepreneurs transmitted the entrepreneurial spirit to Chilean locals. Notably, the transnational entrepreneurs demonstrated that entrepreneurship is not exclusively the right of people with extraordinary talents and capacities but is instead an innovative pursuit open to regular people through entrepreneurial activities.

What transnational entrepreneurs created were not outstanding global success stories but rather moderate successes in their previous or current businesses. For instance, some had recently attracted their first major customers or had sold their previous businesses on a small scale. Others participated in different acceleration programmes or had acquired seed investment. Although the ecosystem literature generally acknowledges that successful role models can inspire future entrepreneurs (Bosma et al. 2012; Roundy 2019; Isenberg 2010), findings from Santiago suggest that entrepreneurial role models represent achievable, small-scale success rather than exceptional, large-scale success.

Transnational entrepreneurs also shared their experiences with dynamic entrepreneurial processes that require resilience. For instance, TE-14, who is an entrepreneur from New Zealand, developed a business idea which he wanted to implement in Chile in 2012. His business failed several times due to the conservative nature of the Chilean market, and each failure forced him to change his focus and business model. This study observed that TE-14 acted as a role model by demonstrating entrepreneurial resilience (Tengeh 2016) in the face of unfavourable market conditions. Furthermore, transnational entrepreneurs presented entrepreneurship as a life option. Despite

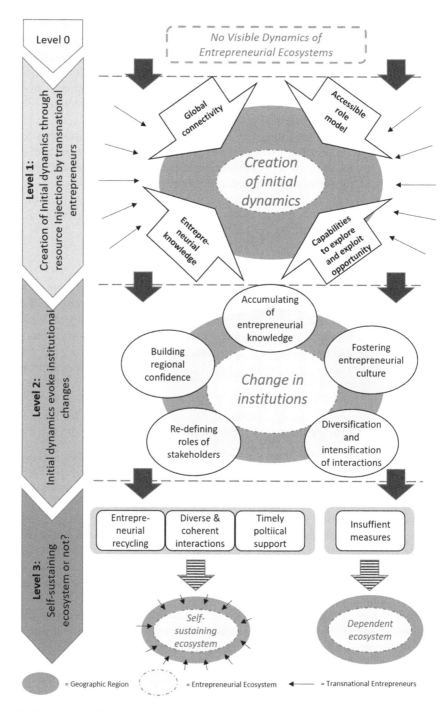

Figure 4. The three-step model for resource injection for the early ecosystem evolution.

numerous other vocational options, they intentionally chose an entrepreneurial career path. Therefore:

RP1-1: Transnational entrepreneurs act as entrepreneurial role models by creating an accessible image of entrepreneurs, demonstrating achievable success in the seed phase, showing entrepreneurial resilience and embodying the entrepreneurial lifestyle.

Table 2. List of selected quotations (Level 1).

RP1-1	Accessible entrepreneurial role model	Experience with the seed phase	• 'During the program what happens was we made our first biggest sale in Dubai. So, we sold around 500 kits to one of the government authorities, so this made us back to Dubai and make things over there' (TE-1) • 'And after that, I went to like from one day to another, I was the most famous entrepreneur in my country' (TE-9) • 'Foreigner founders had more experience in funding, in seed funding, having gone through around and all that. I guess that is also a difference' (CE-2)
		Experience with the dynamic start-up process	• 'Before the hardware company, we have gone through like a lot of ups and downs. The thing is usually like making the product is the easiest thing. Converting the product into MVP is like hard labour.' (TE-1) • 'I started a bakery there, and it was very successful. We initially started with a storefront and a production centre simultaneously, so it was a lot of workloads and then two years after we decided to change our business model and close the storefront and then had only the production centre.' (TE-3)
		Start-up as a vocational choice	• 'We already have people understanding entrepreneurship as a valid way of making a living at this.' (VC-1) • 'A lot of young people in this generation, for me is amazing to know people that are 21 for example and they are already like doing start-ups. When I was 21, I was starting and thinking of getting a job in a company (...), so yes one can learn a lot about those experience.' (CE-2)
RP1-2	Capabilities to explore and exploit unique opportunities	Bring business ideas to the market	• 'I started seeing in Latin America there was a huge phenomenon that is becoming like at really high rates, one of the most obese you know like countries in the world. Chile is the 4th Colombia is going the same direction, we have Costco now like it is crazy the amounts of junk that is sold everywhere. So, I put myself a mission, and it is to change a little bit the whole snacking ecosystem and make it healthier. So, then I realized I could not work for someone and that I had to start my business.' (TE-3)
		Discovery of opportunities in the market	• 'Like maybe people do not have the right type of phones or whatever words Chile seems very developed but then with these random gaps that are just like wide open and you can see what is worked in America you can just copy. So, it seems that there is much opportunity, for example, the banking system is crazy, so there is much opportunity for disruption which we like. (...) Chile seems full of opportunity for entrepreneurs, I think because it's a highly developed economy and everyone has smartphones and you know they have umber and things but then there is also a lot of things that are still quite behind (TE-5).' • 'I saw many failures in co-working here in Chile. I saw a huge opportunity to build this kind of a platform that could eventually support entrepreneurs (EE-7).'
		Alternative ways to exploit opportunities	• 'I think actually the main impact is to help Chilean people and Chilean entrepreneurs to understand the global environment and to get more global and also to like to develop better business. So, exchange experience with Chilean entrepreneurs' (TE-9) • 'And somebody that come from any other country, normally they can see.. I mean a different kind of approaches to some of the markets.' (EE-4)

(Continued)

Table 2. (Continued).

RP.1-3 Dissemination of entrepreneurial knowledge	Start-up know-how	• 'And they have this fail fast way of thinking that worked like we went to the markets, failed, and we tried with bars instead of movies, failed. And then we tried with restaurants, failed, tried with adventures parks, failed. Okay. That.. there is this one market we are being avoiding because it's too big, too concentrated and you're never going to have a chance in there. Like all in. That's our last chance. We went to our tickets and it worked. It was like..it was the best thing we did and the best thing actually was that they told us to destroy our platform. So, we destroyed our platform and made like a shitty landing page..very very..like I would think it was a fraud because our prices were like 7–5% discounted. And the page was very ugly. So, if I was a client I would never buy in that. But somehow people did buy. It worked. And now we are here.' (TE-9)
	Entrepreneurial knowledge	• 'There was some travelling also from the entrepreneurs, they went to the north and to the south. While they were in the south, they will give talks or lectures at the different universities in different areas. That's how it spreads.' (VC-1) • like how to manage the problems that we faced during the logistics happened. Like whenever things like custom stuff and things we don't calculate initially. We discussed about those things." (TE-1)
	Start-up mindset	• 'And I guess the best advice that he gave us was to stay focused and develop one thing right and then maybe think. If you start like thinking about everything you could do, you will finally see that you don't do anything. I guess that was the best thing he could tell us, and I think it's always good to have the opinion of the third party, that is from the outside and even better if you have experience and the kind of experience he has.' (CE-2)
RP1-4 Global connectivity	Global business know-how	• 'So, you think that you're doing something super new and then they tell another tool or another kind of software that you can use or something, they are like opening your mind to another thing. I think that's very valuable and also, they give you a hint for the global market. (...) So, you're always thinking a lot about Spanish speaker or Latin American countries and all of that. And they are like "Okay but how can this work in Europe or how can this work in Asia" and you are like "Ah no idea". I don't know if they have that problem or not so that helps a lot (TE-8).'
	Experience in internationalization	• The wideness of their ambitions. Nobody comes to Chile because it's a big market. So nobody that comes to Chile to start the company, wants to make happen just in Chile.' (VC-2)

Second, the local community was inspired by the presence of so many transnational entrepreneurs, who together demonstrated a diverse range of business ideas that had not yet existed in Chile. For instance, TE-3's familiarity with the healthy snack industry in the US allowed her to recognize this market opportunity in Latin America. Although nutrition and health have become critical issues, for example because of the high obesity rate, the healthy food industry in Latin America is still under-developed. Accordingly, TE-3 decided to develop and launch affordable and approachable healthy snacks in the Chilean market.

Transnational entrepreneurs not only contribute business ideas from outside Chile but also discover untapped opportunities within Chile. Since they have already experienced different institutional settings, these entrepreneurs can recognize the strengths of Chilean institutions and market potentials which are not explicitly visible to local Chileans. In the literature, researchers recommend that entrepreneurs fill institutional voids by uniquely combining resources to develop innovative solutions (Mair and Martí 2006; Garud, Hardy, and Maguire 2002). The diverse interactions among transnational and local entrepreneurs within the Santiago EE made local actors realize where institutional voids existed and how entrepreneurs could address them.

Extant literature explains the skills of transnational entrepreneurs at identifying opportunities in host-country environments that are neglected by locals with the concepts of bifocality (Rouse 1992; Vertovec 2002) and mixed embeddedness (Kloosterman and Rath 2001; Kloosterman, Rusinovic, and Yeboah 2016). Transnational entrepreneurs thus introduce not only business opportunities but also alternative ways to exploit these opportunities. Moreover, by pursuing a large variety of business ideas, transnational entrepreneurs increase the number of knowledge corridors (Ronstadt 1988) and enhance entrepreneurial 'serendipity' (Dew 2009). Consequent exposure to diverse business ideas not only influences the recognition of entrepreneurial opportunities but also accelerates the growth potential of new firms (Gruber, MacMillan, and Thompson 2012).

RP1-2: Transnational entrepreneurs demonstrate different ways to explore and exploit diverse opportunities to the local community by contributing a business idea to the ecosystem from the outside, discovering opportunities within, demonstrating global opportunities, and introducing alternative ways to exploit opportunities.

Third, transnational entrepreneurs contributed both explicit and tacit knowledge related to entrepreneurial activities to Santiago and spread them within the ecosystem. Some entrepreneurs were knowledgeable about technologies applied in the global start-up community. For instance, TE-11 has a virtual reality background and organized the first meeting on this topic for local entrepreneurs in Chile. Another participant, TE-1, possessed extensive knowledge about hardware start-ups (technology, logistics and facilities), which he shared with other entrepreneurs. Other entrepreneurs possessed start-up know-how on useful tools for business development, effective pitching, successful communication with investors and entrepreneurial marketing supported by their own experience. Furthermore, transnational entrepreneurs who had already undergone a dynamic entrepreneurial process also demonstrated an entrepreneurial mindset to local entrepreneurs.

Literature has discussed how a region can gain knowledge from the outside. Motoyama and Knowlton (2016) suggested that government sponsorship could form a cohort of entrepreneurs to design a learning platform. Carayannis, Provance, and Grigoroudis (2016) found that the EE can acquire knowledge from outside the region only after developing formal networks to gain knowledge from more distant regions. This network formation allows knowledge appropriation and develops a region's entrepreneurial capacity to create a critical mass of in-flowing knowledge. To this end, in the Santiago case, the government initiated the Start-Up Chile programme, which formed an extensive network on a regional and global scale. Most of the foreign start-ups came to Santiago through the Start-Up Chile programme, which explicitly encourages participants to transfer their entrepreneurial knowledge and mindset to the local community. This sub-programme of Start-Up Chile, called 'Social Impact/Founders' Lab', encourages transnational entrepreneurs to organize various events and workshops at universities, local schools and companies.

RP1-3: Transnational entrepreneurs contribute both explicit and tacit knowledge related to start-up activities to an emerging ecosystem and disseminate this knowledge within the local community. Formal initiatives and networks that aim at facilitating knowledge transfer are essential for reaching a critical mass.

Fourth, our empirical data revealed that transnational entrepreneurs contributed to enhancing global connectivity within the local ecosystem. On the cognitive level, local entrepreneurs and ecosystem actors have changed their perceptions about global market opportunities, recognizing the feasibility of internationalization due to their daily exposure to many energetic transnational entrepreneurs from all over the world. Dispelling the geographically induced reluctance of Chileans towards internationalization, transnational entrepreneurs have created a somewhat artificial global environment in Santiago, one which has convinced the local community that local start-ups can reach a global market. In a sense, the presence of a temporal global community successfully shortened the psychic distance (cf. Sousa and Bradley 2006; O'Grady and Lane 1996) between the Santiago EE and other EEs in the world.

The high mobility of transnational entrepreneurs can give them an advantage in terms of internationalization strategies, as they can freely move to favourable locations in search of better opportunities. Transnational entrepreneurs shared their knowledge and experience regarding foreign markets and start-up scenes with local Chilean entrepreneurs through formal and informal interactions. In addition to knowledge, transnational entrepreneurs also have unique social capital, such as diaspora networks (Dutia 2012; Kuznetsov 2006) and transnational entrepreneurial networks (Harima 2014). In the observed cases, transnational entrepreneurs opened their connections to foreign investors, accelerators, suppliers, mentors and customers within the Santiago EE.

RP1-4a: The presence of many transnational entrepreneurs creates a temporal global environment, one which reduces the locals' perceived psychic distance between their local ecosystem and the global market. Daily exposure to the global entrepreneurial community helps ecosystem actors to believe in the global potential of local start-ups.

RP1-4b: With the governmental subsidy, regional policymakers attract transnational entrepreneurs, who contribute their experience in foreign markets and their social capital with the global start-up scene to the region.

Although transnational entrepreneurs can create initial dynamics through their presence and interactions with local ecosystem actors, on level 1, changes within the local EE remained rather superficial, and significant transformation of the EE was not yet observable.

Level 2: evoking institutional changes

Five institutional changes induced by initial dynamics characterize level 2: (1) accumulating entrepreneurial knowledge in the region; (2) fostering entrepreneurial culture; (3) diversifying and intensifying interactions; (4) re-defining the roles of ecosystem stakeholders; and (5) building regional confidence. Compared to the initial dynamics on level 1, these five changes took place on the more profound institutional level as an institutional reaction of the Santiago EE to the 'injection' of external entrepreneurial resources. The transition from level 1 to 2 was erratic rather than linear and straightforward. For instance, local participants were at first reluctant to engage in Start-Up Chile's programmes, regarding them as a source for entrepreneurship grants rather than as a platform on which they could interact with foreign entrepreneurs. These different expectations towards the programme between foreign and domestic entrepreneurs can hamper institutional changes. Despite this, the current study did observe institutional changes induced by resource injection.

Institutional theory can offer a meaningful explanation for the transition between levels 1 and 2. The creation of new institutions or the transformation of existing institutions requires legitimacy, which implies that specific actions are considered appropriate and desirable (Dacin and Richard Scott 2002; Delmar and Shane 2004). According to institutional theory, 'institutional entrepreneurs' are agents with the resources and power to change institutions through entrepreneurial actions (Kalantaridis and Fletcher 2012; Levy and Scully 2007). They change institutions by creating a continuous flow of new ideas, theorizing about these ideas, demonstrating that these ideas deserve attention, and disseminating these ideas in the public domain (Svejenova, Mazza, and Planellas 2007). Our Santiago data suggest that transnational entrepreneurs have created numerous new entrepreneurial ideas, have validated their potential to generate success among local partici-pants of the Santiago EE, and have disseminated these ideas within the ecosystem.

Pacheco, York, and Dean (2010) found that collective action, especially by interest groups, is an essential mechanism for institutional change. In Santiago, transnational entrepreneurs, who tem-porarily conducted entrepreneurial activities in the local EE, took collective action as a group of foreign entrepreneurs interested in start-up activities and interactions. Through various interactions, they transmitted their belief in the potential success of start-up activities within the Santiago ecosystem, which in turn stimulated institutional changes. Table 3 compiles a list of selected quotes for each category.

First, the entrepreneurial knowledge contributed by transnational entrepreneurs from the outside has multiplied and accumulated within the Santiago region over time, even after they departed. During their time in Santiago, transnational entrepreneurs transferred both explicit and tacit knowl-edge to the local community via workshops, events and entrepreneurship education. As a result of diverse forms of interaction, an increasing number of local entrepreneurs and ecosystem stake-holders have internalized and transferred important streams of this knowledge to others within the ecosystem. One example is CE-4, who participated in the first Start-Up Weekend organized by transnational entrepreneurs, attended a Start-Up Chile programme, and took over its organizational duties after the entrepreneurs departed.

Transnational entrepreneurs created much commotion in Santiago through their various interactions with the local community. The media recognized the value of such 'noise' and published numerous stories about start-up entrepreneurs, who were depicted differently from conventional small business owners in Chile. Over time, stories about Santiago's ecosystem development spread far beyond the start-up community. The accumulation of entrepreneurial knowledge in the region resulted in the successful education of the masses, who began recognizing the value of start-up activities.

> RP2-1: Transnational entrepreneurs' entrepreneurial knowledge is accumulated within the ecosystem over time through various autonomous interactions among actors, which enhances common understanding of start-up activities and contributions to society.

The second observable change in the Santiago EE was the emergence of an entrepreneurial culture in both the start-up community and Chilean society. In contrast to the conservative Chilean mindset (e.g. strong domestic orientation and risk-aversion; cf. Sepúlveda and Bonilla 2014), transnational entrepreneurs have already stepped out of their comfort zone, crossing borders to pursue opportu-nities. From their global experience, they know that failure is inherent to entrepreneurial processes and serves only as a source for learning opportunities. This optimistic attitude towards entrepre-neurial failures was transmitted to the local Santiago ecosystem.

Another cultural change perceived by respondents was an emergent 'go-global' mindset among local entrepreneurs. Transnational entrepreneurs contributed to the global connectivity of the Santiago EE and, as a result of various interactions within the ecosystem, Chilean entrepreneurs and other ecosystem actors have begun both perceiving global opportunities to be within reach and seeking internationalization as a business expansion strategy. This cultural change was perceptible even outside the entrepreneur community, as notable success stories and entrepreneurial icons were disseminated by the media or in everyday interactions. Consequently, Chilean society's perceptions about entrepreneurs have drastically changed in the last decade. This finding is in line with those of Leatherbee and Eesley (2014), who revealed that social interactions between domestic and foreign entrepreneurs during Start-Up Chile improved Chileans' entrepreneurial behaviours.

Table 3. List of selected quotations (Level 2).

RP1-1	Accessible entrepreneurial role model	Experience with the seed phase	• 'During the program what happens was we made our first biggest sale in Dubai. So, we sold around 500 kits to one of the government authorities, so this made us back to Dubai and make things over there' (TE-1) • 'And after that, I went to like from one day to another, I was the most famous entrepreneur in my country' (TE-9) • 'Foreigner founders had more experience in funding, in seed funding, having gone through around and all that. I guess that is also a difference' (CE-2)
		Experience with the dynamic start-up process	• 'Before the hardware company, we have gone through like a lot of ups and downs. The thing is usually like making the product is the easiest thing. Converting the product into MVP is like hard labour.' (TE-1) • 'I started a bakery there, and it was very successful. We initially started with a storefront and a production centre simultaneously, so it was a lot of workloads and then two years after we decided to change our business model and close the storefront and then had only the production centre.' (TE-3)
		Start-up as a vocational choice	• 'We already have people understanding entrepreneurship as a valid way of making a living at this.' (VC-1) • 'A lot of young people in this generation, for me is amazing to know people that are 21 for example and they are already like doing start-ups. When I was 21, I was starting and thinking of getting a job in a company (...), so yes one can learn a lot about those experience.' (CE-2)
RP1-2	Capabilities to explore and exploit unique opportunities	Bring business ideas to the market	• 'I started seeing in Latin America there was a huge phenomenon that is becoming like at really high rates, one of the most obese you know like countries in the world. Chile is the 4th Colombia is going the same direction, we have Costco now like it is crazy the amounts of junk that is sold everywhere. So, I put myself a mission, and it is to change a little bit the whole snacking ecosystem and make it healthier. So, then I realized I could not work for someone and that I had to start my business.' (TE-3)
		Discovery of opportunities in the market	• 'Like maybe people do not have the right type of phones or whatever words Chile seems very developed but then with these random gaps that are just like wide open and you can see what is worked in America you can just copy. So, it seems that there is much opportunity, for example, the banking system is crazy, so there is much opportunity for disruption which we like. (...) Chile seems full of opportunity for entrepreneurs, I think because it's a highly developed economy and everyone has smartphones and you know they have umber and things but then there is also a lot of things that are still quite behind (TE-5).' • 'I saw many failures in co-working here in Chile. I saw a huge opportunity to build this kind of a platform that could eventually support entrepreneurs (EE-7).'
		Alternative ways to exploit opportunities	• 'I think actually the main impact is to help Chilean people and Chilean entrepreneurs to understand the global environment and to get more global and also to like to develop better business. So, exchange experience with Chilean entrepreneurs' (TE-9) • 'And somebody that come from any other country, normally they can see.. I mean a different kind of approaches to some of the markets.' (EE-4)

(Continued)

Table 3. (Continued).

RP.1-3	Dissemination of entrepreneurial knowledge	Start-up know-how

'And they have this fail fast way of thinking that worked like we went to the markets, failed, and we tried with bars instead of movies, failed. And then we tried with restaurants, failed, tried with adventures parks, failed. Okay. That.. there is this one market we are being avoiding because it's too big, too concentrated and you're never going to have a chance in there. Like all in. That's our last chance. We went to our tickets and it worked. It was like..it was the best thing we did and the best thing actually was that they told us to destroy our platform. So, we destroyed our platform and made like a shitty landing page..very very..like I would think it was a fraud because our prices were like 7-5% discounted. And the page was very ugly. So, if I was a client I would never buy in that. But somehow people did buy. It worked. And now we are here.' (TE-9)

Entrepreneurial knowledge

• 'There was some travelling also from the entrepreneurs, they went to the north and to the south. While they were in the south, they will give talks or lectures at the different universities in different areas. That's how it spreads.' (VC-1)
• 'like how to manage the problems that we faced during the logistics happened. Like whenever things like custom stuff and things we don't calculate initially. We discussed about those things." (TE-1)

Start-up mindset

• 'And I guess the best advice that he gave us was to stay focused and develop one thing right and then maybe think. If you start like thinking about everything you could do, you will finally see that you don't do anything. I guess that was the best thing he could tell us, and I think it's always good to have the opinion of the third party, that is from the outside and even better if you have experience and the kind of experience he has.' (CE-2)

RP1-4 Global connectivity Global business know-how

• 'So, you think that you're doing something super new and then they tell another tool or another kind of software that you can use or something, they are like opening your mind to another thing. I think that's very valuable and also, they give you a hint for the global market. (…) So, you're always thinking a lot about Spanish speaker or Latin American countries and all of that. And they are like "Okay but how can this work in Europe or how can this work in Asia" and you are like "Ah no idea". I don't know if they have that problem or not so that helps a lot (TE-8).'

Experience in internationalization

• 'The wideness of their ambitions. Nobody comes to Chile because it's a big market. So nobody that comes to Chile to start the company, wants to make happen just in Chile.' (VC-2)

Although elite students are more likely to prefer to benefit from their privilege and begin their careers at large companies, entrepreneurship has become a viable vocational option for many Chilean students. The social status elevation of entrepreneurs has given entrepreneurship, and the emerging EE, enhanced legitimacy (Díez-Martín, Blanco-González, and Prado-Román 2016; Kibler, Kautonen, and Fink 2014).

RP2-2a: By getting in touch with transnational entrepreneurs' risk-taking behaviours and strong international entrepreneurial orientation, local entrepreneurs and ecosystem actors develop an entrepreneurial culture in the region with a higher risk tolerance and a stronger global mindset than before.

RP2-2b: By witnessing emerging dynamics within the ecosystem, the social status and image of entrepreneurs has been elevated, which has in turn given the local entrepreneurial ecosystem legitimacy.

Third, the data reveal that interactions among entrepreneurs and related actors within the ecosystem have become more diverse and intensified over time due to the proliferation of stakeholders and the emergence of independent networks. Respondents recalled the situation around 2010, when only a few organizations offered support for entrepreneurial activities in Santiago. Along with the emergence of the Santiago EE, the number of support organizations, such as accelerators, incubators and investors, has increased, as has the variety of support they can offer. For instance, many universities in Santiago now 'have their own accelerators that are running correctly' (VC-1). There are now 'at least thirteen' (VC-2) accelerators in Santiago.

The initial dynamics on level 1 have also attracted private investors, like business angels and venture capitalists. Despite the favourable environment for investors, both formal and informal equity funding in Chile are regarded as rather incipient and precarious in Chile (Romaní, Amorós, and Atienza 2008). Although foreign investors continue to observe the development of the Santiago ecosystem to evaluate its investment potential, some Chilean investors have already made small-scale investments in emerging start-ups. Brown and Mason (2017) argued that financial providers, including banks, venture capital firms, business angels and accelerators, are vital for enabling the transfusion of resources into successful start-ups, calling them as 'ecosystem resource providers'. Roundy (2017) similarly explained that variations in the hybrid support organizations available in an EE can lead to the diversification of its entrepreneurial activities.

Another indicator of strengthened interactions are emerging, autonomous networks as sources of social capital for entrepreneurs and stakeholders (Alvedalen and Boschma 2017). However, the linkage between entrepreneurial stakeholders in Chile has remained underdeveloped, resulting in insufficient social capital in the Santiago ecosystem (Klerkx, Álvarez, and Campusano 2015; Bernasconi 2005). Participants in this study commonly described Start-Up Chile as the largest and most active global network in Santiago's start-up scene. Start-Up Chile has an extensive list of global alumni, many of whom remain connected via virtual channels (e.g. Facebook, WhatsApp) and often act as mentors for current participants of Start-Up Chile. Furthermore, Start-Up Chile is partnered with accelerators and incubators in many countries, thereby supporting the market entrance of its alumni. Apart from Start-Up Chile networks, some formal organizations are connecting ecosystem actors horizontally. For instance, ASECH (Associación de Emprededores de Chile), Chile Global Angels and ACVC (Associación Chilena de Venture Capital) are newly established formal networks aimed at connecting ecosystem stakeholders. Furthermore, ecosystem actors also organize small-scale networks of a more informal nature, such as learning groups, small workshops and groups of entrepreneurs from similar regions. The emergence of different types of social networks represents a critical step for ecosystem development, as the connectivity, density and strength of these networks among stakeholders determine the inclusivity of the EE (Neumeyer, Santos, and Morris 2018).

Start-up events, such as meet-ups, are also a critical component in ecosystem development, as they facilitate various types of interactions and create 'weak ties' among actors (Granovetter 1973). These events also facilitate opportunities for vicarious learning, as entrepreneurs can share stories of their entrepreneurial processes among each other (Holcomb et al. 2009; Roundy 2019).

RP2-3: Initial dynamics within the ecosystem emerging through resource injections by transnational entrepreneurs multiply entrepreneurial resource providers, diversify ecosystem stakeholders, and lead to the emergence of autonomous networks and start-up events, which in turn intensify and diversify the connectivity, density and strengths of interactions within the EE.

Fourth, in response to the initial dynamics created by transnational entrepreneurs on level 1, existing stakeholders, such as universities, financial institutions, media, corporate actors and policymakers, have recognized the potentials of start-ups. This has resulted in the re-definition of their role within the EE. Before the initial ecosystem dynamics became visible, universities, banks and private firms had been silent observers (Poblete and Amorós 2013; Bernasconi 2005). Since they were not familiar with start-ups, such organizational actors took considerable time to define their new position as active agents within the ecosystem. While banks and companies are still prudent about start-up involvement, a few signs of their emerging interest were observable. It has become standard for local universities to offer entrepreneurship education and for media to frequently report local entrepreneurial success stories. The literature also suggests that universities and multinational enterprises play essential roles in the ecosystem (Ghio, Guerini, and Rossi-Lamastra 2019; Bhawe and Zahra 2019).

RP2-4: The emergence of initial dynamics within the ecosystem convinced other institutional actors, such as universities, the government, private corporations, banks and media, of the potentials of start-ups, which led them to re-define their role to become more actively involved in the ecosystem.

Finally, we observed that the earlier dynamics triggered by transnational entrepreneurs in Santiago helped build confidence at the regional level. Departing from the strong domestic orientation of Chileans and their tendency to admire products, services and behaviours from outside the country (Gómez 2001), CORFO has made substantial efforts to build global connections by, for instance, attracting international venture capital (Agosin, Grau, and Larrain 2010). This has opened the door to the internationalization of Chilean entrepreneurial activities. In this respect, global interest in Chilean entrepreneurship policies and in the Santiago EE was sparked by the reputation of Start-Up Chile, brought about by extensive global marketing. Transnational entrepreneurs with the Start-Up Chile imprint also contributed to establishing the global reputation of the Santiago EE ('Chilecon Valley') by word of mouth. As a consequence, the global start-up community has begun considering Santiago as one of the most rapidly growing EEs on a global scale (Startup Genome 2017). When Chileans heard about the achievements of the Santiago ecosystem and witnessed the large number of transnational entrepreneurs coming to Chile to pursue entrepreneurial opportunities, they began to believe in the massive potential and uniqueness of the EE in their region. Subsequent exposure to diverse transnational entrepreneurs created an environment in which locals could experience entrepreneurial energy every day.

Notably, ecosystem stakeholders and entrepreneurs know full well the position of the Santiago ecosystem and pursue realistic goals by taking advantage of regional characteristics. For instance, transnational entrepreneurs and investors have repeatedly mentioned that Santiago is a perfect place to test minimum viable products before expanding to the wider Latin American market. They have also acknowledged other regional characteristics, like the supportive entrepreneurial policy and the low cost of developers and entrepreneurial human resources. The fact that Chile shares a time zone with North America represents a favourable condition for start-ups planning to enter the North American market. This awareness of regional strengths may be attributable to the perceptions of transnational entrepreneurs who have experienced different EEs worldwide. Transnational entrepreneurs have the cognitive flexibility to compare their transnational experiences (Rouse 1992) in Santiago with those of other ecosystems, which could in turn help them identify the unique strengths of the Santiago ecosystem.

RP2-5a: The increasingly global and domestic reputation of the local ecosystem, as well as the presence of numerous energetic transnational entrepreneurs, can help build regional confidence.

RP2-5b: Transnational entrepreneurs can recognise the strengths of an entrepreneurial ecosystem by comparing it with other ecosystems in other countries, which can help the region build substantial regional confidence.

On level 2, the community started working as an EE with the five institutional changes evoked by the initial dynamics on level 1. Although there have been some visible institutional changes, empirical evidence shows that the Santiago EE is not yet considered a self-sustaining ecosystem due to its heavy reliance on governmental support.

Level 3: on the path to establishing a resilient ecosystem

The Santiago ecosystem is now approaching a crossroads: it will either become a sustainable scale-up ecosystem, or it will not. This section presents the Santiago ecosystem at present and discusses how it can possibly step away from dependence on governmental support based on current empirical evidence.

The Santiago ecosystem is still entirely dependent on governmental support, as TE-7 mentioned in an interview: 'everything here is CORFO'. EE-7 carefully assumed that at least 90% of start-up funding is subsidized by the government. Start-Up Chile, which is fully backed by CORFO, has successfully attracted many transnational entrepreneurs. On the flip side, many transnational entrepreneurs would not have come to Chile without governmental incentives. Without CORFO, there would be far fewer transnational entrepreneurs in the ecosystem, which would in turn reduce the intensity of ecosystem interactions. More proof of the ecosystem's dependence is that most stakeholders rely on various policy instruments offered by CORFO. Interview respondents explained that many venture capitalists and other support organizations would not exist without governmental subsidies. CORFO's intensive start-up support measures thus represent a two-edged sword. On the one hand, such support was necessary to create initial dynamics. On the other, it created a public support-centred ecosystem in which entrepreneurs and stakeholders competed over the acquisition of public subsidies. Additionally, the availability of extensive equity-free investment can reduce the entrance motivation of angel investors, who offer equity funding. In this respect, Chile especially needs informal investors to overcome equity gaps (Romaní, Amorós, and Atienza 2008).

The current situation of the Santiago EE can best be described as 'embryonic' according to the typology of Brown and Mason (2017). To become a resilient ecosystem, one which can 'weather challenges, such as the loss of a major anchor employer, an exogenous economic shock, or the change of a technological paradigm' (Spigel and Harrison 2018, 161), the Santiago EE must therefore take additional steps.

First, some large exits of so-called 'blockbuster entrepreneurship' (Brown and Mason 2017) are needed in the Santiago ecosystem. Such major exits would not only represent start-up success stories in the region but would also stimulate entrepreneurial recycling (Mason and Harrison 2006). Moreover, the region needs both successful and failed narratives of mature, skilful, highly qualified and experimental start-ups, which would generate rich entrepreneurial knowledge on the regional level and encourage the next generation to 'recycle' such knowledge. This knowledge accumulation process entails an important resource flow within ecosystems (Spigel and Harrison 2018; Roundy 2019). Furthermore, the creation of some visible global success stories is a prerequisite for attracting transnational entrepreneurs and foreign entrepreneurial resource providers (Brown and Mason 2017).

Second, interactions and networks must be both more diverse and coherent to enact and maintain the resilience of the EE (Roundy, Brockman, and Bradshaw 2017) – but they also need to be developed autonomously. One type of interaction that is critical to ecosystem development but is currently insufficient in the Chilean context is the one between private corporations and the start-up scene. Although Chilean private firms have started to change their perceptions, they generally remain reluctant to take concrete actions in start-up engagement through, for instance, corporate venture capital and accelerators (Kanbach and Stubner 2016; Kupp, Marval, and Borchers 2017). As long as corporate actors do not proactively participate in entrepreneurial activities in the region, its ecosystem will not reach a critical mass of interactions (Ghio, Guerini, and Rossi-Lamastra 2019).

Third, it is essential that CORFO revises the role and strategy of public actors in the ecosystem. While CORFO's political measures have achieved specific results in the early phase of ecosystem evolution, it is meaningful to critically question their current and previous measures according to the evolutionary stage of the Santiago ecosystem. In the initial stage, the primary political objective was to generate a greater number of entrepreneurial activities, which was outstandingly achieved. However, the numerous entrepreneurs and stakeholder interactions in the ecosystem cannot survive without governmental support. Thus, the next vital step is to switch the political focus to the creation of high-profile start-ups, which can facilitate entrepreneurial recycling, to make existing actors and stakeholders less dependent on governmental subsidies, and to encourage corporate actors to be more active within the EE.

RP3: To become a resilient ecosystem, the ecosystem must facilitate mechanisms of entrepreneurial recycling as well as diverse and coherent interactions with strong corporate participation. In this process, public actors can continuously re-define their roles and strategies according to the ecosystem's evolution.

Conclusion

Research contribution

The findings of this study contribute to recent scholarly discussions on ecosystem evolution in several ways. The mechanisms of resource injections presented in this study focus on 'temporary imports' of transnational entrepreneurs. The results offer novel insights, particularly regarding the early evolution of EEs and the role the national government may play in different phases. At the same time, this study also discussed critical aspects of this 'top-down approach' to governing EEs (Colombo et al. 2019). The empirical case revealed an ecosystem dilemma, as the region cannot sustain the driving force of ecosystem evolution without entrepreneurial resources artificially created by public support. The consequent over-reliance on policy instruments creates a vicious cycle, one which strengthens the dependency relationship and prevents the region from transforming into a self-sustaining and resilient ecosystem.

Notably, one important side-story relates to a particular type of ecosystem actor – namely a public accelerator – that coordinates the flow of resources contributed by transnational entrepreneurs. The public accelerator can be considered an 'anchor tenant', which refers to a central player spurring ecosystem creation and development (Colombelli, Paolucci, and Ughetto 2019). While different types of individuals and organizations (business angels, universities, corporates) can become anchor tenants to facilitate resource injections, the strategic aims of public accelerators have a particular synergy, as they seek to stimulate entrepreneurial activities in a certain territory to develop the regional economy (Aernoudt 2004; Pauwels et al. 2016). The import of entrepreneurial resources alone does not necessarily evoke institutional changes and ecosystem evolution, since entrepreneurial resources need to be transferred to other ecosystem stakeholders and must be embedded in institutional environments. Public accelerators can coordinate interactions to efficiently disseminate resources and multiply the regional entrepreneurial resource base.

Practical implications

Our research implies that political initiatives can attract transnational entrepreneurs who could contribute entrepreneurial resources to a region. To facilitate the successful emergence of initial dynamics, policymakers should be aware of some issues. First, a larger number of transnational entrepreneurs is needed to create a critical mass of resources. Second, policymakers should offer soft-landing support, as well as community and networking services, so that transnational entrepreneurs can overcome institutional barriers. Third, transnational entrepreneurs should have the capacity to interact with the local community to transfer their resources. This study also highlights the importance of anchor tenants as facilitators and coordinators of interactions among ecosystem stakeholders. In the presented case, the anchor tenant was Start-Up Chile, a public accelerator. Policymakers should build support organizations, such as public accelerators, with the specific objective of developing a regional EE.

Limitations

There are several limitations to our study. First, since our research was conducted in a single ecosystem, we could not examine regional differences. Second, although we collected data at three different time points (2015, 2017 and 2019), our study neither adequately considered developments after 2017 nor conducted a longitudinal analysis, which would have enabled us to trace ecosystem evolution from 2010. We instead relied on retrospective views from interviewees and secondary data. Third, this study employed a snowballing strategy for data collection, which may have caused selection bias among the respondents. EX-1 pointed out the potential risk of including multiple interviewees who were involved in Start-Up Chile or with other policy instruments. Fourth, the intercultural setting created an unavoidable risk for biases and missing information due to linguistic barriers. Finally, this study used Start-Up Chile as a focal policy instrument for investigation, even though CORFO has been offering a wide range of entrepreneurial support. Due to the complex nature of EEs, isolating the most influential mechanisms in their evolution is nearly impossible, and as such this study should not be regarded as comprehensive with respect to all the factors contributing to ecosystem development.

Future perspectives

We recommend that future research investigates mechanisms of ecosystem emergence or resource injections in other newly emerging resource-scarce ecosystems and under different institutional conditions, such as rural areas in developed countries or EEs in countries with weak institutions. Furthermore, we encourage further investigation of the future development of the Santiago EE, as it is now entering a critical phase. Should the region overcome its resiliency dilemma and transform from an artificially created to a self-sustaining ecosystem, then future research on this transformation could offer valuable insights for policymakers in emerging countries as well as for EE researchers.

This study revealed the critical role of ecosystem governance through top-down approaches. Some interesting follow-up questions in this regard lude: How do private anchor tenants govern an EE through a top-down approach? In which ways can EEs be governed? Can future research specify the nature and drivers of ecosystem evolution, and can such research determine the strength of the imprint of a given regional structure when it comes to resource injection by transnational entrepreneurs as well as how such injections are used to evoke momentum in EEs?

Acknowledgement

We appreciate Startup Chile, CORFO, and all the other stakeholders of the Santiago entrepreneurial ecosystem for their generous support, which enabled us to conduct this study. We also thank our colleagues at the Chair in Small Business & Management (LEMEX), University of Bremen, Thomas Baron, Manal Haimour, Tatevik Narimanyan, Quynh Duong Phuong, and Tenzin Yeshi for providing us with valuable and critical comments as friendly reviewers.

Disclosure statement

No potential conflict of interest was reported by the authors.

ORCID

Aki Harima ⓘD http://orcid.org/0000-0001-7499-3488
Jan Harima ⓘD http://orcid.org/0000-0001-9042-0225
Jörg Freiling ⓘD http://orcid.org/0000-0001-6922-9805

References

Acs, Z. J., E. Autio, and L. Szerb. 2014. "National Systems of Entrepreneurship: Measurement Issues and Policy Implications." *Research Policy* 43 (3): 476–494. doi:10.1016/j.respol.2013.08.016.

Acs, Z. J., E. Stam, D. B. Audretsch, and A. O'Connor. 2017. "The Lineages of the Entrepreneurial Ecosystem Approach." *Small Business Economics* 49: 1–10. doi:10.1007/s11187-017-9864-8.

Adner, R. 2006. "Match Your Innovation Strategy to Your Innovation Ecosystem." *Harvard Business Review* 84 (4): 1–11.

Adner, R. 2017. "Ecosystem as Structure: An Actionable Construct for Strategy." *Journal of Management* 43 (1): 39–58. doi:10.1177/0149206316678451.

Aernoudt, R. 2004. "Incubators: Tool for Entrepreneurship?" *Small Business Economics* 23 (2): 127–135. doi:10.1023/B:SBEJ.0000027665.54173.23.

Agosin, M., N. Grau, and C. Larrain. 2010. "Industrial Policy in Chile." *IDB-WP-170. IDB Working Paper Series.* doi:10.1111/j.1813-6982.1994.tb01228.x.

Almeida, P., and B. Kogut. 1999. "Localization of Knowledge and the Mobility of Engineers in Regional Networks." *Management Science* 45 (7): 905–917. doi:10.1287/mnsc.45.7.905.

Alvedalen, J., and R. Boschma. 2017. "A Critical Review of Entrepreneurial Ecosystems Research: Towards A Future Research Agenda." *European Planning Studies* 25 (6): 887–903. doi:10.1080/09654313.2017.1299694.

Amorós, J. E., C. Felzensztein, and E. Gimmon. 2013. "Entrepreneurial Opportunities in Peripheral versus Core Regions in Chile." *Small Business Economics* 40 (1): 119–139. doi:10.1007/s11187-011-9349-0.

Asheim, B. T., and A. Isaken. 2002. "Regional Innovation Systems: The Integration of Local 'Sticky' and Global 'Ubiquitous' Knowledge." *Journal of Technology Transfer* 27: 77–86. doi:10.1023/A:1013100704794.

Audretsch, D. B., and A. N. Link. 2019. "Embracing an Entrepreneurial Ecosystem: An Analysis of the Governance of Research Joint Ventures." *Small Business Economics* 52: 429–436. doi:10.1007/s11187-017-9953-8.

Audretsch, D. B., and M. Belitski. 2016. "Entrepreneurial Ecosystems in Cities: Establishing the Framework Conditions." *Journal of Technology Transfer* 1–22. doi:10.1007/s10961-016-9473-8.

Auerswald, P. E., and L. Dani. 2017. "The Adaptive Life Cycle of Entrepreneurial Ecosystems: The Biotechnology Cluster." *Small Business Economics* 49: 97–117. doi:10.1007/s11187-017-9869-3.

Bagwell, S. 2015. "From Mixed Embeddedness to Transnational Mixed Embeddedness: An Exploration of Vietnamese Businesses in London." *International Journal of Entrepreneurial Behavior & Research* 24: 104–120.

Bahrami, H., and S. Evans. 1995. "Flexible Re-Cycling and High-Technology Entrepreneurship." *California Management Review* 37 (3): 62–89. doi:10.2307/41165799.

Baltar, F., and I. B. Icart. 2013. "Entrepreneurial Gain, Cultural Similarity and Transnational Entrepreneurship." *Global Networks* 13 (2): 200–219. doi:10.1111/glob.12020.

Baron, T., and A. Harima. 2019. "The Role of Diaspora Entrepreneurs in Start-up Ecosystem Development - a Berlin Case Study." *International Journal of Entrepreneurship and Small Business* 36 (1/2): 74–102. doi:10.1504/IJESB.2019.096968.

Baron, T., and J. Freiling. 2019. "Blueprint Silicon Valley? Explaining Idiosyncrasy of Startup Ecosystems." *Problemy Zarzadzania* 1/2019 (81): 57–76. doi:10.7172/1644-9584.81.3.

Bas, G., E. A. Tomas, and M. Kunc. 2008. "Innovation, Entrepreneurship and Clusters in Latin America Natural Resource - Implication and Future Challenges." *Journal of Technology Management & Innovation* 3 (3): 52–65. doi:10.4067/S0718-27242008000200005.

Bernasconi, A. 2005. "University Entrepreneurship in a Developing Country: The Case of the P. Universidad Católica de Chile, 1985–2000." *Higher Education* 50 (2): 247–274. doi:10.1007/sl0734-004-6353-l.

Bhawe, N., and S. A. Zahra. 2019. "Inducing Heterogeneity in Local Entrepreneurial Ecosystems: The Role of MNEs." *Small Business Economics* 52: 437–454. doi:10.1007/s11187-017-9954-7.

Bischoff, K., C. K. Volkmann, and D. B. Audretsch. 2017. "Stakeholder Collaboration in Entrepreneurship Education: An Analysis of the Entrepreneurial Ecosystems of European Higher Educational Institutions." *The Journal of Technology Transfer.* doi:10.1007/s10961-017-9581-0.

Bolund, P., and S. Hunhammar. 1999. "Ecosystem Services in Urban Areas." *Ecological Economics* 29: 293–301. doi:10.1016/S0921-8009(99)00013-0.

Bosma, N., J. Hessels, V. Schutjens, M. Van Praag, and I. Verheul. 2012. "Entrepreneurship and Role Models." *Journal Of Economic Psychology* 33 (2): 410-424.

Brown, R., and C. Mason. 2017. "Looking inside the Spiky Bits: A Critical Review and Conceptualisation of Entrepreneurial Ecosystems." *Small Business Economics* 49: 11–30. doi:10.1007/s11187-017-9865-7.

Brown, R., S. Mawson, N. Lee, and L. Peterson. 2019. "Start-up Factories, Transnational Entrepreneurs and Entrepreneurial Ecosystems: Unpacking the Lure of Start-up Accelerator Programmes." *European Planning Studies* 27 (5): 885–904. doi:10.1080/09654313.2019.1588858.

Bruns, K., N. Bosma, M. Sanders, and M. Schramm. 2017. "Searching for the Existence of Entrepreneurial Ecosystems: A Regional Cross-Section Growth Regression Approach." *Small Business Economics* 49: 31–54. doi:10.1007/s11187-017-9866-6.

Büchi Buc, H. 2006. How Chile successfully transformed its economy. No. 1958 (September 19, 2006). The Heritage Foundation. (Online publication) https://www.heritage.org/international-economies/report/how-chile-successfully-transformed-its-economy

Carayannis, E. G., M. Provance, and E. Grigoroudis. 2016. "Entrepreneurship Ecosystems: An Agent-Based Simulation Approach." *The Journal of Technology Transfer* 41 (3): 631–653. doi:10.1007/s10961-016-9466-7.

Carmel, E., and J. Richman. 2013. "Building International Social Capital at the Startup Chile Accelerator. 2326003". *SSRN Electronic Journal*. doi:10.2139/ssrn.2326003.

Cavallo, A., A. Ghezzi, and R. Balocco. 2018. "Entrepreneurial Ecosystem Research: Present Debates and Future Directions." *International Entrepreneurship and Management Journal* 1–31. doi:10.1007/s11365-018-0526-3.

Chandra, A., and M. A. Medrano Silva. 2012. "Business Incubation in Chile: Development, Financing and Financial Services." *Journal of Technology Management and Innovation* 7 (2): 1–13. doi:10.4067/S0718-27242012000200001.

Chanra, A., and M. Narczewska. 2009. "Business Incubator Financing and Financial Services in Chile." *2009-WP-2. Networks Financial Institute Working Paper*. doi:10.1108/01409171011011599.

Charmaz, K. 2008. "Grounded Theory as an Emergent Method." In *Handbook of Emergent Methods*, edited by S. N. Hesse-Biber and P. Leavy, 155–170. New York: Guilford Press.

Cohen, B. 2006. "Sustainable Valley Entrepreneurial Ecosystems." *Business Strategy and the Environment* 15 (1): 1–14. doi:10.1002/bse.428.

Colombelli, A., E. Paolucci, and E. Ughetto. 2019. "Hierarchical and Relational Governance and the Life Cycle of Entrepreneurial Ecosystems." *Small Business Economics* 52: 505–521. doi:10.1007/s11187-017-9957-4.

Colombo, M. G., G. B. Dagnino, E. E. Lehmann, and M. Salmador. 2019. "The Governance of Entrepreneurial Ecosystems." *Small Business Economics* 52: 419–428. doi:10.1007/s11187-017-9952-9.

Contreras, S., and A. Greenlee. 2018. "The Effectiveness of Microenterprise Policies in Chile: The Case of Entrepreneurship Center – ChileCompra." *SSRN Electronic Journal* 0–3. doi:10.2139/ssrn.3276199.

Costello, L., M. L. McDermott, and R. Wallace. 2017. "Netnography: Range of Practices, Misperceptions, and Missed Opportunities." *International Journal of Qualitative Methods* 16 (1): 1–12. doi:10.1177/1609406917700647.

Côté, R., and J. Hall. 1995. "Industrial Parks as Ecosystems." *Journal of Cleaner Production* 3 (1): 41–46. doi:10.1016/0959-6526(95)00041-C.

Crosling, G., M. Nair, and S. Vaithilingam. 2015. "A Creative Learning Ecosystem, Quality of Education and Innovative Capacity: A Perspective from Higher Education." *Studies in Higher Education* 40 (7): 1147–1163. doi:10.1080/03075079.2014.881342.

Dacin, M. T., and W. Richard Scott. 2002. "Institutional Theory and Institutional Change: Introdcution to the Special Research Forum." *Academy of Management Journal* 45 (1): 45–56. doi:10.5465/amj.2002.6283388.

Delmar, F., and S. Shane. 2004. "Legitimating First: Organizing Activities and the Survival of New Ventures." *Journal of Business Venturing* 19 (3): 385–410. doi:10.1016/S0883-9026(03)00037-5.

Dew, N. 2009. "Serendipity in Entrepreneurship." *Organization Studies* 30 (7): 735–753. doi:10.1177/0170840609104815.

Díez-Martín, F., A. Blanco-González, and C. Prado-Román. 2016. "Explaining Nation-Wide Differences in Entrepreneurial Activity: A Legitimacy Perspective." *International Entrepreneurship and Management Journal* 12 (4): 1079–1102. doi:10.1007/s11365-015-0381-4.

Drori, I., B. Honig, and M. Wright. 2009. "Transnational Entrepreneurship: An Emergent Field of Study." *Entrepreneurship Theory and Practice* 33 (5): 863–891. doi:10.1111/etap.12026.

Dube, R. 2015. "Chile Keeps Nurturing Seeds for 'Chilecon Valley'.." *The Wall Street Journal*, August 23. https://www.wsj.com/articles/chile-keeps-nurturing-seeds-for-chilecon-valley-1440371282

Dutia, S. G. 2012. "Diaspora Networks: A New Impetus to Drive Entrepreneurship." *Innovations: Technology, Governance, Globalization* 7 (1): 65–72. doi:10.1162/INOV_a_00116.

Eckhardt, J. T., M. P. Ciuchta, and M. Carpenter. 2018. "Open Innovation, Information, and Entrepreneurship within Platform Ecosystems." *Strategic Entrepreneurship Journal* 12 (3): 369–391. doi:10.1002/sej.1298.

Egusa, C., and V. O'Shee. 2016. "A Look into Chile's Innovative Startup Government." *Techcrunch*, https://techcrunch.com/2016/10/16/a-look-into-chiles-innovative-startup-government/?guccounter=1

Feld, B. 2012. *Startup Communities: Building an Entrepreneurial Ecosystem in Your City*. Hoboken, NJ: John Wiley & Sons, Inc.

Fraiberg, S. 2017. "Start-Up Nation: Studying Transnational Entrepreneurial Practices in Israel's Start-Up Ecosystem." *Journal of Business and Technical Communication* 31 (3): 350–388. doi:10.1177/1050651917695541.

Garud, R., C. Hardy, and S. Maguire. 2002. "Institutional Entrepreneurship as Embedded Agency : An Introduction to the Special Issue." doi:10.1177/0170840607078958.

Ghio, N., M. Guerini, and C. Rossi-Lamastra. 2019. "The Creation of High-Tech Ventures in Entrepreneurial Ecosystems: Exploring the Interactions among University Knowledge, Cooperative Banks, and Individual Attitudes." *Small Business Economics* 52: 523–543. doi:10.1007/s11187-017-9958-3.

Gilbert, B. A., P. P. McDougall, and D. B. Audretsch. 2008. "Clusters, Knowledge Spillovers and New Venture Performance: An Empirical Examination." *Journal of Business Venturing* 23 (4): 405–422. doi:10.1016/j.jbusvent.2007.04.003.

Gioia, D. A., K. G. Corley, and A. L. Hamilton. 2013. "Seeking Qualitative Rigor in Inductive Research." *Organizational Research Methods* 16 (1): 15–31. doi:10.1177/1094428112452151.

Global Entrepreneurship Research Association. 2018. "Global Entrepreneurship Monitor 2017/2018". *Global Entrepreneurship Monitor.* http://www.gemconsortium.org/report/50012

Gómez, C. F. 2001. "Chilean Culture: Entrepreneurs and Workers." *The Asian Journal of Latin American Studies* 14 (2): 113–160.

Gonder, T. 2012. "An Early Assessment of Start-Up Chile." *Innovations: Technology, Governance, Globalization* 7 (2): 29–32. doi:10.1162/INOV_a_00126.

Gonzalez-Uribe, J., and M. Leatherbee. 2018. "The Effects of Business Accelerators on Venture Performance: Evidence from Start-Up Chile." *Review of Financial Studies* 31 (4): 1566–1603. doi:10.1093/rfs/hhx103.

Goswami, K. J., R. Mitchell, and S. Bhagavatula. 2018. "Accelerator Expertise: Understanding the Intermediary Role of Accelerators in the Development of the Bangalore Entrepreneurial Ecosystem." *Strategic Entrepreneurship Journal* 12 (1): 117–150. doi:10.1002/sej.1281.

Granovetter, M. S. 1973. "The Strength of Weak Ties." *American Journal of Sociology* 78 (6): 1360–1380. doi:10.1086/225469.

Gruber, M., I. C. MacMillan, and J. D. Thompson. 2012. "Escaping the Prior Knowledge Corridor: What Shapes the Number and Variety of Market Opportunities Identified before Market Entry of Technology Start-Ups?" *Organization Science* 24 (1): 280–300. doi:10.1287/orsc.1110.0721.

Harima, A. 2014. "Network Dynamics of Descending Diaspora Entrepreneurship: Multiple Case Studies with Japanese Entrepreneurs in Emerging Economies." *Journal of Entrepreneurship, Management and Innovation* 10 (4): 65–92. doi:10.7341/jemi.

Holcomb, T. R., R. Duane Ireland, R. M. Holmes Jr, and M. A. Hitt. 2009. "Architecture of Entrepreneurial Learning: Exploring the Link among Heuristics, Knowledge, and Action." *Entrepreneurship Theory and Practice* 33 (1): 167–192. doi:10.1111/j.1540-6520.2008.00285.x.

Housley, W., B. Dicks, K. Henwood, and R. Smith. 2017a. "Qualitative Methods and Data in Digital Societies." *Qualitative Research* 17 (6): 607–609. doi:10.1177/1468794117730936.

Housley, W., H. Webb, A. Edwards, R. Procter, and M. Jirotka. 2017b. "Digitizing Sacks? Approaching Social Media as Data." *Qualitative Research* 17 (6): 627–644. doi:10.1177/1468794117715063.

Iansiti, M., and R. Levien. 2004. "Strategy as Ecology." *Harvard Business Review* 82 (3): 68–81.

Isenberg, D. J. 2010. "The Big Idea: How to Start an Entrepreneurial Revolution." *Harvard Business Review* 88: 6. doi:10.1353/abr.2012.0147.

Isenberg, D. J. 2011. "The Entrepreneurship Ecosystem Strategy as a New Paradigm for Economic Policy: Principles for Cultivating Entrepreneurship." *The Babson Entrepreneurship Ecosystem Project.* Vol. 1. Presentation at the Institute of International and European Affairs. doi:10.1093/rfs/hhr098.

Kalantaridis, C., and D. Fletcher. 2012. "Entrepreneurship and Institutional Change: A Research Agenda." *Entrepreneurship & Regional Development* 24 (3–4): 199–214. doi:10.1080/08985626.2012.670913.

Kanbach, D. K., and S. Stubner. 2016. "Corporate Accelerators as Recent Form of Startup Engagement: The What, the Why, and the How." *Journal of Applied Business Research* 32 (6): 1761–1776. doi:10.19030/jabr.v32i6.9822.

Kantis, H., J. Federico, and S. I. García 2018. Opening the black box of ecosystem diversity around the globe: The index of dynamic entrepreneurship (IDE). (1. ed.) - Rafaela: Associación Civil red Pymes Mercosur.

Kibler, E., T. Kautonen, and M. Fink. 2014. "La Légitimité Sociale Régionale de l'entrepreneuriat: Les Conséquences Pour Les Intentions Entrepreneuriales et Le Comportement de Démarrage." *Regional Studies* 48 (6): 995–1015. doi:10.1080/00343404.2013.851373.

Klerkx, L., R. Álvarez, and R. Campusano. 2015. "The Emergence and Functioning of Innovation Intermediaries in Maturing Innovation Systems: The Case of Chile." *Innovation and Development* 5 (1): 73–91. doi:10.1080/2157930X.2014.921268.

Kloosterman, R., and J. Rath. 2001. "Immigrant Entrepreneurs in Advanced Economies: Mixed Embeddedness Further Explored." *Journal of Ethnic and Migration Studies* 27 (2): 189–201. doi:10.1080/13691830123940.

Kloosterman, R., K. Rusinovic, and D. Yeboah. 2016. "Super-Diverse Migrants—Similar Trajectories? Ghanaian Entrepreneurship in the Netherlands Seen from a Mixed Embeddedness Perspective." *Journal of Ethnic and Migration Studies* 42 (6): 913–932. doi:10.1080/1369183X.2015.1126091.

Krishna, H. S., and M. H. Bala Subrahmanya. 2015. "Transnational Entrepreneurship and Indian High-Tech Start-up Survival: An Empirical Investigation." *South Asian Journal of Management* 22 (2): 81–98. http://search.ebscohost.com/login.aspx?direct=true&db=buh&AN=109221253⟨=pt-br&site=ehost-live

Kupp, M., M. Marval, and P. Borchers. 2017. "Corporate Accelerators: Fostering Innovation while Bringing Together Startups and Large Firms." *Journal of Business Strategy* 38 (6): 47–53. doi:10.1108/JBS-12-2016-0145.

Kuznetsov, Y. 2006. *Diaspora Networks and the International Migration of Skills. How Countries Can Draw on Their Talent Abroad.* Washington, DC: World Bank Publications.

Leatherbee, M., and C. E. Eesley. 2014. "Boulevard of Broken Behaviors: Socio-Psychological Mechanisms of Entrepreneurship Policies". *SSRN* August: 1–28. doi:10.2139/ssrn.2488712.

Levy, D., and M. Scully. 2007. "The Institutional Entrepreneur as Modern Prince: The Strategic Face of Power in Contested Fields." *Organization Studies* 28 (7): 971–991. doi:10.1177/0170840607078109.

Mack, E., and H. Mayer. 2016. "The Evolutionary Dynamics of Entrepreneurial Ecosystems." *Urban Studies* 53 (10): 2118–2133. doi:10.1177/0042098015586547.

Mair, J., and I. Martí. 2006. "Social Entrepreneurship Research: a Source Of Explanation, Prediction, and Delight." *Journal Of World Business* 41 (1): 36-44.

Malecki, E. J. 2018. "Entrepreneurship and Entrepreneurial Ecosystems." *Geography Compass* 12: 1–21. doi:10.1111/gec3.12359.

Mason, C. M., and R. Brown. 2014. "Entrepreneurial Ecosystems and Growth Oriented Entrepreneurship." In *Background Paper Prepared for the Workshop Organised by the OECD LEED Programme and the Dutch Ministry of Economic Affairs on Entrepreneurial Ecosystems and Growth Oriented Entrepreneurship.* doi:10.1017/CBO9781107415324.004.

Mason, C. M., and R. T. Harrison. 2006. "After the Exit: Acquisitions, Entrepreneurial Recycling and Regional Economic Developmen." *Regional Studies* 40: 55–73. doi:10.1080/00343400500450059.

Melo, H. 2012. "Prosperity through Connectedness - Innovations Case Narrative: Start-Up Chile." *Innovations* 7 (2): 19–23. https://www.mitpressjournals.org/doi/pdf/10.1162/INOV_a_00124

Motoyama, Y., and K. Knowlton. 2016. "From Resource Munificence to Ecosystem Integration: The Case of Government Sponsorship in St. Louis." *Entrepreneuriship Research Journal* 28 (5–6): 448–470. doi:10.2139/ssrn.2498226.

Neck, H. M., G. Dale Meyer, B. Cohen, and A. C. Corbett. 2004. "An Entrepreneurial System View of New Venture Creation." *Journal of Small Business Management* 42 (2): 190–208. doi:10.1111/j.1540-627X.2004.00105.x.

Neumeyer, X., S. C. Santos, and M. H. Morris. 2018. "Who Is Left Out: Exploring Social Boundaries in Entrepreneurial Ecosystems". *Journal of Technology Transfer*, no. 0123456789. doi:10.1007/s10961-018-9694-0.

Newland, K., and H. Tanaka. 2010. "Mobilizing Diaspora Entrepreneurship for Development." *Diaspora & Development Policy Project.* Washington. http://www.migrationpolicy.org/pubs/diasporas-entrepreneurship.pdf

Nylund, P. A., and B. Cohen. 2017. "Collision Density: Driving Growth in Urban Entrepreneurial Ecosystems." *International Entrepreneurship Management Journal* 13 (3): 757–776. doi:10.1007/s11365-016-0424-5.

O'Connor, A., and G. Reed. 2018. "Theorizing the University Governance Role in an Entrepreneurial Ecosystem." In *Entrepreneurship Ecosystems: Place-Based Transformations and Transitions*, edited by A. O'Connor, E. Stam, F. Sussan, and D. B. Audretsch, 81–100. Cham, Switzerland: Springer International Publishing.

O'Grady, S., and H. W. Lane. 1996. "The Psychic Distance Paradox." *Journal of International Business Studies* 27 (2): 309–333. doi:10.1057/palgrave.jibs.8490137.

Pacheco, D. F., J. G. York, and T. J. Dean. 2010. "The Coevolution of Instituiona Entrepreneurship: A Tale of Two Theories." *Journal of Management* 36 (4): 974–1010. doi:10.1177/0149206309360280.

Pauwels, C., B. Clarysse, M. Wright, and V. H. Jonas. 2016. "Understanding a New Generation Incubation Model: The Accelerator." *Technovation* 50–51: 13–24. doi:10.1016/j.technovation.2015.09.003.

Poblete, C., and J. E. Amorós. 2013. "University Support in the Development of Regional Entrepreneurial Activity: An Exploratory Study from Chile." *Investigaciones Regionales* 26: 159–177.

Porter, M. E. 2000. "Location, Competition, and Economic Development: Local Clusters in a Global Economy." *Economic Development Quarterly* 14 (1): 15–34. doi:10.1177/089124240001400105.

Qian, H., Z. J. Acs, and R. R. Stough. 2013. "Regional Systems of Entrepreneurship: The Nexus of Human Capital, Knowledge and New Firm Formation." *Journal of Economic Geography* 13 (4): 559–587. doi:10.1093/jeg/lbs009.

Romaní, G., J. E. Amorós, and M. Atienza. 2008. "Formal and Informal Equity Funding in Chile." *Estudios de economia* 35 (2): 179–194.

Romaní, G., M. Atienza, and J. E. Amorós. 2013. "The Development of Business Angel Networks in Latin American Countries: The Case of Chile." *Venture Capital* 15 (2): 95–113. doi:10.1080/13691066.2013.788822.

Ronstadt, R. 1988. "The Corridor Principle." *Journal of Business Venturing* 3: 31–40. doi:10.1016/0883-9026(88)90028-6.

Roundy, P. T. 2016. "Start-up Community Narratives: The Discursive Construction of Entrepreneurial Ecosystems." *Journal of Entrepreneurship* 25 (2): 232–248. doi:10.1177/0971355716650373.

Roundy, P. T. 2017. "Hybrid Organizations and the Logics of Entrepreneurial Ecosystems." *International Entrepreneurship and Management Journal* 13 (4): 1221–1237. doi:10.1007/s11365-017-0452-9.

Roundy, P. T. 2019. "Rust Belt or Revitalization: Comparing Narratives in Entrepreneurial Ecosystems." *Management Research Review* 42 (1): 102–121. doi:10.1108/MRR-09-2015-0216.

Roundy, P. T., B. K. Brockman, and M. Bradshaw. 2017. "The Resilience of Entrepreneurial Ecosystems." *Journal of Business Venturing Insights* 8 (May): 99–104. doi:10.1016/j.jbvi.2017.08.002.

Roundy, P. T., M. Bradshaw, and B. K. Brockman. 2018. "The Emergence of Entrepreneurial Ecosystems: A Complex Adaptive System Approach." *Journal of Businss Research* 86 (1): 1–10. doi:/10.2139/.

Rouse, R. 1992. "Making Sense of Settlement : Class Transformation, Cultural Struggle, and Transnationalism among Mexican Migrants inthe United States." *Annals New York Academy of Sciences 645 (1)*, 25–52.

Saxenian, A. 1990. "Regional Networks and the Resurgence of Silicon Valley." *California Management Review* 33 (1): 89–112. doi:10.2307/41166640.

Saxenian, A. 2001. "The Silicon Valley-Hsinchu Connection: Technical Communtiies and Industrial Upgrading." *Berkely Planning Journal* 15 (1): 3–31.

Saxenian, A. 2002. "Silicon Valley's New Immigrant High-Growth Entrepreneurs." *Economic Development Quarterly* 16 (1): 20–31. doi:10.1177/0891242402016001003.

Saxenian, A. 2005. "From Brain Drain to Brain Circulation: Transnational Communities and Regional Upgrading in India and China." *Studies in Comparative International Development* 40 (2): 35–61. doi:10.1007/BF02686293.

Saxenian, A. 2006. *The New Argonauts: Regional Advantage in a Global Economy*. Cambridge, UK: Harvard University Press.

Schäfer, S., and S. Henn. 2018. "The Evolution of Entrepreneurial Ecosystems and the Critical Role of Migrants. A Phase-Model Based on A Study of IT Startups in the Greater Tel Aviv Area." *Cambridge Journal of Regions, Economy and Society* 11 (2): 317–333. doi:10.1093/cjres/rsy013.

Schuetz, A. 1945. "On Multiple Realities." *Philosophy and Phenomenological Research* 5 (4): 533–576. doi:10.2307/2102818.

Schwellnus, C. 2010. "Chile: Boosting Productivity Growth by Strengthening Competition, Entrepreneurship and Innovation." *785. OECD Economics Department Working Papers*.

Sepúlveda, J. P., and C. A. Bonilla. 2014. "The Factors Affecting the Risk Attitude in Entrepreneurship: Evidence from Latin America." *Applied Economics Letters* 21 (8): 573–581. doi:10.1080/13504851.2013.875104.

Sousa, C. M. P., and F. Bradley. 2006. "Cultural Distance and Psychic Distance: Two Peas in a Pod?" *Journal of International Marketing* 14 (1): 49–70. doi:10.1509/jimk.14.1.49.

Spigel, B. 2016. "Developing and Governing Entrepreneurial Ecosystems: The Structure of Entrepreneurial Support Programs in Edinburgh, Scotland." *International Journal of Innovation and Regional Development* 7 (2): 141. doi:10.1504/IJIRD.2016.077889.

Spigel, B. 2017. "The Relational Organization of Entrepreneurial Ecosystems." *Entrepreneurship Theory and Practice* 41 (1): 49–72. doi:10.1111/etap.12167.

Spigel, B., and R. Harrison. 2018. "Toward a Process Theory of Entrepreneurial Ecosystems." *Strategic Entrepreneurship Journal* 12 (1): 151–168. doi:10.1002/sej.1268.

Stam, E. 2015. "Entrepreneurial Ecosystems and Regional Policy: A Sympathetic Critique." *European Planning Studies* 23 (9): 1759–1769. doi:10.1080/09654313.2015.1061484.

Stam, E., . 2017. *Measuring Entrepreneurial Ecosystems*. Utrecht: Tjalling C. Koopmans Research Institute.

Startup Genome. 2017. *Global Startup Ecosystem Report 2017*.

Sussan, F., and Z. J. Acs. 2017. "The Digital Entrepreneurial Ecosystem." *Small Business Economics* 49: 55–73. doi:10.1007/s11187-017-9867-5.

Svejenova, S., C. Mazza, and M. Planellas. 2007. "Cooking up Change in Haute Cuisine: Ferran Adrià as an Institutional Entrepreneur." *Journal of Organizational Behavior* 28: 539–561. doi:10.1002/()1099-1379.

Tansley, A. G. 1935. "TThe Use and Abuse of Vegetational Concepts and Terms." *Ecology* 16 (3): 284–307. doi:10.2307/1930070.

Tengeh, R. K. 2016. "Entrepreneurial Resilience: The Case of Somali Grocery Shop Owners in a South African Township." *Problems and Perspectives in Management* 14 (4): 203–211. doi:10.21511/ppm.14(4-1).2016.09.

Theodoraki, C., K. Messeghem, and M. P. Rice. 2018. "A Social Capital Approach to the Development of Sustainable Entrepreneurial Ecosystems : An Explorative Study." *Small Business Economi* 51: 153–170. doi:10.1007/s11187-017-9924-0.

Thompson, T. A., J. M. Purdy, and M. J. Ventresca. 2018. "How Entrepreneurial Ecosystems Take Form: Evidence from Social Impact Initiatives in Seattle." *Strategic Entrepreneurship Journal* 12 (1): 96–116. doi:10.1002/sej.1285.

Valdez, J. 1988. "The Entrepreneurial Ecosystem: Toward a Theory of New Business Formation." In *Proceedings of the Small Business Institute Director's Association, Jude, University of Texas*. University of Texias.

Van De Ven, H. 1993. "The Development of an Infrastructure for Entrepreneurship." *Journal of Business Venturing* 8 (3): 211–230. doi:10.1016/0883-9026(93)90028-4.

Vertovec, S. 2002. "Transnational Networks and Skilled Labour Migration." *02–02. Transnational Communities Working Paper (University of Oxford, an ESRC Research Programme)*.

Vertovec, S. 2004. "Migrant Transnationalism and Modes of Transformation." *International Migration Review* 38 (3): 970–1001. doi:10.1111/j.1747-7379.2004.tb00226.x.

Yun, J. J., D. Won, K. Park, and J. Yang. 2017. "Growth of a Platform Business Model as an Entrepreneurial Ecosystem and Its Effects on Regional Development." *European Planning Studies* 25 (5): 805–826. doi:10.1080/09654313.2017.1282082.

Unhelpful help: The state of support programmes and the dynamics of entrepreneurship ecosystems in Ethiopia

Ashenafi Biru, David Gilbert ⓘ and Pia Arenius

ABSTRACT

Entrepreneurship support programmes are a major component of the entrepreneurship ecosystem. Through these programmes, stakeholders, often government-affiliated, aim to facilitate and enhance productive entrepreneurship practices within start-ups. However, the effectiveness of these support programmes is often considered in isolation from other entrepreneurship ecosystem domains, ignoring how the programmes impact the dynamics of the entrepreneurship ecosystem as a whole. This paper investigates how the structure and implementation of entrepreneurship support programmes in Ethiopia influence the entrepreneurial behaviours of firms within the ecosystem, thus extending previous research that has questioned the effectiveness of entrepreneurship support programmes in producing productive entrepreneurial ecosystems. Through a qualitative research methodology, consisting of 36 in-depth, semi-structured interviews with firm founders in the manufacturing sector in Ethiopia, we show that entrepreneurship support programmes that do not prioritize innovative and competitive firms when distributing resources, can dissuade firms from being entrepreneurial and pushing forward in the market. In the absence of competition-based resource distribution, firms focus on their survival rather than taking risks to expand their operations and this may impede the effort to create successful entrepreneurial ecosystems. Based on our findings, we offer a more pragmatic role for support programmes in creating entrepreneurial ecosystems within developing economies.

Introduction

Scholars and policy makers agree that entrepreneurship is a driving force across advanced and developing economies due to its role in facilitating sustainable economic growth through employment creation, innovation and business diversification (Dorado and Ventresca 2013; Edoho 2015). Considering this pivotal role, it is not surprising that governments and other stakeholders all over the world are proposing, formulating and implementing policies and strategies for the creation of an entrepreneurship-enabling environment. An enabling environment can unleash productive entrepreneurship, thereby accelerating a country's industrial and economic growth, as well as creating critical pillars necessary for the commercialization of innovations (Acs, Szerb, and Lloyd 2017b; Nambisan and Baron 2013). Research into entrepreneurial ecosystems has been at the forefront of the efforts exploring enabling environments and how entrepreneurship can be boosted across a wide variety of contexts (Audretsch et al. 2019).

An entrepreneurship ecosystem encompasses the coordination of interdependent actors and factors in a way that facilitates productive entrepreneurship practice within a certain location (Spigel 2017). A productive ecosystem prioritizes the agency of the entrepreneurs, inclusive leadership, high network density between the various actors in the ecosystem and ready access to relevant resources such as capital, services and talent, with a facilitating role of government in the background (Feld 2012). One of the primary factors within an entrepreneurship ecosystem is the role entrepreneurship support programmes play in fostering entrepreneurship within start-ups and small firms (Isenberg 2010; Spigel 2017). According to Autio et al. (2014), successful entrepreneurship ecosystems require many well-respected stakeholders to take an active role (or provide substantial support) in guiding entrepreneurial activities across all stages, sectors, demographics, and geographies and within an effective and well-integrated governance structure. Similarly, Spigel (2016) emphasizes that entre-preneurship support programmes run by either the government or other stakeholders are a key driving force in the creation of entrepreneurial ecosystems. Hence, governments have devoted considerable resources to developing programmes to boost entrepreneurial activity within their economies through the establishment and promotion of incubators, accelerators, activators and entrepreneurship training forums (Malecki 2018; Mason and Brown 2013).

This study seeks to understand why in Ethiopia, despite the intense efforts by governments to promote entrepreneurship, entrepreneurship supports are not yet yielding productive entrepreneurial ecosystems. While some regions have seen successful entrepreneurial ecosystems emerge, such as Silicon Valley and Boston, in the United States; Cambridge in the United Kingdom, and the Danish start-up ecosystem, other regions, especially those in developing economies have not experienced such success. Despite significant policy and investment efforts aimed at creating enabling environments to promote an entrepreneurship culture across regions, sub-Saharan African countries still maintain one of the lowest rates for start-up success and ecosystem performance (Ács et al. 2018). Reviewing the Global Start-up Ecosystems Report (2018), which lists current entrepreneurship hotspots around the world, Africa remains unrepresented. The empirical context of our study, Ethiopia, is now considered as one of the more stable countries in Africa (OECD 2013) and has relative similarity with other sub-Saharan Africa nations in terms of socio-economic status, economic growth and government policies focused on the development of entrepreneurship and micro and small enterprises (Moller and Wacker 2017). As such, this study's findings are to some extent generalizable to other sub-Saharan contexts.

By studying how the structure and governance of Ethiopia's entrepreneurship support pro-grammes impact the success of the country's entrepreneurial ecosystems, we contribute to an emerging understanding that such systems need to be examined through a broad and integrated lens. Firstly, we outline a more nuanced perspective of how entrepreneurship support programmes shape the nature of entrepreneurship ecosystems in a developing country. Although scholars and policymakers in the field of entrepreneurship have questioned the effectiveness of entrepreneurship support programmes, research on their effect on the productiveness of entrepreneurial ecosystems is limited, particularly in developing country settings (Sheriff and Muffatto 2015). Secondly, we contribute empirical evidence to assist in understanding the effectiveness of entrepreneurship support programmes in encouraging entrepreneurship in environments like Ethiopia, where the institutional settings are nascent, and the overall environment is predominantly constraining (Eyana, Masurel, and Paas 2018). Where past studies have tended to take a static approach to the study of the role of support programmes within entrepreneurial ecosystems, by largely ignoring both their origins and governance, our study focuses on these aspects and pays particular attention to the processes by which support programmes facilitate (or not), firm autonomy and viability. We argue that the structure of the Ethiopian support programmes and the way such programmes are administered may actually impede the effectiveness and level of success of the support programmes within the ecosystem. Entrepreneurship support programmes that are poorly designed and deliv-ered with little regard for the wider ecosystem may not only slow efforts to boost entrepreneurship within an ecosystem but may also bring about an ecosystem dominated by businesses that add little or no value to the economy.

Literature review

The spread of industrial clusters as drivers of industrialization

Prior to the conceptualization of the entrepreneurship ecosystem to discuss localized entrepreneurship, cluster theory was the dominant paradigm, driven by the work of Porter (1990) and others on the relationship of clusters, innovation and competitive advantage of nations. Industrial clusters have been discussed as the concentration of groups of enterprises engaged in similar activities (Porter 1998), geographically defined production (Torre 2006) and market organizations (Maskell and Lorenzen 2004). The theory has centred on the geographical proximity of similar firms under the assumption that operational closeness engenders the sharing of industry specific knowledge, creating a localized environment primed for innovation (Brekke 2015; Jaffe, Trajtenberg, and Henderson 1993). From this standpoint, industrial clusters were entrenched as the blueprint for a core economic development model, prioritizing localized industrial innovation at the sub-national level (Feldman 2014). Considering private-public partnerships as the central strategy, the 2013 UN economic report for Africa pointed to the formation of industrial clusters. The textile and apparel, leather and leather products, agro-processing, pharmaceuticals and other industries that emerged in Ethiopia since the 1990s had their foundations in such industrial clusters.

The growth of industrial clusters in developing countries, particularly in sub-Saharan Africa countries, has come hand in hand with a growing dependency on official development assistance (ODA) and charity transfers from non-government organizations. African countries are the major recipients of ODA. The 2014 UN report on trade and development noted that over the preceding decade the net ODA flowing to African countries increased from 20 USD.4 billion in 2002 to a peak of 50 USD.7 billion in 2011. While one of the purposes of ODA is to improve the business environment for investments in developing countries, empirical studies have presented mixed results on the impact of aid on investment in Africa. A study by Juselius, Framroze, and Tarp (2011) that considered 36 African countries, found a positive impact of ODA on investment in 33 of the 36 countries. In contrast, using data of 52 African countries for the period of 1996–2010, Asongu (2012) found that ODA has fuelled corruption in the African continent. Dependence on ODA has meant cluster strategies have come to focus on industries capable of bringing wealth into the region from outside. According to Mendes, Bertella, and Teixeira (2014), the industrialization policy of nations in sub-Saharan Africa has failed on account of the predominant focus on capital-intensive production processes rather than the enhancement of human capital and natural resources. The relationship of economic development efforts to the exploration of local opportunities, sustainable job creation and the cultivation of local innovation remains unclear. Hence, although scholars have argued that public policies and strategies focused on industrial clusters have created success in privileging certain sectors (Rocha and Sternberg 2005), the capitalization of internal innovation has been far less successful.

When considered in relation to entrepreneurship, the conceptual foundation of industrial clusters has only a tentative relationship with entrepreneurial activity. Cluster theory focuses on economies of scale (the ability of the ventures as a group in producing goods or services at lower cost) rather than a comprehensive comparative framework among the firms (Pitelis 2012). And though more recently, focus has begun to shift towards a view of clusters as environments that facilitate innovation and transaction activities (Li and O'Connor 2015), when applied to entrepreneurship, the emphasis on co-working spaces and social embeddedness downplays the entrepreneurs and entrepreneurial activity of the firms located in the cluster (Pitelis 2012).

Entrepreneurship ecosystems

The concept of entrepreneurial ecosystems emerged in order to reinforce the pivotal role of entrepreneurs in a geographical setting, as well as to reinforce the importance of other stakeholders and environmental factors such as policy and entrepreneurship support programmes in the creation of a conducive environment for high-growth entrepreneurship. Spilling (1996, 91) noted that entrepreneurial ecosystems are the 'complexity and diversity of actors, roles and environmental factors that interact to determine the entrepreneurial performance of a region or locality'. When functioning effectively, entrepreneurial ecosystems enhance innovation and high-growth start-ups through the facilitation of a favourable economic and social environment that surrounds and supports the entrepreneurship process (Spigel 2017). In recent years, the concept of entrepreneurial ecosystems has gained popularity due to the attention paid in the mainstream business and entrepreneurship literature to a number of prominent localized success stories (Feld 2012; Isenberg 2010), predominantly or almost exclusively found in advanced countries.

Although there are now a number of models of entrepreneurial ecosystems, the framework developed by Isenberg (2011) on *'entrepreneurship ecosystem strategy for economic development'* has emerged as a cost-effective strategy for stimulating economic prosperity and has recently received traction among scholars in entrepreneurship. In his framework, Isenberg (2011) identified six domains within the entrepreneurial system: culture, policy, finance, human capital, market, and institutional supports. These six domains comprise multiple interdependent elements that help facilitate productive entrepreneurship in a regional territory. By prioritizing the effort and entrepreneurial drive of new ventures and emphasizing the dynamic and systemic inter-relationship of multiple stakeholders, the ecosystem concept has shifted some emphasis away from cluster theory. According to Isenberg (2011), this framework may replace the concepts of industrial cluster strategies, innovation systems, knowledge economy and national competitiveness policies. The re-focus on the entrepreneur is of central importance, particularly in developing countries, where entrepreneurship is rarely celebrated (Vershinina, Woldesenbet Beta, and Murithi 2018). Facilitating the development of supportive entrepreneur-focused ecosystems helps innovative and growth-oriented entrepreneurs by, firstly, normalizing entrepreneurial activities through increasing the number of entrepreneurs, start-ups and investors visibly engaging in entrepreneurial activity (Brown and Mason 2017); and, secondly, increasing entrepreneurs' and start-ups' ability to expand and grow by providing the opportunity to draw on resources such as knowledge spillovers, networking, investment capital, and expert guidance and mentorship (Audretsch, Aldridge, and Sanders 2011).

With respect to the policy and leadership domain in the entrepreneurial ecosystem framework, the role of government and other institutional stakeholders is to facilitate the entrepreneurial activities of high-growth firms by improving the environment in which they operate (Mason and Brown 2014). In developing countries where firms fail to attain high levels of internal capability (Ngobo and Fouda 2012), Isenberg's (Isenberg 2010) concept that creating an environment that supports and facilitates the growth of entrepreneurial capabilities is especially vital. Mason and Brown (2013) also note that government and other major stakeholders need to work together to create a supportive environment for entrepreneurs in order to help them recognize market opportunities and identify ways of exploiting them. However, in the extant literature, it is not clear how government intervention can be used to successfully promote the emergence of entrepreneurial ecosystems or to stimulate the key processes of spin-offs and the emergence of entrepreneurial support in its various forms.

Entrepreneurship support programmes

Of the six domains set out in Isenberg's framework, the government is the central actor of influence in the policy domain and contributes directly to the entrepreneurship ecosystem through regulatory and other institutional initiatives. Government-led entrepreneurship support programmes are increasingly popular in developing countries, where institutional settings are still nascent, as a means to support entrepreneurs and start-ups, which in turn advance industrialization and wealth creation. Entrepreneurial support programmes share similarities; the majority are now structured around supporting entrepreneurs with a small range of business models including fee-for-service, free/rent-for-workspace, equity-for-seed investments and benevolent donations. Cancino, Bonilla, and Vergara (2015) note that entrepreneurship support programmes may play a part in encouraging entrepreneurs to start a business or to improve their business performance. Thus, considering the relevance of entrepreneurship support programmes in nurturing entrepreneurial activity, it is important that research focuses on how support programmes can drive the formation of productive entrepreneurial ecosystems (Isenberg 2010; Spigel 2016).

The extant literature presents entrepreneurship support programmes and policies as integral components in the structure of the entrepreneurial ecosystem (Doh and Kim 2014; Spigel 2016). Spigel (2016) reinforces the role of public and private organizations within the ecosystem in fostering entrepreneurship within start-ups and small firms through support programmes. Beyond the immediate impact of these support programmes on the ventures themselves, they potentially also create strong networks of entrepreneurs, investors and advisors (Feldman 2014); encourage research-intensive universities that produce new technological innovations and encourage entrepreneurs (Schaeffer and Matt 2016); and open sections of the market by lowering regulatory barriers (Ackermann 2012). These contributions help to build the momentum of entrepreneurs in the ecosystem, increasing the number of ambitious entrepreneurs by encouraging risk-taking and innovative activities and improving the survival and growth prospects of new firms through their influence on the wider institutional environment (Acs et al. 2017a, 2017b).

Though multiple studies have stressed that entrepreneurship is a local phenomena and subject to boundary and social context (Aldrich 2010; Baumol 1990), national entrepreneurship cultures across developing countries have been found to be relatively similar (Minkov and Hofstede 2012). The literature has sought to address the issue of culture (Spigel 2013) and this is a prevalent concern in countries like Ethiopia where a career as an entrepreneur is rated poorly, often seen by society as the choice of last resort (Gebremichael 2014; Lindvert, Patel, and Wincent 2017). Within these economies, government support programmes to promote entrepreneurial activities are increasingly being implemented across developing countries, and they tend to be structured and administered mainly in an effort to drive self-employment in job creation (Cho and Honorati 2013).

Recent studies have also examined the nature of entrepreneurship relative to the level of national economic development (Du and O'Connor 2018; Prieger et al. 2016; Wennekers et al. 2005). Drawing a distinction between necessity and opportunity entrepreneurship, Wennekers et al. (2005) found a U-shaped relationship between the rate of nascent entrepreneurship and the level of economic development of a country. According to their findings, low per capita income economies see high rates of necessity nascent entrepreneurship, and that the impact of this activity in terms of economic growth can be negative. However, further studies in developing economies have suggested that when the entrepreneurial activities are focused on opportunity, small entrepreneurial start-ups can play significant positive role in countries' economic advancement (Du and O'Connor 2018; Prieger et al. 2016). Prieger et al. (2016) suggested that small entrepreneurial firms with the ability to discover opportunities and willingness to take risks play a greater role in developing countries, where entrepreneurship is yet to reach its optimal level. Similarly, Du and O'Connor (2018) found a positive relationship between opportunity-driven start-ups and national-level economic efficiency. Although necessity-driven entrepreneurship could be the solution for unemployment in developing countries, if economic growth remains stagnant, entrepreneurship can become a welfare substitution (Du and O'Connor 2018).

These findings are pertinent when considering efforts to generate entrepreneurial ecosystems through support programmes. According to Sheriff and Muffatto (2015), despite the availability of policies and programmes essential for the creation of an entrepreneurship ecosystem within developing countries, the creation of self-sustaining entrepreneurship ecosystems may be hampered due to the lack of proper coordination and governance. Entrepreneurial ecosystems, as Spigel (2016) noted, are by their nature not centrally governed. In actuality, at least in their early stages, in developing countries such as Ethiopia, entrepreneurial ecosystems largely involve the participation of government, and are therefore, to a greater extent, governed centrally.

Study context

The Ethiopian business environment

According to the World Bank report (2018), real GDP growth in Ethiopia averaged 10.3 percent between 2006 and 2016, resulting in one of the fastest-growing economies globally. Like many developing countries, micro and small enterprises (MSEs) make up around 99 percent of all businesses in Ethiopia and they are increasingly being recognized not only as productive drivers of economic growth and development, but also as a means for social and political stability in the region (Ayyagari, Beck, and Demirguc-Kunt 2007; Bekele and Worku 2008a). Fostering entrepreneurship has therefore been a focus of the Ethiopian government in structuring the institutional arrangements to promote new business ventures and the overall performance of MSEs (Bekele and Worku 2008b). Despite the significant contribution of MSEs to Ethiopian economic growth, such enterprises perform poorly in terms of entrepreneurial practice (Eyana, Masurel, and Paas 2018).

In international comparisons, the Ethiopian business environment and regulatory systems stand out as unfavourable. In 2019, the World Bank ranked 190 countries on the ease of doing business; Ethiopia ranked 159. Similarly, using the GEM dataset, Gebrewolde and Rockey (2016) reported that unfavourable economic conditions, inconsistent policies, difficulty in accessing credit facilities, high costs of doing business, corruption and poor social and political attitudes towards MSEs present obstacles for Ethiopian enterprises. These problems persist, despite concerted efforts from the government to stimulate an entrepreneurial economy, and MSEs continue to be uncompetitive in the domestic and international market (Ayyagari, Demirguc-Kunt, and Maksimovic 2014). At the same time, as noted in the World Bank report, Ethiopia has made significant reforms – making it easier to start a business, by removing the need to obtain a certificate of competence for certain business types; to obtain construction permits, by reducing the time needed to obtain planning consent; and to enforce contracts, by establishing specialized benches to resolve commercial cases (World Bank 2019). Hence, we are presented an intriguing study context in Ethiopia, a low GDP economy that has experienced double digit growth for over a decade but performs poorly when measured on the ease of doing business.

Entrepreneurship support programmes and the nature of entrepreneurship in ethiopia

Ethiopia's entrepreneurship development policy aims at not only reducing poverty and creating more employment opportunities, but also nurturing entrepreneurship and laying the foundation for entrepreneurial ecosystems. This policy runs in parallel with the current Growth and Transformation Plan II (GTP II) (2015/16-2019/20), a national five-year plan created by the Ethiopian Government to advance the country's economy by achieving a projected GDP growth of 10–15% per year. Entrepreneurship is a vital component of economic growth and development and it is a major factor for the development of vibrant and innovative ventures – the core of most competitive economies (Ayyagari, Beck, and Demirguc-Kunt 2007).

The Ethiopian government's recognition of the strategic importance of promoting entrepreneurial ventures has translated into extensive support for start-ups, with the intention of enabling enterprises to contribute to the social and economic development of the nation (Assefa, Bienen, and Ciuriak 2013). The government has asserted that MSEs are the solution to accelerating the industrial transformation and enabling Ethiopia to join the middle-income countries within a short period of time (Sapovadia 2015). As such, the government affords entrepreneurship prominent attention in its efforts to create jobs, generate income, and establish a foundation for the industrialization of the nation (Assefa, Bienen, and Ciuriak 2013). Ethiopia has implemented a support policy package called 'Micro and Small Enterprises (MSEs) Graduation Programme' to promote the development of entrepreneurial ventures. The aim of the graduation programme is to assist start-ups to grow into self-sustainable and competitive businesses, usually within a timeframe of 3 to 5 years. While in the programme, the businesses benefit from access to markets; tax exemption and priority in government contracts; access to finance; access to working space, and technological support. The government has a set of size-related criteria used for administering this graduation process and has established in every local government office a steering committee to assess the readiness of the businesses to graduate.

Though support programmes have played a significant role in creating job opportunities in Ethiopia and a substantial number of start-ups, entrepreneurship still carries a social stigma (Amentie and Lalise Kumera 2016). An extensive body of research now supports the view that culture is intrinsically linked to entrepreneurial endeavours through the legitimization of the entre-preneurial process (Fayolle, Basso, and Bouchard 2010) and through the social and regulatory structures in which the entrepreneurial process is carried out (Abdi and Aulakh 2012). Based on Hofstede's (1984, 1991) well established classification framework, cultures with high individualism, low power distance, low uncertainty avoidance, and high masculinity have been found as most conducive conditions for productive entrepreneurship (Hayton, George, and Zahra 2002). The culture of Ethiopia, the context for this case study, is not overly aligned to this profile. Measured on Hofstede's original four dimensions Ethiopia's culture is categorized as masculine in motivation and intermediate in terms of uncertainty avoidance, low on individualism and high on power distance. On two of the cultural dimensions, the Ethiopian culture appears appropriately conducive to productive entrepreneurship, whereas the remaining two dimensions seem more likely to inhibit entrepreneurial activity. We note that on the two additional dimensions Hofstede later added to his classification (long-term orientation and indulgence vs self-restraint), Ethiopia has not yet been classified.

This translates to a conflicting context for entrepreneurs and small business owners in Ethiopia. Entrepreneurs are discouraged by the negative social perception and lack of community support (Brixiova and Ncube 2013). Ethiopian society at large still considers corporate jobs as the 'golden path' to success, job security and wealth, while entrepreneurship is considered by many to be a last resort. Given Ethiopia is a collectivist and family-oriented society (Hofstede 2018), entrepreneurial careers are not viewed as a feasible means for anyone wishing to lead a strong, settled family life. Paradoxically, those Ethiopian entrepreneurs who do achieve success are afforded legitimacy and community respect (Biru, Gilbert, and Arenius 2017).

Methodology

Research design

We adopted an exploratory qualitative approach in our investigation of entrepreneurs in micro and small enterprises. We engaged this approach as it allows us to seek explanation for how the structure and nature of entrepreneurship support programmes impact the dynamics of the entrepreneurial ecosystem in a developing country context. Creswell (2013) notes that qualitative data provides clear understanding of the research problem in a natural setting where the researcher collects data through open-ended questions, analyses them empirically, focuses on the meaning of participants and explains the outcomes. This assists in the interpretation and understanding of the complex reality of a given situation, and is effective in detecting intangible factors and research issues that may not be readily apparent (Richards 2014). We drew the sample for the qualitative interviews from the registry of the Ethiopian Trade and Industry Development Agency. We selected manufacturing firms from four regional ecosystems clusters in Ethiopia: Oromia; Amhara; Tigray; and Southern Nations, Nationalities and Peoples' Region (SNNP) where the majority of MSEs in the country are based as detailed by the Federal Micro and Small Enterprise Development Agency (FeMSEDA (2014). We selected the manufacturing sector due to its reputation for being an innovative, exported oriented sector at the forefront of the Ethiopian government's ambitious industrialization agenda (Shiferaw 2017). Within the sector, we selected start-up founders/operators who had been running their current business for more than three years, to ensure that they had sufficient business experience to share with us.

Data collection and analysis

We conducted 36 in-depth semi-structured interviews with start-ups in the manufacturing sector, with each interview ranging from 90 minutes to two hours. We conducted all interviews with the intention of exploring how the entrepreneurship support programmes in Ethiopia promote and/or impede the formation of functional ecosystems. As suggested by Gioia, Corley, and Hamilton (2013), we explored the issues raised during the early interviews in further interviews. We identified these emerging issues during the concurrent data collection, coding and analysis of the interview transcripts. In addition to the face-to-face interviews with entrepreneurs, we conducted an additional four interviews with experts in the graduation programme (entrepreneurship promotion agents) within the local offices. This was important for assessing whether, and in what form, the entrepreneurship support programmes enabled or constrained the productive entrepreneurial activity of start-ups in the ecosystem.

Moreover, we triangulated this data with archival data from FeMSEDA and regional offices including annual and committee reports. We analysed this archival data to obtain an understanding of the structure and governance of the support programmes within the Ethiopian context. Table 1 displays a detailed list of all data sources and Table 2 provides the data structure of our findings.

Our interpretive approach involved a process of simultaneously collecting and analysing the data, reassessing our findings and going back into the field to collect further data until we reached data saturation, thereby eliciting sufficiently detailed responses from the respondents with no additional data of relevance presenting. We recorded the interviews with the interviewees' consent and subsequently transcribed and coded the responses to identify themes and connections between themes. We analysed the data through thematic analysis following the procedures recommended by Braun and Clarke (2006) and Boyatzis (1998). We based our interpretation of interview transcripts on multiple readings of each transcript in order to capture a holistic image of participants' experiences, followed by a part-by-part interpretation of key concepts throughout each transcript. We treated each transcript as part of a larger whole, comprised of multiple transcripts. In all cases, we continuously compared the interpretations of parts to each other and to the whole. We associated our interpretations with specific words and lines within the transcripts, allowing for constant refinement of concept definitions. We integrated all codes, categories, and interpretations to demonstrate a holistic picture of the entrepreneurial ecosystem in the Ethiopian context.

Table 1. Details of data sources.

Data type	Quantity	Original Sources	Original purpose
Interviews	36 start-ups, 33.5 hours in total	Owners and operators of start-ups	Analysis for the study
Interviews	4 experts, 6.5 hours in total	Start-up development experts/ agents	Analysis for the study
Federal and regional strategic reports	237 pages	Start-ups development committees, FeMSEDA and Regional Bureau	Record keeping of the federal and regional government offices
Archival records (meeting minutes, notes, copies of speeches and memos)	Approximately 172 documents	Federal and regional committees, letters and directives to regional and local leaders	For the records of the committee members and attendees
Observation and informal talks, investigator's note from two conferences and visits to businesses	Approximately 11 hours	Written by the investigator	Analysis for the study

Table 2. Data structure: First-order codes, second order themes and aggregate dimensions based on interviews.

1st Order Concepts	2nd Order Themes	Aggregate Dimensions
• Many people I know are starting businesses. It is a kind of trend now. • At this time, it is easy to start a firm. All you need is a business idea. There are support services available to walk you through the process. • The government is encouraging me to be self-employed by providing loans, tax exemptions and a place to manufacture our products.	Emergence of new start-ups	Consequences of meritless access
• I started my business because I couldn't get salaried employment. Before it was easy to get a job in government or private companies. There are no many paid jobs out there anymore. • Many people are starting businesses until they get a corporate job. I am one of them. I am doing this because I couldn't get a job after I graduated from college. • I started my business, so I could support my family. I don't know about the future but now it is hand to mouth.	Attraction of necessity start-ups	
• I plan to stay small so that I can access support. The government supports and prioritizes only MSEs. • I tried to get all the supports the government offers. It is a huge part of our profits. • I don't want to graduate to a medium-sized firm. Graduating to medium sized firm means you have to start paying tax and interest on loans from the bank and compete with the big companies all by yourself. Who wants that?	High exploitation of the system	
• We all have to queue at the registry to get a loan. It is a kind of first come first served. • There is not special treatment or priority for innovative firms. I have so many innovate prototypes that I want to produce, but I can't get the loan on time. It is frustrating when you see un-entrepreneurial people take the resources that are supposed to be for innovative entrepreneurs.	Lack of recognition for innovative firms	
• The government provides all types of support to MSEs. Finance, training, market information etc • Political affiliation matters when gaining access to government support.it is up to the government who should be supported and who is not.	High involvement of government	Nature of stakeholder collaboration in the ecosystem
• Other organizations require government recommendations to provide support. • The processes for government and non-government support are the same.	Dependency of other stakeholders	
• Firms receive relatively similar loan terms and training. • Training is mandatory; whether you need it or not, you have to attend. • Some training we attend does not benefit our firm's performance.	Lack of demand-driven support	Structure and governance of the support programmes
• You have to bribe officials if you want fast services. If I do not pay my way through, the authorities can make me wait indefinitely. • There is unfair distribution of support by local offices. Who you know in the administration really matters when it comes to accessing government resources • If you do not pay the officials, you do not receive access to working space on time.	Corruption	
• There is no more support if you graduate to a medium-sized firm. • The government mainly supports start-ups. That's why no wants to grow.	Lack of support for medium and large sized firms	

Findings

From the outset, almost all of the participants noted the significant number of new start-ups that have been established in the past few years. Many attributed this directly to the Ethiopian government's encouraging policies. The participants echoed the general view that MSEs, and start-ups in general, are a powerful springboard for rapid economic growth. In line with the government's stated aims, participants noted the contribution of MSEs to employment, innovation and diversified business activities, and described the extent to which the government appears committed to facilitating the ideal environment for small businesses to grow and prosper. This speaks to the extent to which the government has promoted its agenda.

> The government considers the MSEs as drivers of job creation and a means to minimize the income distribution gap, to encourage competition, identify and exploit niche markets, introduce technical change and enhance productivity, and through all of these fuel economic growth. *Government agent at the federal agency, Addis Ababa*

With this common starting point, the participants' opinions of the entrepreneurship support pro-grammes and the overall entrepreneurship ecosystems largely overlapped. In the course of the interviews, we identified three main factors that describe and distinguish the current entrepreneur-ship ecosystem in the Ethiopian context: (i) the equality of access to government resources and the ramifications of this for the ecosystem; (ii) the manner in which the various stakeholders work together to deliver support and how this impacts entrepreneurs; and (iii) the manner in which the support programmes are administered and the constraining pressure this exerts on start-ups.

Merit-free access to support programmes: All entrepreneurs have equal access to start-up support resources

A common reason given by participants for their entry into the market was the pressure they felt in finding a means to survive. Entrepreneurship provided many with a practical alternative to paid employment, as there are generally limited jobs in the market, a situation that is worsening due to the growing population of educated employment-age Ethiopians (Di Nunzio 2015). With Ethiopia's higher education system expanding extensively in the last ten years, a record-level of university graduates have entered the job market. The overall number of tertiary students in both public and private institutions increased by more than 2,000 percent, from 34,000 in 1991 to 757,000 in 2014, per UIS data. As the experiences of multiple participants describe, the corporate market is not growing fast enough to absorb the employable workforce.

> After graduation from college, I was desperate to find a job and get settled in life, but jobs were nowhere to be found. I became a cigarette, khat and alcohol addict and unfortunately, I ended up in prison. Although I came back home empty handed, while I was in prison, I received vocational training in fashion design and sewing. At that time, I was aware of the government's initiative to support anyone who wants to start a business by providing them with workplace sheds and other support services like money to set up and train. So, I immediately jumped onto the wagon and here I am now a business owner. *Start-up owner, Oromia region*

Many participants went further and attributed their decision to become one of the many new start-ups in the market to the availability of the government support itself. These participants noted that starting a business represented one of the few feasible means of income-generation for the country's youth. Participants frequently remarked how the government entrepreneurship support pro-grammes facilitated their jump into the small business world: a participant from Tigray started her house appliance business so that she could afford to raise her young sister and support her sick mother; a participant from Oromia established an app developing and repair of mobile devices firm to generate income after graduating from university. Multiple participants made mention that their foray into business was not their intended path and many still see it as a stepping stone or stop-gap till they can secure a corporate or government position. In the view of many of the participants, self-employment provides a certain degree of social legitimacy while they work towards their ultimate aim of a corporate job.

> I was hoping to get a nice job and help my parents, once I graduated from university, but I was not lucky. I have a degree in engineering but no job or money, and it was everyone's hope that I would be taking care of my

sibling and my parents. So, the only option I had was to start a small manufacturing business. It was not hard to start as the government offered us operating capital, training and a working space. Although, being an entrepreneur was not my dream job and I am still looking for a nice job, I am doing great. I'm happy that the government creates a job for us. *Start-up co-founder, Amhara region*

This proliferation of necessity entrepreneurs was also related, in a more general sense, by participants who identified as opportunity driven-entrepreneurs; a participant from Tigray, whose cement manufacturing business was beginning to gain traction noted that he was surrounded by small business owners who had no intention to grow and were satisfied with their access to the government's coffers.

The equal access to support had many of our interviewees, including the experts in the field, professing scepticism as to whether the entrepreneurship support programmes attracted the 'best and the brightest' into entrepreneurial ventures. Multiple participants criticized the government for focusing on the quantity rather than the quality of start-ups.

Although I appreciate what the government is doing to support us and help us to grow, it is discouraging when you see people with no interest in doing business and start-ups with no intention to grow, stay in business comfortably because they manage to piggyback on the government support programmes. *Small business owner, Tigray region*

The impact of flooding the ecosystem with what could broadly be described as non-entrepreneurial start-ups, is being felt by those start-ups seeking to grow and be successful. One participant from SNNP region was concerned by the intense competition with other firms to access the government support and cited difficulty in competing for financial loans, as impeding her ambition to achieve high growth and to go global with her textile business. Her frustration stemmed from the way the government provides financial credit to firms without having any specific criteria, which she believed robs her high-performing business of the advantage it would have were firms required to compete on innovative or growth-oriented grounds. She felt resources are being given over to business owners who only seek government credit as a form of temporary income, which effectively drains the funds that she could be putting towards creating high-quality garments to meet the demands of her growing domestic and foreign customer base.

Multiple participants stressed their desire for a competitive engagement model. Many recognized that the government's intention to foster start-up innovation, vertical growth and eventual market competition has been the driving force behind the MSE graduation programme since its instigation in 2006, but most agreed that this goal has, as yet, not been achieved. In evaluating the current state of the support programmes, the participants gave numerous examples of how the support programmes fail to recognize and reward start-ups that invest their efforts in innovation and entrepreneurial activity. Those participants who did not already see this happening, predicted its impending effect.

With the current rapid advancement of technology, the market requires agile, innovative and risk-taking start-ups. If the government keeps treating everyone equally without prioritizing the most innovative and entrepreneurial start-ups when providing financial access and technical support, then I think the programme will become a hoarding place for unproductive start-ups and this will undermine the creative and innovative enterprises. *Start-up founder, Oromia region*

The frustration voiced by many participants at the government's equal allocation of support regularly tended towards resignation. This discouragement with the system went hand in hand with a concern that non-entrepreneurial practices are gradually being legitimized. The provision of unrestricted support appeared to be a disincentive to entrepreneurial activity and favour those firms that aim to be profitable through accessing support without any growth intention. One participant explicitly detailed how this approach is inhibiting the entrepreneurial nature of the ecosystem by creating an environment where new start-ups are pressured into mimicking the strategies of unproductive firms around them.

One of the first things you need to know when you're starting out is how other firms run their business. In addition to being legally compliant, as a small business owner, you are very curious to learn the tricks others use in business to be more profitable. One of the things people in the business will tell you is how to take advantage of the support programmes. *Small business owner, Amhara region*

Participants who self-identified as entrepreneurs eagerly put forward plans favouring competitiveness, noting that reallocating resources to innovative and potentially high-growth firms could help their firms to be more specialized and more focused on their core competencies. An entrepreneur in traditional Ethiopian textile designs from Tigray suggested she would use capital to access export chains; a metal and wood work entrepreneur from SNNP region was competing for a grant to build a machine to create unique designs; and a food processing entrepreneur from Tigray region was struggling to secure funding which would allow her to produce a variety of traditional food ingredients. Interestingly, many participants linked their propositions back to the government's entrepreneurship building goals of job creation and expanded industrialization. The government's apparent inability to capitalize on this goal-oriented business planning was a major source of frustration among the entrepreneurs.

Imbalance of actors: Centralization and its impacts on the collaboration of stakeholders within the ecosystem

The issue of non-competitive access to government support programmes is exacerbated by the centralization of governance in Ethiopia. Participants related their experiences of government interaction that reinforces the government as the primary point of control for entrepreneurship support. Participant experiences ranged from having to deal with single departments for multiple requirements to meeting resistance on aspects of their business process that they felt should fall outside the purview of the government. For example, a participant from Tigray region pointed out how the inefficient bureaucracy in the local government offices had become an obstacle to the effective management of the business, and in doing so described the reach of the government's responsibilities.

The people in the local agencies are overloaded with many things and because of this they fail to implement the policies properly. It is the local office that processes the business registrations, facilitates business training, processes business loan applications, and follows-up on loan applications and repayments. To get one thing done, it takes a long time and with this situation, it is very difficult for us to grow, let alone to accelerate the industrial transformation of the country. *Small business owner, Tigray region*

It is interesting to note that participants rarely spoke of actors other than the government in the entrepreneurship ecosystem. When prompted, participants described the reasons why they could not obtain resources from other alternative sources such as universities, microfinance institutions, international projects (e.g. UNIIDO) and other non-profit organizations that support entrepreneurship development in the country. Some participants reported that these secondary stakeholders were passive and did not take the initiative in supporting entrepreneurs. In fact, many participants declared that other stakeholders avoided undertaking independent action in the entrepreneurship field and only provided support in line with government directives. In some situations, participants described gatekeeper processes on the part of the government. A small business owner from Amhara region described a situation where she was keen to access support offered to her business venture, which would have meant she could effect a radical change to make a sustainable business model. As part of the application process, she was required to obtain a recommendation from the local authorities in order to access the resources from the Canadian-based organization. Many participants described how this process is used by the government to enforce broadened access to resources, to the point that innovative firms are no longer prioritized since local authorities give a recommendation letter to anyone who wants to access resources from non-government stakeholders. A small business entrepreneur from SSNP described how this process operates on a national scale:

> A year ago, a Canadian based organization announced a financial credit for small businesses with feasible and innovative business plans. The requirement was a business plan and a recommendation letter from the regional micro and small business development agency. It was a good opportunity for us because we are in the furniture business and we have some innovative designs that we want to manufacture to boost customer demand. We submitted our application along with many other firms but during the process they changed their original requirements because the Ethiopian government asked them to accommodate as many firms as possible. Ultimately, they ended up offering Birr 5000 –10,000 ($190-$380) for all the applicants regardless of the innovativeness and feasibility of their business plan. We did not accept the credit because it was 20 times less than what we applied for and that amount of money would not have made any change at all. *Small business owner, SNNP*

We also learnt from our participants' accounts that stakeholders, such as financial institutions and universities, were unwilling to prioritize innovative, risk-taking firms in their provision of financial and technical support without government surety. Without the government's acknowledgement that it would bear responsibility for the start-ups failure to repay loans or budget for the universities to provided technical support, support was not forthcoming. This reticence was cited by some participants as a reason for their decreasing motivation to pursue their more innovative business projects.

Structure and governance of the entrepreneurship support programmes

In Ethiopia, the government is the primary stakeholder in all entrepreneurship development. Our review of archival data from FeMSEDA confirms that, in line with the entrepreneurship development policy, Ethiopia now boasts strong concentrations of start-ups in the main cities of four major regions. These are the regions represented in our sample of participating founders and business owners, Amhara, Oromia, Tigray and SSNP. As described by our participants, the delegation of entrepreneurship development responsibilities to the regional governments has seen the government take on an expansive role in these ecosystems. The government, FeMSEDA, distributed more than 150 USD million USD in aid and grants to start-ups in 2015–16, with a particular focus on the manufacturing sector (FeMSEDA 2017). Our participants accessed this support through dozens of schemes that are run mainly by the regional agencies. Some of these support programmes offer generic guidance for entrepreneurs in all sectors while others provide targeted support for enterprise in government priority sectors.

Training and skill development are a key focus of government support programmes. Despite the government's effort to provide different support packages to support the start-ups in their entrepreneurial activity, the participants appeared to doubt the merits of the type of resources and training they had been offered. They felt that they were offered non-relevant training. Participants described instances where the courses provided by the government were delivered on a mass scale, which they suggested was for the sake of economies of scale. Overall, the participants tended to view the training programmes as a waste of time and resources, as their 'one-size-fits-all' design and the mandatory attendance requirement were not something they appreciated.

> My firm received a letter of invitation from the MSE development agency to attend a training programme about 'book keeping' for two consecutive days, I called the office and told them I have a diploma in accounting and I have adequate know-how on how to maintain my firm's books. But, they said it was mandatory training for all start-ups in the city and if I did not attend the training, they would not send my loan application to the microfinance office for further processing. *Entrepreneur, Oromia region*

Participants describe duplication and inefficiency across a range of support programmes. A handicraft producer from Tigray region was forced into accepting government-purchased materials, which she did not require; an entrepreneur from SNNP described the microfinance department's inability to structure a loan to suit her actual needs; and another entrepreneur from Amhara region detailed his struggle with the government's insistence that he has to participate in meetings that have nothing to do with his business activities.

Many participants considered that the lack of support for medium and large sized firms discourages small businesses from growing. FeMSEDA archival data confirms that while the government aims to graduate more than 10% of start-ups every year, so far only 1% of start-ups each year have actually graduated from the programme. Many of the participants reported that they do not want to graduate to independence for fear that they might lose the government support. Start-ups perceived the graduation programme as a safe zone, a place to avoid business failure, lighten competition and to more easily access government support.

> To be honest, we exceeded the graduation criteria two years ago, but we preferred to stay as a small enterprise. It might seem a bit selfish that I still get some support from the government even though my business is doing great. I am so afraid we will eventually lose the business if we graduate and the government support ends. I know many firms which graduated to medium sized level, but they really regret it because it is very hard to get resources on your own. *Entrepreneur, Tigray region*

Participants highlighted the aims of the support programmes as a rationale for the instigation of a competitive system of distribution; many also extended this to take in the enforcement of graduating criteria so that the start-ups accessing resources are actually start-ups. Many participants noted that the government's support for firms that are not contributing to the overall entrepreneurship ecosystem was creating a false economy.

> We are a poor country and the government cannot afford to finance every individual who wants to start a business. I strongly believe that the country will be better off with few effective entrepreneurial start-ups rather than with thousands of firms which rely on the government support for their survival. The moment you stop the support, they will be out of business, we will be back to zero growth and unemployment will be rampant. *Entrepreneur, Amhara region*

While some of the participants detailed how the support programme provides them with the opportunity to build business capabilities and financial potential before they are exposed to heightened market competition from larger firms, many others noted the programmes' lack of flexibility once start-ups matured. A number of participants linked this lack of post-start-up support to the government's focus on employment creation, which they saw as being at odds with market sustainability.

> When we started our business, the government gave us special attention and provided us with technical and financial support. Under the graduation programme, we were nurtured and trained very well. But, things are getting messy and it is now very difficult to access these supports on time, as the government tries to accommodate everyone. *Start-up founder, Tigray region*

With little incentive to grow, many participants repeatedly returned to the fact that the government's entrepreneurship support programme does not appear to be governed in a way that replicates the necessary environment to foster entrepreneurship.

Discussion

In this study, we argue that understanding how entrepreneurship support programmes in Ethiopia impact the dynamics of the entrepreneurial ecosystem provides insights into why the country, and potentially other sub-Saharan African countries, struggle to establish entrepreneurial ecosystems that promote productive entrepreneurship. We have adopted the *Institutional Analysis and Development framework (IAD)* introduced by Ostrom (2011, Ostrom 1999) to conceptualize the impact of entrepreneurship support programmes on the overall entrepreneurship ecosystem dynamics in the case of Ethiopia (Figure 1). The IAD framework focuses on the environmental context, the nature of interactions and outcomes generated by actors in particular decision-making settings (Ostrom 2011). Considering the basic characteristics of actors' interdependence and their interaction when administering and implementing entrepreneurship support programmes helps us to understand how the nature and structure of the support programmes impact the overall

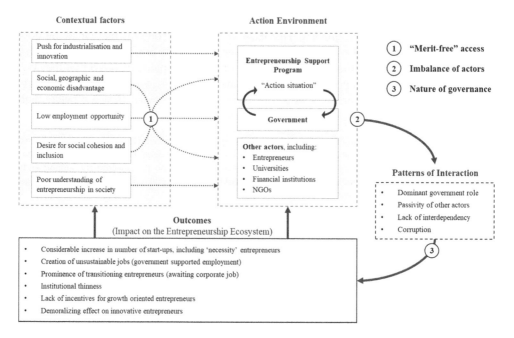

Figure 1. The nature of entrepreneurship ecosystem as a result of stakeholder's interaction dynamics in the support programme.

ecosystem. We draw this framework from economics and policy literature, where comparable contexts are discussed, and institutional analysts often refer to dysfunctional situations similar to those presented in our context (Adam and O'Connell 1999; Ostrom 2011). Similar to our context, scholars utilizing this framework argue that such problems or dysfunctionality in actors' interaction may generate counter-intentional and counterproductive outcomes for the actors within them and for others affected by them; in our case, entrepreneurs or their ventures. This cycle is therefore useful for guiding our discussion concerning the relationship between the key insights of our study.

The first insight of our study concerns the context of the entrepreneurial ecosystem. Our findings point to the existence of merit-free access to support. This is an outcome of the government's interest in achieving broad social and economic goals via the entrepreneurship support pro-grammes. The desire to improve economic growth and accelerate job creation by facilitating entrepreneurship and innovation has been a common theme of policy in developing countries like Ethiopia, that have high rates of unemployment and are attempting to catch-up to the devel-oped economies (Moller and Wacker 2017). However, the underlying motivations for establishing entrepreneurship support programmes in Ethiopia are, according to our findings, much broader and include desires (i) to enhance innovation and the industrial transformation process of the country, (ii) to address social, geographical and economic disadvantage across the society, (iii) to facilitate job creation, (iv) to enhance social cohesion and inclusion and (v) to reorient society's attitudes regard-ing the desirability of founding and growing a start-up business. Of these various contextual factors, three (ii, iii and iv) have a clear impact on the government's decision to structure their entrepreneur-ship support programme to be a 'merit-free access' support programmes that can be accessed by all type of individuals involved in start-up activities.

According to the IAD framework, the entrepreneurship support programme is impacted by both the contexts within which it has been developed, as discussed before, and the interaction of the stakeholders (actors) putting it into practice. This engagement takes place in what Ostrom (2002, 2011) conceived as the 'action situation', where all the stakeholders interact in multiple fields, including policy, finance, training, marketing and other aspects where the stakeholders seek to solve the common problem to hand. Our findings revealed that there is an imbalance of actors' roles, with the Ethiopian government having a dominant presence in most aspects of the entrepreneurship support programme. While entrepreneurship support programmes do not create an entrepreneurial ecosystem by themselves, they are often the heart of an entrepreneurial ecosystem by facilitating new start-ups to overcome their obstacles such as lack of resources, capabilities, financing and access to market (Brown and Mason 2017; Stam and Spigel 2016). However, the diffuse nature of power across the entrepreneurial activities makes the way support programmes are administered and implemented a critical issue. Spigel (2016) notes that while government support is critical in building entrepreneurial ecosystems, governments cannot determine and direct how entrepreneurs act about establishing and operating a business nor can it dictate entrepreneurs' behaviours towards risk and investment. Rather, scholars (see, e.g. Amezcua et al. 2013) argue that support programmes should be administered and implemented within existing social frameworks and in collaboration with other stakeholders, and be mainly entrepreneur-led.

According to Brown and Mason (2017), patterns of interaction within successful entrepreneurship ecosystems assume actors are both active and are able to compromise in situations where the nature of interaction does not satisfy all actors involved. In the Ethiopian case, however, of these stakeholders, the government is the instigator and primary stakeholder of the support programme as it provides the full-fledged financial and technical support. Other stakeholders have lesser roles and act at the direction of the government when participating in the entrepreneurship support programme. As a result, the patterns of interaction between the stakeholders appear to be dependent on one dominant stakeholder (government), with all other stakeholders' passive or dependent to various degrees. This has impacted the way in which the support programme is structured and the governance and operation of the entrepreneurial ecosystem. Within the support programme, entrepreneurs note that the distribution of support services is dependent on bribes and cronyism, and that the support that is more readily accessed is not fit for purpose. Beyond the support programme, there is little support offered for 'graduating' firms, which appears to create a reticence on the part of the entrepreneurs to grow beyond the bounds of the support programmes.

We devote the remainder of this discussion to the impacts the Ethiopian support programme structure has on the overall entrepreneurial ecosystem, closing the cycle presented above. We focus our discussion on those outcomes raised by our respondents as impacting on their entrepreneurial performance: (i) the prevalence of necessity entrepreneurs in the ecosystem; (ii) the lack of institutional thickness; and (iii) the lack of focus on high performing entrepreneurs. We explain how these outcomes have shaped the entrepreneurial ecosystem in Ethiopia and inform our observations with the current literature.

The prevalence of necessity entrepreneurs. Although the prioritization of the job creation aspect of entrepreneurship is important, given the country's growing youth population and the limited availability of jobs in corporate and government institutions, the resulting impact of this singular focus is producing an ecosystem that is non-entrepreneurial in nature. The ongoing and considerable investment in the support programmes to help new entrepreneurs create new self-employment ventures has seen the ecosystem become overcrowded with individuals who just want to start a business as a means of employment, either as a stepping stone until they get a job in the corporate world or out of necessity as a means to survive. These entrepreneurs have little intention of growing their venture, and start-ups with entrepreneurial intentions struggle to scale up in an overcrowded landscape. So, while the current ecosystem shaped via the support programmes increases the number of start-ups in the short term, our results suggest current practices are not achieving sustainable entrepreneurship. Primarily this is due to the nature of the start-ups encouraged into the ecosystem under the programme. Our evidence indicates that many firm owners start their venture not because they have the interest or intention to carry out business activities and entrepreneurship, but because of the support the government is providing. The life span of such ventures will therefore be largely determined by the duration of the support programmes.

Our findings align with previous studies that focus on ecosystem performance. Stam (2015) noted that entrepreneurial ecosystems should produce innovative and high-growth firms. Similarly,

Henrekson and Sanandaji (2014) suggested, to strengthen entrepreneurial ecosystems, the focus should be beyond the traditional measures such as self-employment and new business formation. As the support programmes are not designed to be accessible forever, we argue that many of these enterprises may weaken and sustainability of jobs may erode should the policy to continuously support the start-ups change. We found that the resulting ecosystem was marked by a high level of dependency, in conflict with the expectation that entrepreneurs should retain the agency to develop and lead the ecosystem, while the government supports and facilitates from the background (Spigel 2016; Stam and Spigel 2016).

Lack of institutional thickness. In Ethiopia, as in many developing economies around the world, entrepreneurs face institutional arrangements that are absent or weak (Mair and Marti 2009; Peng 2003) and limited access to resources or alternative sources of finance. Thus, government support programmes have become the major source of resources that entrepreneurs require. In line with this, we found that the centralization of government control over the design and implementation of the entrepreneurship support programme has seen the government taking on multiple roles within the ecosystem. These roles extend from encouraging people to form a business, directing training, creating financial and marketing access and offering tax exemptions, with little or no collaboration with other actors and agents in the ecosystem. Actors such as universities and financial institutions wait for direction from the government with regards to how to support the start-ups and promote entrepreneurship. In creating a productive entrepreneurial ecosystem, institutional thickness, which refers to the high level of interaction and collaboration among stakeholders or agents within the ecosystem, is vital (Spigel 2016). Although the concept of institutional thickness was introduced via early thinking on the clusters within a globalized economy by Amin and Thrift (1995), the entrepreneurial ecosystem approach literature has adopted the concept of institutional thickness to emphasize the interdependence between actors and factors (Acs et al. 2017b). Embracing this notion, scholars (see, e.g. Audretsch et al. 2019; Mason and Brown 2014; Spigel 2017; Stam 2015) argue that successful ecosystems are not defined by high rates of start-ups but rather by the quality of the interactions between actors and factors. It is these interactions that create supportive regional environments able to increase the competitiveness of new ventures.

In contrast, we found that most of the start-ups in the graduation programmes depend largely on government contributions for their business survival. These government-controlled contributions include access to information, marketing, finance and even means of training and other human capital development. While these programmes are a way to channel resources and guidance to entrepreneurs, they do not in and of themselves establish an entrepreneurial ecosystem. Stam and Spigel (2016) suggest that beyond the quantity of support programmes, establishing coordinated connections between support programmes organized by government and other agents in the ecosystem can enhance institutional thickness and thereby help preserve the entrepreneurs' competitive advantage. The support programme cannot provide all the resources and support start-ups need, especially as the firms progress through various entrepreneurial pathways. Rather, the support options available to firms need to come through collaboration with other actors in the market. Stronger stakeholder links foster institutional thickness and constitute an enabling business environment (Aidis, Estrin, and Mickiewicz 2008).

Demotivation of high potential entrepreneurs. The lack of attention paid to innovative and high-growth firms pushes the firms to compete for the support offered by the government and other institutions, such as universities, and discourages entrepreneurs from pursuing innovation. Entrepreneurs witnessing the negative consequences of entrepreneurship practice in their environment (dependency, remaining micro or small for a long period, lack of recognition for innovation and creativity, corrupt behaviours of entrepreneurs without being held accountable etc.), experience decrease in their entrepreneurial ambition. The findings from this study suggest a more focused entrepreneurship support approach that looks beyond the employment-drive of increasing the number of start-ups and embraces and prioritizes innovative and high-growth entrepreneurial ventures. This suggestion is made in line with scholars who have theorized that support programmes need to focus on highly innovative entrepreneurship that facilitates the foundation of a strong entrepreneurial culture and preserves the attractiveness of the ecosystem as a place for vibrant entrepreneurs (Acs, Szerb, and Lloyd 2017b; Audretsch and Belitski 2017; Kantis and Federico 2012; Voelker 2012). Similarly, Isenberg (2010) suggests, in discussing the concept of the entrepreneurial ecosystem, public leaders should favour high-potential entrepreneurs in building successful entrepreneurial ecosystems. Supporting studies show that while high-growth firms contribute to a large share of gross jobs gained (Davidsson and Delmar 2006), they are also powerful engines of job and output growth, and create positive spillovers for other businesses along the value chain (Grover, Medvedev, and Olafsen 2018).

Given the economic capacity of Ethiopia and the limited available resources, we argue that a competency-based support approach is necessary to support innovative and high-growth ventures at all stages of development. Based on their findings of a U-shaped relationship between a country's level of economic development and its rate of entrepreneurial dynamics, Wennekers et al. (2005) suggested that developing countries are better off focusing on economic efficiency by investing in large businesses and fostering foreign investment, whereas improving incentive structures for start-ups is a promising public policy approach for advanced nations. However, we argue that, considering Ethiopia has been experiencing rapid economic growth, the country may benefit more by focusing resources on innovative and growth-oriented firms. Our argument is consistent with findings of recent studies suggesting that developing countries should focus on promoting more innovative start-ups (Du and O'Connor 2018; Prieger et al. 2016). In particular, Du and O'Connor (2018) suggested that government emphasis on increasing the number of start-ups by implementing 'race to the bottom' policy without a focus on innovate and opportunity-driven entrepreneurship may impede the improvement of country level economic efficiency. Considering this together with our findings, we contend that prioritizing innovative and high-growth entrepreneurs may increase the number of jobs generated within the country (in line with the goals of the government's support programmes), with the additional benefit that these jobs will no longer be directly dependent on government support.

We also seek to reinforce the role of the entrepreneur. As noted previously, it is difficult to create entrepreneurial ecosystems through the support programmes in isolation, especially when the role of the entrepreneurial actors themselves is not emphasized. Pervasive top-down governance goes against the systemic nature of the entrepreneurship ecosystem and undermines, and in some instances overrides, the role of other important stakeholders in the ecosystem. Responsibility for the creation of an entrepreneurial ecosystem sits with multiple actors; entrepreneurs themselves are responsible for implementing entrepreneurial business operations. Other actors, such as government agencies, can support start-ups in their business activity, but these actors cannot offer entrepreneurial passion and interest. In creating successful entrepreneurial ecosystems, it may be necessary for the government to be less interventionist – more a facilitator than a manager. Innovative and growth-oriented firms are inherently risky and typically unique (Mason and Brown 2013). Supporting such firms to succeed is more about eliminating obstacles to their growth such as unfair taxation, cumbersome red tape, lack of skilled employees and investment capital, anti-competitive practices, or lack of access to markets. This may provide the opportunity for local success stories to become celebrated role models for others and facilitate pathways to build more productive entrepreneurial ecosystems (Mason and Brown 2014).

More resources and support cannot bring about an effective entrepreneurial ecosystem without the entrepreneurs' aspiration to grow and take more entrepreneurial pathways (innovative, risky and proactive). Isenberg (2010) argues that flooding the system with too much easy money, such as government grants, may inhibit the success of any entrepreneurship ecosystem. The government, if it wants to bring about a more entrepreneurial ecosystem, may need to disrupt the current patterns of interaction and to incentivize (rather than subsidize) entrepreneurs. What is important is to encourage firms that can sustain their own growth as much as possible before seeking additional support from the government or other stakeholders (Audretsch et al. 2019; Isenberg 2010). We note that in the absence of competitive-based resource distribution, firms often revert to a survival-focused mode. Thus, until a support programme framework that encourages and rewards firms for being innovative and competitive is developed, Ethiopia's entrepreneurial ecosystem may struggle to flourish.

Implications and further research

Our study has empirically examined entrepreneurial ecosystems through the impact of entrepreneurial support programmes. As a contribution to theory development of entrepreneurial ecosystems, we shed light on an example of how entrepreneurship support programmes developed to foster entrepreneurship can have unintended consequences within the overall entrepreneurial dynamics due to their governance and structure. We observed that when government support programmes are structured and administered with the intent of increasing the number of start-ups as a means to reduce unemployment, they discourage entrepreneurial firms from pursuing innovative and growth-oriented pathways and impede the development of successful entrepreneurial ecosystems. Whilst our context of Ethiopia provided a fruitful ground for study, the gap between theory and practice is evident. With respect to the applicability of this case study to wider contexts, while we acknowledge context will matter, we would expect future research teams to encounter comparable phenomena in environments displaying similar cultural dimensions (high power distance, collectivist, masculine societies). For instance, while cultural and formal institutional differences separate the sub-Saharan Africa nations, each has substantial challenges characterized by the lack of well-established entrepreneurship ecosystems (Sheriff and Muffatto 2015).

Our study opens up several avenues for future research. First, we have shown that government support programmes that aim to address unemployment rather than the proliferation of high-growth start-ups may impede the effort to build entrepreneurial ecosystems that can sustain themselves and add value to the economy. Consistent with our findings, research on entrepreneurial ecosystems has suggested that government and non-government support services should focus and prioritize high-growth start-ups, claiming that ambitious and high potential entrepreneurial ventures are an important source of innovation, productivity growth, and employment (Isenberg 2010; Mason and Brown 2014; Nylund and Cohen 2017). Taken together, we have shown that when support services predominantly focus on self-employment, they may attract individuals with little or no entrepreneurial intention to launch business ventures, thus diminishing access to the pool of resources available for entrepreneurs. This appears to create an ecosystem dominated by inefficient and unproductive businesses with little value to offer. Moreover, in our study, we provide some evidence of how equal treatment of entrepreneurs with no consideration for their innovativeness and growth potential, actually discourages entrepreneurs from engaging in innovative, risky and proactive business activities. This effectively impedes the programme's efforts to build entrepreneurial ecosystems despite their intended goals. Addressing these issues will require a longitudinal approach that explores how employment-oriented support programmes shape the overall entrepreneurship ecosystems in the region. Our results should not be viewed as advocating a reduction in government efforts to promote self-employment policies. Rather, we suggest that support programmes would be more effective in promoting entrepreneurial ecosystems by prioritizing innovative and growth-oriented firms.

In addition to this, though beyond the purview of this study, the government's role in buttressing the broader economy could be considered. The lack of support for medium to large sized firms (in comparison to the support provided to MSEs) was raised by the respondents in our study and may be a constraining factor in firms deciding to stay small (and protected). If firms are to be incentivized to expand beyond the confines of the government's direct support, some form of economic concession may be necessary to further smooth this transition. More empirical research is necessary to evaluate if the current government-led support programmes are effective in creating and sustaining successful entrepreneurial ecosystems across the country over the medium to long term. Further research may examine the connections between entrepreneurship support programmes and the extent to which the aim to form a productive entrepreneurial ecosystem is shared by other important stakeholders. Future research may also focus on how entrepreneur-led ecosystems can be fostered and how entrepreneurial ventures can work with support programmes led by government and non-government organizations in order to develop their skills, extend their networks and obtain resources. This may provide critical insights into the overall role of entrepreneurship support programmes in shaping vibrant, high-value and self-supporting entrepreneurial ecosystems.

Disclosure Statement

No potential conflict of interest was reported by the authors.

ORCID

David Gilbert (iD) http://orcid.org/0000-0003-0586-8733

References

Abdi, M., and P. S. Aulakh. 2012. "Do Country-level Institutional Frameworks and Interfirm Governance Arrangements Substitute or Complement in International Business Relationships?" *Journal of International Business Studies* 43 (5): 477–497. doi:10.1057/jibs.2012.11.

Ackermann, S. 2012. *Are Small Firms Important? Their Role and Impact*. New York: Springer Science & Business Media.

Acs, Z. J., E. Stam, D. B. Audretsch, and A. O'Connor. 2017a. "The Lineages of the Entrepreneurial Ecosystem Approach." *Small Business Economics* 49 (1): 1–10. doi:10.1007/s11187-017-9864-8.

Acs, Z. J., L. Szerb, and A. Lloyd. 2017b. "Enhancing Entrepreneurial Ecosystems: A GEI Approach to Entrepreneurship Policy." In *Global Entrepreneurship and Development Index 2017*, 81–91. Springer.

Ács, Z. J., L. Szerb, E. Lafuente, and A. Lloyd. 2018. "What Can We Do to Improve the Entrepreneurial Ecosystem?" In *Global Entrepreneurship and Development Index 2018*, 55–63. Switzerland: Springer Nature.doi.org/10.1007/978-3-030-03279-1_5.

Adam, C. S., and S. A. O'Connell. 1999. *Aid, Taxation, and Development: Analytical Perspectives on Aid Effectiveness in Sub-Saharan Africa*. Washington, DC: World Bank.

Aidis, R., S. Estrin, and T. Mickiewicz. 2008. "Institutions and Entrepreneurship Development in Russia: A Comparative Perspective." *Journal of Business Venturing* 23 (6): 656–672. doi:10.1016/j.jbusvent.2008.01.005.

Aldrich, E. H. 2010. "Beam Me Up, Scott(ie)! Institutional Theorists' Struggles with the Emergent Nature of Entrepreneurship." *Research in the Sociology of Work* 21 (1): 329–364.

Amentie, E. N., and C. Lalise Kumera. 2016. "The Effects of Firms Characteristics on the Growth of Medium and Small Business in Developing Country (Case Study Ethiopia)." *Global Journal of Management and Business Research* 16: 6.

Amezcua, A. S., M. G. Grimes, S. W. Bradley, and J. Wiklund. 2013. "Organizational Sponsorship and Founding Environments: A Contingency View on the Survival of Business-incubated Firms, 1994–2007." *Academy of Management Journal* 56 (6): 1628–1654. doi:10.5465/amj.2011.0652.

Amin, A., and N. Thrift. 1995. "Globalisation, Institutional 'Thickness' and the Local Economy." In *Managing Cities: The New Urban Context*, edited by P. Healey, S. Cameron, S. Davoudi, S. Graham, and A. Madani-Pour, 91–108. Chichester: New Urban Context John Wiley & Sons.

Asongu, S. 2012. "On the Effect of Foreign Aid on Corruption." *Economics Bulletin* 32 (3): 2174–2180.

Assefa, H., D. Bienen, and D. Ciuriak. 2013. "Ethiopia's Investment Prospects: A Sectoral Overview." *African Review of Economics and Finance* 4 (2): 203–246.

Audretsch, D. B., J. A. Cunningham, D. F. Kuratko, E. E. Lehmann, and M. Menter. 2019. "Entrepreneurial Ecosystems: Economic, Technological, and Societal Impacts." *The Journal of Technology Transfer* 44 (2): 313–325.

Audretsch, D. B., and M. Belitski. 2017. "Entrepreneurial Ecosystems in Cities: Establishing the Framework Conditions." *The Journal of Technology Transfer* 42 (5): 1030–1051. doi:10.1007/s10961-016-9473-8.

Audretsch, D. B., T. T. Aldridge, and M. Sanders. 2011. "Social Capital Building and New Business Formation: A Case Study in Silicon Valley." *International Small Business Journal* 29 (2): 152–169. doi:10.1177/0266242610391939.

Autio, E., M. Kenney, P. Mustar, D. Siegel, and M. Wright. 2014. "Entrepreneurial Innovation: The Importance of Context." *Research Policy* 43 (7): 1097–1108. doi:10.1016/j.respol.2014.01.015.

Ayyagari, M., A. Demirguc-Kunt, and V. Maksimovic. 2014. "Who Creates Jobs in Developing Countries?" *Small Business Economics* 43 (1): 75–99. doi:10.1007/s11187-014-9549-5.

Ayyagari, M., T. Beck, and A. Demirguc-Kunt. 2007. "Small and Medium Enterprises across the Globe." *Small Business Economics* 29 (4): 415–434. doi:10.1007/s11187-006-9002-5.

Baumol, W. J. 1990. "Entrepreneurship: Productive, Unproductive, and Destructive." *Journal of Business Venturing* 11: 3–22. doi:10.1016/0883-9026(94)00014-X.

Bekele, E., and Z. Worku. 2008a. "Factors that Affect the Long-Term Survival of Micro, Small and Medium Enterprises in Ethiopia." *South African Journal of Economics* 76 (3): 548–568. doi:10.1111/saje.2008.76.issue-3.

Bekele, E., and Z. Worku. 2008b. "Women Entrepreneurship in Micro, Small and Medium Enterprises: The Case of Ethiopia." *Journal of International Women's Studies* 10 (2): 3–19.

Biru, A. G., D. Gilbert, and P. M. Arenius. 2017. "The Viability of Small Businesses in Ethiopia: An Institutional Perspective." *Academy of Management Proceedings* 2017 (1): 15111. Briarcliff Manor, NY 10510: Academy of Management. doi:10.5465/AMBPP.2017.15111abstract.

Boyatzis, R. E. 1998. *Transforming Qualitative Information: Thematic Analysis and Code Development*. London: Sage.

Braun, V., and V. Clarke. 2006. "Using Thematic Analysis in Psychology." *Qualitative Research in Psychology* 3 (2): 77–101. doi:10.1191/1478088706qp063oa.

Brekke, T. 2015. "Entrepreneurship and Path Dependency in Regional Development." *Entrepreneurship & Regional Development* 27 (3–4): 202–218. doi:10.1080/08985626.2015.1030457.

Brixiova, Z., and M. Ncube 2013. Entrepreneurship and the Business Environment in Africa: An Application to Ethiopia.

Brown, R., and C. Mason. 2017. "Looking inside the Spiky Bits: A Critical Review and Conceptualisation of Entrepreneurial Ecosystems." *Small Business Economics* 49 (1): 11–30. doi:10.1007/s11187-017-9865-7.

Cancino, C. A., C. A. Bonilla, and M. Vergara. 2015. "The Impact of Government Support Programs for the Development of Businesses in Chile." *Management Decision* 53 (8): 1736–1754. doi:10.1108/MD-06-2014-0428.

Cho, Y., and M. Honorati. 2013. *Entrepreneurship Programs in Developing Countries: A Meta Regression Analysis*. Washington, DC: World Bank.

Creswell, J. W. 2013. *Research Design: Qualitative, Quantitative, and Mixed Methods Approaches*. Thousand Oaks, CA: Sage publications.

Davidsson, P., and F. Delmar. 2006. "High-growth Firms and Their Contribution to Employment: The Case of Sweden 1987–96." In *Entrepreneurship and the Growth of Firms*, 156–178. Cheltenham, UK: Edward Elgar Publishing Ltd.

Di Nunzio, M. 2015. "What Is the Alternative? Youth, Entrepreneurship and the Developmental State in Urban Ethiopia." *Development and Change* 46 (5): 1179–1200. doi:10.1111/dech.2015.46.issue-5.

Doh, S., and B. Kim. 2014. "Government Support for SME Innovations in the Regional Industries: The Case of Government Financial Support Program in South Korea." *Research Policy* 43 (9): 1557–1569. doi:10.1016/j.respol.2014.05.001.

Dorado, S., and M. J. Ventresca. 2013. "Crescive Entrepreneurship in Complex Social Problems: Institutional Conditions for Entrepreneurial Engagement." *Journal of Business Venturing* 28 (1): 69–82. doi:10.1016/j.jbusvent.2012.02.002.

Du, K., and A. O'Connor. 2018. "Entrepreneurship and Advancing National Level Economic Efficiency." *Small Business Economics* 50 (1): 91–111. doi:10.1007/s11187-017-9904-4.

Edoho, F. M. 2015. "Entrepreneurialism: Africa in Transition." *African Journal of Economic and Management Studies* 6: null. doi:10.1108/AJEMS-03-2015-0038.

Eyana, S. M., E. Masurel, and L. J. Paas. 2018. "Causation and Effectuation Behaviour of Ethiopian Entrepreneurs: Implications on Performance of Small Tourism Firms." *Journal of Small Business and Enterprise Development* 25 (5): 791–817. doi:10.1108/JSBED-02-2017-0079.

Fayolle, A., O. Basso, and V. Bouchard. 2010. "Three Levels of Culture and Firms' Entrepreneurial Orientation: A Research Agenda." *Entrepreneurship and Regional Development* 22 (7–8): 707–730. doi:10.1080/08985620903233952.

Feld, B. 2012. *Startup Communities: Building an Entrepreneurial Ecosystem in Your City*. Hoboken, NJ: John Wiley & Sons.

Feldman, M. P. 2014. "The Character of Innovative Places: Entrepreneurial Strategy, Economic Development, and Prosperity." *Small Business Economics* 43 (1): 9–20. doi:10.1007/s11187-014-9574-4.

FeMSEDA. 2014. "Federal Micro and Small Enterprises Development Sector: Annual Statitical Report." *Information and Technology Directorare, Addis Ababa* 2: 42–50.

Gebremichael, B. A. 2014. "The Impact of Subsidy on the Growth of Small and Medium Enterprises (Smes)." *Journal of Economics and Sustainable Development* 5 (3): 178–188.

Gebrewolde, T. M., and J. Rockey. 2016. "*The Effectiveness of Industrial Policy in Developing Countries: Causal Evidence from Ethiopian Manufacturing Firms.*" Brussels, Belgium: Université Libre de Bruxelles.

Gioia, D A.., K G.. Corley, and A L.. Hamilton. 2013. "Seeking Qualitative Rigor in Inductive Research: Notes on The Gioia Methodology." *Organizational Research Methods* 16 (1): 15-31. doi:10.1177/1094428112452151.

Grover, A., D. Medvedev, and E. Olafsen. 2018. *High-Growth Firms*. Washington, DC: World Bank.

Hayton, J. C., G. George, and S. A. Zahra. 2002. "National Culture and Entrepreneurship: A Review of Behavioral Research." *Entrepreneurship Theory and Practice* 26 (4): 33–52. doi:10.1177/104225870202600403.

Henrekson, M., and T. Sanandaji. 2014. "Small Business Activity Does Not Measure Entrepreneurship." *Proceedings of the National Academy of Sciences* 111 (5): 1760–1765. doi:10.1073/pnas.1307204111.

Hofstede, G. 1984. "Values and Culture." In *Culture's Consequences: International Differences in Work-related Values* 5. Newbury Park, CA: Sage.

Hofstede, G. 1991. "Cultures and Organizations: Software of the Mind." In *Airaksinen*, edited by House, R. J., Hanges, P. J., Javidan, M., Dorfman, P. W., and Gupta, V., 1–25. London and New York: McGraw Hill.

Hofstede, G. 2018. "Hofstede Insights." *Recuperado De*. www. Hofstedeinsights. Com/models/national-culture

Isenberg, D. 2011. "The Entrepreneurship Ecosystem Strategy as a New Paradigm for Economic Policy: Principles for Cultivating Entrepreneurship." In *Presentation at the Institute of International and European Affairs*. Babson Park, MA: Babson Entrepreneurship Ecosystem Project, Babson College.

Isenberg, D. J. 2010. "How to Start an Entrepreneurial Revolution." *Harvard Business Review* 88 (6): 40–50.

Jaffe, A. B., M. Trajtenberg, and R. Henderson. 1993. "Geographic Localization of Knowledge Spillovers as Evidenced by Patent Citations." *The Quarterly Journal of Economics* 108 (3): 577–598. doi:10.2307/2118401.

Juselius, K., N. Framroze, and F. Tarp 2011. "The Long-run Impact of Foreign Aid in 36 African Countries." UNU-WIDER Working Paper vol 51.

Kantis, H. D., and J. S. Federico. 2012. "Entrepreneurial Ecosystems in Latin America: The Role of Policies." In *International Research and Policy Roundtable*. 1–15. Liverpool, UK: Kauffman Foundation.

Li, H., and A. O'Connor. 2015. "Do Clusters Matter to the Entrepreneurial Process?." *Welcome to the Electronic Edition of Integrating Innovation* 1: 119 –158.

Lindvert, M., P. C. Patel, and J. Wincent. 2017. "Struggling with Social Capital: Pakistani Women Micro Entrepreneurs' Challenges in Acquiring Resources." *Entrepreneurship & Regional Development* 29 (7–8): 759–790. doi:10.1080/08985626.2017.1349190.

Mair, J., and I. Marti. 2009. "Entrepreneurship in and around Institutional Voids: A Case Study from Bangladesh." *Journal of Business Venturing* 24 (5): 419–435. doi:10.1016/j.jbusvent.2008.04.006.

Malecki, E. J. 2018. "Entrepreneurs, Networks, and Economic Development: A Review of Recent Research." In *Reflections and Extensions on Key Papers of the First Twenty-Five Years of Advances* 20: 71–116. Wagon Lane, UK: Emerald Publishing Limited.

Maskell, P., and M. Lorenzen. 2004. "The Cluster as Market Organisation." *Urban Studies* 41 (5–6): 991–1009. doi:10.1080/00420980410001675878.

Mason, C., and R. Brown. 2013. "Creating Good Public Policy to Support High-growth Firms." *Small Business Economics* 40 (2): 211–225. doi:10.1007/s11187-011-9369-9.

Mason, C., and R. Brown. 2014. "Entrepreneurial Ecosystems and Growth Oriented Entrepreneurship." *Final Report to OECD, Paris* 30 (1): 77–102.

Mendes, A. P. F., M. A. Bertella, and R. F. Teixeira. 2014. "Industrialization in Sub-Saharan Africa and Import Substitution Policy." *Brazilian Journal of Political Economy* 34 (1): 120–138. doi:10.1590/S0101-31572014000100008.

Minkov, M., and G. Hofstede. 2012. "Is National Culture a Meaningful Concept? Cultural Values Delineate Homogeneous National Clusters of In-country Regions." *Cross-Cultural Research* 46 (2): 133–159. doi:10.1177/1069397111427262.

Moller, L. C., and K. M. Wacker. 2017. "Explaining Ethiopia's Growth Acceleration—The Role of Infrastructure and Macroeconomic Policy." *World Development* 96: 198–215. doi:10.1016/j.worlddev.2017.03.007.

Nambisan, S., and R. A. Baron. 2013. "Entrepreneurship in Innovation Ecosystems: Entrepreneurs' Self–regulatory Processes and Their Implications for New Venture Success." *Entrepreneurship Theory and Practice* 37 (5): 1071–1097. doi:10.1111/etap.2013.37.issue-5.

Ngobo, P. V., and M. Fouda. 2012. "Is 'Good'governance Good for Business? A Cross-national Analysis of Firms in African Countries." *Journal of World Business* 47 (3): 435–449. doi:10.1016/j.jwb.2011.05.010.

Nylund, P. A., and B. Cohen. 2017. "Collision Density: Driving Growth in Urban Entrepreneurial Ecosystems." *International Entrepreneurship and Management Journal* 13 (3): 757–776. doi:10.1007/s11365-016-0424-5.

OECD. 2013. *African Economic Outlook: Structural Transformation and Natural Resources*. OECD publishing. https://read.oecd-ilibrary.org/development/african-economic-outlook-2013

Ostrom, E., 1999. "An assessment of the institutional analysis and development framework". *Theories of the Policy Process*, edited by Paul A. Sabatier, 1 (2). New York: Routledge.

Ostrom, E. 2002. *Aid, Incentives, and Sustainability: An Institutional Analysis of Development Cooperation. Main Report* (1): 117–144. Oxford Press, UK: Sida.

Ostrom, E. 2011. "Background on the Institutional Analysis and Development Framework." *Policy Studies Journal* 39 (1): 7–27. doi:10.1111/psj.2011.39.issue-1.

Peng, M. W. 2003. "Institutional Transitions and Strategic Choices." *Academy of Management Review* 28 (2): 275–296. doi:10.5465/amr.2003.9416341.

Pitelis, C. 2012. "Clusters, Entrepreneurial Ecosystem Co-creation, and Appropriability: A Conceptual Framework." *Industrial and Corporate Change* 21 (6): 1359–1388. doi:10.1093/icc/dts008.

Porter, M. E. 1990. *The Competitive Advantage of Nations*. London: Macmillan.

Porter, M. E. 1998. *Clusters and the New Economics of Competition*. Vol. 76. Boston: Harvard Business Review.

Prieger, J. E., C. Bampoky, L. R. Blanco, and A. Liu. 2016. "Economic Growth and the Optimal Level of Entrepreneurship." *World Development* 82: 95–109. doi:10.1016/j.worlddev.2016.01.013.

Richards, L. 2014. *Handling Qualitative Data: A Practical Guide*. 3rd edition. London, UK: Sage.

Rocha, H. O., and R. Sternberg. 2005. "Entrepreneurship: The Role of Clusters Theoretical Perspectives and Empirical Evidence from Germany." *Small Business Economics* 24 (3): 267–292. doi:10.1007/s11187-005-1993-9.

Sapovadia, V. K. 2015. "Analyzing Challenges & Opportunities of Ethiopian SMEs: Micro & Macro Economic Drivers." *Available at SSRN 2589674*. doi:10.2139/ssrn.2589674.

Schaeffer, V., and M. Matt. 2016. "Development of Academic Entrepreneurship in a Non-mature Context: The Role of the University as a Hub-organisation." *Entrepreneurship & Regional Development* 28 (9–10): 724–745. doi:10.1080/08985626.2016.1247915.

Sheriff, M., and M. Muffatto. 2015. "The Present State of Entrepreneurship Ecosystems in Selected Countries in Africa." *African Journal of Economic and Management Studies* 6 (1): 17–54. doi:10.1108/AJEMS-10-2012-0064.

Shiferaw, A. 2017. "Productive Capacity and Economic Growth in Ethiopia." *UNDP CDP Backroung Paper* 34: 24.

Spigel, B. 2013. "Bourdieuian Approaches to the Geography of Entrepreneurial Cultures." *Entrepreneurship & Regional Development* 25 (9–10): 804–818. doi:10.1080/08985626.2013.862974.

Spigel, B. 2016. "Developing and Governing Entrepreneurial Ecosystems: The Structure of Entrepreneurial Support Programs in Edinburgh, Scotland." *International Journal of Innovation and Regional Development* 7 (2): 141–160. doi:10.1504/IJIRD.2016.077889.

Spigel, B. 2017. "The Relational Organization of Entrepreneurial Ecosystems." *Entrepreneurship Theory and Practice* 41 (1): 49–72. doi:10.1111/etap.12167.

Spilling, O. R. 1996. "The Entrepreneurial System: On Entrepreneurship in the Context of a Mega-event." *Journal of Business Research* 36 (1): 91–103. doi:10.1016/0148-2963(95)00166-2.

Stam, E. 2015. "Entrepreneurial Ecosystems and Regional Policy: A Sympathetic Critique." *European Planning Studies* 23 (9): 1759–1769. doi:10.1080/09654313.2015.1061484.

Stam, F., and B. Spigel 2016. "Entrepreneurial Ecosystems." *USE Discussion Paper Series* 16 (13).

Torre, A. 2006. "Collective Action, Governance Structure and Organizational Trust in Localized Systems of Production. The Case of the AOC Organization of Small Producers." *Entrepreneurship and Regional Development* 18 (1): 55–72. doi:10.1080/08985620500467557.

Vershinina, N., K. Woldesenbet Beta, and W. Murithi. 2018. "How Does National Culture Enable or Constrain Entrepreneurship? Exploring the Role of Harambee in Kenya." *Journal of Small Business and Enterprise Development* 25 (4): 687–704. doi:10.1108/JSBED-03-2017-0143.

Voelker, T. A. 2012. "Entrepreneurial Ecosystems: Evolutionary Paths or Differentiated Systems?" *Business Studies Journal* 4 (2): 43–61.

Wennekers, S., A. Van Wennekers, R. Thurik, and P. Reynolds. 2005. "Nascent Entrepreneurship and the Level of Economic Development." *Small Business Economics* 24 (3): 293–309. doi:10.1007/s11187-005-1994-8.

World Bank. February 2018. *Ethiopia Economic Update: Reform Imperatives for Ethiopia's Services Sector*. World Bank. https://www.worldbank.org/en/country/ethiopia/publication/ethiopia-economic-update-reform-imperatives-for-ethiopias-services-sector

World Bank. June 2019. *Doing Business*. World Bank. http://www.doingbusiness.org/

Index

For Product Safety Concerns and Information please contact our
EU representative GPSR@taylorandfrancis.com Taylor & Francis
Verlag GmbH, Kaufingerstraße 24, 80331 München, Germany